PITTSBURGH THEOLOGICAL MONOGRAPHS

New Series

Dikran Y. Hadidian
General Editor

15

Coleridge as Poet and Religious Thinker

Also by David Jasper

IMAGES OF BELIEF IN LITERATURE (*editor*)

COLERIDGE AS POET AND RELIGIOUS THINKER

By

David Jasper

PICKWICK PUBLICATIONS
Allison Park, Pennsylvania
1985

First published in Great Britain in 1985 by
THE MACMILLAN PRESS LTD

and in the USA in 1985 by
PICKWICK PUBLICATIONS
4137 Timberlane Drive
Allison Park, PA 15101

Printed in Hong Kong

Library of Congress Cataloging in Publication Data
Jasper, David .
Coleridge as poet and religious thinker.
(Pittsburgh theological monographs. New
Series; 15).
1. Coleridge, Samuel Taylor – Knowledge –
Literature
I. Title
820.9   PR4487.L5
ISBN 0–915138–70–0

For Alison

Revealed truth does not lie in propositions or sentences or concepts, but in images that are related, compared, and interwoven by inspired imagination

Charles C. Hefling, *Jacob's Ladder* (1979)

Contents

Contents

Preface

I am grateful for the help which I have received in preparing this study from the Durham University Library; the British Library, Department of Manuscripts; the Bodleian Library, Oxford; the English Faculty Library, Oxford; and the Devon Record Office. To Hatfield College, Durham, I am obliged for the research fellowship which enabled me to undertake the work in the first place, and for continuous help and encouragement during the years of its development. I am indebted also to the Cleaver Trustees for their generous support. My wife and I owe to Lord and Lady Coleridge the memory of a delightful visit to their house in Ottery St Mary, where the hospitality was matched by their patience in answering questions about Samuel Taylor Coleridge.

Part of Chapter 4 has been published in J. R. Watson (ed.), *An Infinite Complexity: Essays in Romanticism* (Edinburgh, 1983); material from Chapter 6 in *The Modern Churchman*, XXVI (1983); and material from Chapter 7 in *The Durham University Journal*, LXXVI (Dec 1983).

My thanks are due to the many individuals who have assisted me by letter or in conversation, and particularly to Dr John Coulson, Dr F. W. Dillistone, Dr Stephen Prickett, Dr Geoffrey Rowell and Dr Kathleen Wheeler. Dr David Whewell of the Department of Philosophy, Durham University, patiently helped me with my reading of Kant. James Green, of the Division of Religion and Philosophy, Sunderland Polytechnic, enabled me to refer to information on material in current research in Britain stored in the Polytechnic computer. Mr Jack Priestly of the School of Education, Exeter University, introduced me to Lord and Lady Coleridge. Mrs Jane Bonner helped me with the German translations, which, with translations from French, are my own unless otherwise acknowledged in the notes. I am grateful to Mrs Frances Durkin for undertaking the laborious task of typing the final draft. Most of all, however, whatever I have achieved is due to the energy and enthusiasm of Dr Ann Loades of the Department of Theology, Durham University – a fine scholar, a wise teacher and a good friend.

Finally, the unfailing support of my parents and my wife, Alison, through the years deserves more gratitude than I have words to express.

Hatfield College   D.J.

Abbreviations and Primary Sources

AR(I)	*Aids to Reflection*, 7th edn, ed. Derwent Coleridge (London, 1854)
AR(II)	*Aids to Reflection*, with James Marsh's 'Preliminary Essay' of 1840 (London, 1913)
Bibliography I	Thomas J. Wise, *A Bibliography of the Writings in Prose and Verse of S. T. Coleridge* (London, 1913)
Bibliography II	Richard and Josephine Haven, and Maurianne Adams (eds), *Samuel Taylor Coleridge: An Annotated Bibliography of Criticism and Scholarship*, vol. I: *1793–1899* (Boston and London, 1976)
Bibliography III	Jefferson D. Caskey and Melinda M. Stapper (eds), *Samuel Taylor Coleridge: A Selective Bibliography of Criticism, 1935–77* (Westport and London, 1978)
BL	*Biographia Literaria*, ed. J. Shawcross, 2 vols (Oxford, 1907)
BL.MSS.ADD 47496–47550	Manuscript notebooks in the British Library
Church and State	*On the Constitution of the Church and State According to the Idea of Each*, ed. John Barrell (London: Everyman, 1972)
CL	*Collected Letters*, ed. E. L. Griggs, 6 vols (Oxford, 1956–71)
CN	*The Notebooks of Samuel Taylor Coleridge*, ed. Kathleen Coburn, 3 parts in 6 vols, 1794–1819 (London and New York, 1957–73)

Confessions	*Confessions of an Inquiring Spirit*, ed. Henry Nelson Coleridge, 1840 (Menston, Yorks.: Scholar Press, 1971)
Devon Record Office 121Z/F4	Small collection of letters and papers relating to Coleridge
Friend(CC)	*The Friend*, ed. Barbara E. Rooke, 2 vols, in *Collected Coleridge*, vol. 4 (London and Princeton, 1969)
Imagination	*Imagination in Coleridge*, ed. John Spencer Hill (London and Basingstoke, 1978)
IS	*Inquiring Spirit: A New Presentation of Coleridge from his Published and Unpublished Prose Writings*, ed. Kathleen Coburn, rev. edn (Toronto, 1979)
Lay Sermons(CC)	*Lay Sermons*, ed. R. J. White, in *Collected Coleridge*, vol. 6 (London and Princeton, 1972)
Lectures(CC)	*Lectures 1795: On Politics and Religion*, ed. Lewis Patton and Peter Mann, in *Collected Coleridge*, vol. 1 (London and Princeton, 1971)
Logic	*Logic*, ed. J. R. de J. Jackson, in *Collected Coleridge*, vol. 13 (London and Princeton, 1981)
Marginalia	*Marginalia*, vol. 1, ed. George Whalley, in *Collected Coleridge*, vol. 12 (London and Princeton, 1980)
Misc. Crit.	*Miscellaneous Criticism*, ed. T. M. Raysor (London, 1936)
Omniana	Robert Southey and S. T. Coleridge, *Omniana, or Hores Otiosiores*, ed. Robert Gittings (Carbondale, Ill., 1969)
PC	*The Portable Coleridge*, ed. I. A. Richards (Harmondsworth, 1977)
Phil. Lect.	*The Philosophical Lectures*, ed. Kathleen Coburn (London, 1949)

Poems	*Poems*, selected and ed. John Beer (London, 1974)
PW	*Poetical Works*, ed. Ernest Hartley Coleridge (Oxford, 1969)
17 Cent.	*Coleridge on the Seventeenth Century*, ed. Roberta Florence Brinkley (Durham, NC, 1955)
Sh.	*Coleridge on Shakespeare*, ed. Terence Hawkes (Harmondsworth, 1969)
Sh. Crit.	*Shakespearean Criticism*, ed. T. M. Raysor, 2 vols, 2nd edn (London, 1960)
Theory of Life	*Hints towards the Formation of a more Comprehensive Theory of Life*, ed. Seth B. Watson, 1848 (Farnborough, 1970)
TT	*Passages from the Prose and Table Talk of Coleridge*, ed. W. H. Dircks (London, 1894)

Additional Coleridge material

Essays on His Times 3, ed. David V. Erdman, in *Collected Coleridge*, vol. 3 (London and Princeton, 1978)

The Literary Remains of Samuel Taylor Coleridge, ed. H. N. Coleridge, 4 vols (London, 1836–9)

Marginalia in Robert Southey, *The Life of John Wesley* (1820), ed. Maurice H. Fitzgerald (Oxford, 1925)

Prefaces to editions of poetry, 1794–1834, *Poetical Works*, 2 vols (Oxford, 1912) vol. II, pp. 1135–61.

'Selection from Mr Coleridge's Literary Correspondence, no. 1', including 'On the Philosophic Import of the Words Object and Subject', *Blackwood's Edinburgh Magazine*, X (1821) 243–63.

Specimens of the Table Talk of S. T. Coleridge, ed. H. N. Coleridge (London, 1851)

1 Introduction

Many years ago, when I was looking over Piranesi's *Antiquities of Rome*, Mr. Coleridge, who was standing by, described to me a set of plates by that artist, called his *Dreams*, and which record the scenery of his own visions during the delirium of a fever. Some of them (I describe only from memory of Mr. Coleridge's account) represented vast Gothic halls: on the floor of which stood all sorts of engines and machinery, wheels, cables, pulleys, levers, catapults, &c. &c. expressive of enormous power put forth and resistance overcome. Creeping along the sides of the walls, you perceived a staircase; and upon it, groping his way upwards, was Piranesi himself: follow the stairs a little further, and you perceive it come to a sudden abrupt termination, without any balustrade, and allowing no step onwards to him who had reached the extremity, except into the depths below. Whatever is to become of poor Piranesi, you suppose, at least, that his labours must in some way terminate here. But raise you eyes, and behold a second flight of stairs still higher: on which again Piranesi is perceived, by this time standing on the very brink of the abyss. Again elevate your eye, and a still more aerial flight of stairs is beheld: and again is poor Piranesi busy on his aspiring labours: and so on, until the unfinished stairs and Piranesi both are lost in the upper gloom of the hall. With the same power of endless growth and self-reproduction did my architecture proceed in dreams.[1]

A search through Coleridge's writings, in published form and in the still unpublished British Library notebooks, has yielded only one reference to the work of the Venetian architect and engraver Giovanni Battista Piranesi (1720–78). In a letter of 3 November 1814 to the poet John Kenyon, Coleridge describes Jeremy Taylor's 'Letter on original sin' as, in one sense, a 'Countenance that looks towards his Followers–. . . all weather-eaten, dim, noseless, a *Ghost in Marble* – such as you may have seen represented in many of Piranesi's astounding Engravings from Rome & the Campus Martius.'[2] Taylor on Original Sin is discussed at great length in *Aids to Reflection* (1825). Piranesi's etchings of ancient and modern Rome and the *Carceri d'Invenzione* (begun *c.* 1745,

1

reworked 1761), or *The Prisons*, became known in England through the admiration of English art connoisseurs on the Grand Tour. His exaggerated visions of grandeur were carried into English romanticism by their recognition in the writings of William Beckford (1759–1844), J. M. W. Turner (1775–1851) and Horace Walpole (1717–97), who, in 1771, wrote of 'the sublime dream of Piranesi . . . he has imagined scenes that would startle geometry, and exhaust the Indies to realize'.[3] Piranesi's *Prisons*, called by De Quincey his 'Dreams', have frequently been compared with Edmund Burke's *Philosophical Enquiry into the Origin of our Ideas of the Sublime and the Beautiful* (1757) as analyses of the effect of 'infinity and things multiplied without end', and of the relationship between the finite and the infinite.[4]

Coleridge, in his turn, was affected by these extraordinary etchings, expressions of a deep spiritual conflict which, in many ways, matches his own. Philip Hofer describes how Piranesi's

> etched lines dance and soar, stimulating the beholder's imagination at the same time that they fill him with wonder, a deep sadness and a sense of mystery. Where do these immense vaults actually end? To what further fastnesses do the innumerable staircases and balconies lead? What tortures are suggested by the projecting beams, wheels, ropes, chains and less clearly defined means of punishment? Who are those wretched beings one occasionally glimpses chained and fastened to the great rings in the walls! By whose authority were they put there, and for what cause? For all Piranesi's barely outlined and emaciated, ragged figure subjects defy analysis[5]

If De Quincey's report is to be trusted, Coleridge seems to have placed Piranesi within the prison, and identified himself with Piranesi. The great pieces of machinery express power exercised against power in a series of counterbalances, tensioned like the poles of a vast magnet. He himself, an insignificant and indistinct figure, is seen toiling up a staircase which ascends mysteriously and infinitely into the vaulted recesses. Aspiration matches the endlessness of a prison which both traps the artist in his finitude and suggests a possible escape into infinity for the man who would persevere against terrible odds. The toils of mortality are dreadful engines of torture and chains which hang heavily, yet aspiration is infinite and hope endless. The prison itself, and its staircases, is unfinished, an emblem of endless growth and possibilities; the artist is repeatedly rediscovered, his figure reflected time and again until lost in the indistinctness of the upper vault.

Such an image of Coleridge as artist lies at the heart of the present study. Through such an image will be examined Coleridge's religious and theological conclusions, in the belief that art and aesthetics can illuminate and refresh the religious life. Obversely, theology may be the conserving source for a theory of the almost limitless freedom of the artist as inspired creator. In Coleridge's own time, De Quincey was aware of tensions in his thought between aesthetics and poetry, Christianity and philosophy, 'their occasional connections or approaches, and their constant mutual repulsions'.[6] Archdeacon Julius Hare, a theological commentator, caught the tone of Piranesi's influence and characterized the conflicts of Coleridge's concerns as a spiritual quest. He dedicated his book *The Mission of the Comforter* (1846) 'To the honoured memory of Samuel Taylor Coleridge, the Christian philosopher, who through dark and winding paths of speculation was led to the light, in order that others by his guidance might reach that light.'[7] Later in the nineteenth century a clear schism occurred between those who read Coleridge as a religious writer and those who read him as a poet and literary critic. It was most clearly focused in an acrimonious debate in the *Fortnightly Review* in 1885 between John Tulloch and H. D. Traill.[8] Tulloch, who had emphasized Coleridge's place in the religious history of his century in *Movements of Religious Thought in Britain during the Nineteenth Century* (1885), defended Coleridge as a 'spiritual thinker' in the tradition of Hooker, Milton and Jeremy Taylor. Traill, whose *Coleridge* was published a year earlier, dismisses Coleridge's religious thought as confused mysticism, detached, unsystematic and insubstantial. Among theologians and in the literary fraternity, Coleridge continued to be a source of inspiration, and occasionally the link between his imaginative insight and his sense of the divine in the work of theology was recognized. A. C. Swinburne wrote that 'the ardour, delicacy, energy of his intellect, his resolute desire to get at the root of things and deeper yet, if deeper might be, will always enchant and attract all spirits of like mould and temper'.[9] Nevertheless, the sense of ruined genius and of what might have been, and the image of, in Lamb's words, 'an Archangel a little damaged',[10] remained. Leslie Stephen described Coleridge's career as 'the history of early promise blighted and vast powers all but running hopelessly to waste'.[11]

There is, of course, truth in what Stephen says. Yet, as in Piranesi's etchings, the sense of unfinished ruin is a necessary element in Coleridge's task. For if it were finished and achieved, the book would be closed and infinity foreshortened. The dispute continues in our own time. Some have rightly warned against the tendency to regard Coleridge as the omnicompetent master of all that he attempted. Thus, recognizing the poor quality of the political *Essays on His Times* which have been republished in the *Collected Coleridge*, E. P. Thompson has remarked that 'it is altogether proper that this inflated reputation should be so damaged'.[12] Nevertheless, such criticism becomes misguidedly destructive when, as in the case of Norman Fruman's *Coleridge: The Damaged Archangel* (London, 1972), the obsession with sources, Coleridge's plagiarisms and eclecticism and his personal shortcomings, serves merely to obscure the entelechy governing the diversity of his pursuits. For his notions of symbol and imagination give an integrity to his attention to religion (where they find their origin), aesthetics, literature, ethics and politics. Furthermore, his experience as a poet seems to have suggested an analogy between the poetic mind and the mind which is imaginatively responsive to the fundamental mystery of divine inspiration. The common rhetoric for which Coleridge laboured in all his writings has been well characterized by Stephen Happel – 'words made beautiful by grace'.[13]

Coleridge's position between literature and religion might be illustrated by reference to a paper by Mary Midgley in her book *Heart and Mind* (1981), entitled 'Creation and Originality'. Mary Midgley denies the notion of creating or inventing new moral values through the will, for what *generates* thoughts is the imagination.[14] Furthermore, thoughts are generated within an unbroken continuum, so that new thoughts develop from what has gone before, and old thoughts do not become obsolete. In what sense, however, can the imagination be said to generate or create, on the religious model of divine creation, since people are not gods?

Midgley is specifically using Nietzsche and Sartre in giving a religious reference to the notion of creation, describing man as God's successor (p. 46). She raises two problems from this description. First, that God's creation is complete and finished. By analogy, therefore, each of us adds not to a developing continuum of creation, but creates an individual, self-sufficient and solipsistic world with self at the centre. Second, the point of ascribing the task of creation to God at all arises out of its essential mysteriousness. Is it helpful to transfer such mysteriousness to the human craftsman, for do we not therefore end up by simply saying that we do not understand at all how it is done, whether it be art or the creation of moral values? Agnosticism has merely spread from the divine to the human.

In response to these problems Mary Midgley suggests that talk of creating values through the will necessarily involves the aping, even the outdoing, of God (p. 48). Nietzsche and Sartre are simply trying to fit man into the God-shaped hole, left after the death of God. Turning more positively to the mystery of human originality, she addresses herself first to the fact of *individuality* – that everyone is different. From this she draws the expression 'the world is always being created anew' (p. 52), since each person's vision of the public world is unique, unparalleled, and irreplaceable, and she refers to Chesterton's remark that the suicide destroys not just one man but the whole world, since *his* world can never come again.

From the activity of the individual in the world, Midgley examines the nature of genius in the individual. What is special about Blake, Socrates, or – we might add – Coleridge? Using the image of the mine, and of the individual digging within the self, she stresses that, though hard work may be necessary, the great artist like Blake or Shakespeare will eventually produce what seems much more found than deliberately fashioned (p. 55). Thus many artists speak of inspiration, and thus it would be odd to make the will central, although a willed act of perseverance may be necessary. She then makes the important distinction between the individual who stands out because merely eccentric and the genius whose originality is worth following. Properly, artistic creativity is valuable to and addresses humanity as a whole, just as does the act of divine creation.

Creation, therefore, Mary Midgley begins to conclude, is something less pretentious than a single, splendid act, but is going on all the time, moving and developing. Such creation

> demands chiefly courage and clear-headedness. Innovators in this field innovate by their acts, not by new intellectual feats or by talk. Workers of art are, I think, just a special class of such acts. . . . It is the combination that is new, not the elements. (pp. 57–8)

In Coleridge, however, we take an important further step. For Midgley's artist is no more than the 'maker' described by Plato in the *Timaeus*, who follows the demiurgus or supreme artisan in bringing order out of a pre-existent chaos.[15] His faculty Coleridge might characterize as the secondary Imagination. The primary Imagination, however, as 'the repetition in the finite mind of the eternal act of creation in the infinite I AM',[16] lies in the Judaeo-Christian theory of God's creativity *ex nihilo* and dependent upon no prior, logical necessity. This tradition of Genesis, St Athanasius and St Augustine sets before the artist the tremendous image of God's creation.

In his division of the Imagination into primary and secondary, Coleridge sets the creative artist between these two traditions, the Platonic and the Judaeo-Christian. The result is described by Milton Nahm.

> From the perspective of such a reconciliation, the value of the theory of unlimited and unrestricted creative power . . . may be discerned. As philosophic issues, the ideas of pure creativity, the unique individual, and absolute freedom are for the artist and for the aesthetic percipient limiting conceptions. By using them in this way, man may at once measure his present achievement in terms of perfection and give himself a goal of value, definable, unattainable, but progressively approachable without limit. By means of such limiting conceptions, the artist adjusts the infinitely variable and flexible instruments of art to the artistic structure and to the aesthetic end.[17]

The discipline of art, therefore, opens the particular to the universal and the finite to the infinite. The Bible, so often described by Coleridge in the context of literary genius, 'contains a Science of *Realities*: and therefore each of its Elements is at the same time a living GERM, in which the Present involves the Future, and in the Finite the Infinite exists potentially'.[18] In the creativity of the artist is born the 'symbol', 'that most glorious birth of the God-like within us'.[19] As in the symbol, heaven itself may be imaged in a dew-drop, so in reflection upon the nature and genius of the artist – or, for Coleridge, in self-reflection – may be perceived something of the nature of God's original creating power and of the divine revelation to our 'inward experience'.

Although this study will follow a rough chronological course through Coleridge's life, its purpose is in no sense biographical. Of necessity, each chapter deals with much the same issues as its predecessors, since Coleridge's opinions and beliefs were a development from, and construction of, a fundamental position, adopted early and constant through his life. The result here is, perhaps, a series of different perspectives on a few common issues, a number of aids to reflection. Very close to the heart of the study is Coleridge's developing 'Polar Logic', which issued finally in the Trinitarianism of his later years. A similar centrality was given to polarity by Owen Barfield in his book *What Coleridge Thought* (1971), most particularly in his chapter 'Man and God', where he concludes that only in the recognition of tri-unity, the three 'in' one and one 'in' three, do we come to recognize and become conscious of our real selves, and begin to apprehend the nature of the divinity.[20]

The concluding chapter focuses upon specific examples of how what is examined in this study may be of importance for both the nineteenth and twentieth centuries. There is little evidence that Austin Farrer was particularly influenced by Coleridge, but the relevance of the debate arising out of *The Glass of Vision* (1948) to central issues in Coleridge is striking. Other examples from twentieth-century theology might have been chosen. For instance, Pamela Vermes's description of the perfection of human nature through the imitation of God, as described in the writings of Martin Buber, bears comparison with Coleridge's sense of the divine perceived through the nature of man made in God's image. In her book *Buber on God and the Perfect Man* (1980), she describes the idea of divine revelation not as a fixed image but in deed and action.[21] More recently, Northrop Frye's study of the Bible and literature, *The Great Code* (1982), establishes a series of bases for discussion remarkably consonant with those which direct Coleridge's religious thinking and reflections on literature: the nature of the observer as observed and artist as spectator; the understanding of language, and particularly the word 'God', as a process ever 'accomplishing itself'; the rejection of a notion of revelation as simply the conveyance of information from an objective divine source to a subjective human receptor.[22]

What is here undertaken, therefore, is not simply an historical study of an episode in English literature and theology. It is pursued in the belief that Coleridge's experience and practice as poet, critic, theologian and philosopher represents matter of universal importance in all these fields, which each generation must rediscover and attend to for itself.

2 The Romantic Context

Norman Fruman's *Coleridge: The Damaged Archangel* (1972) stands as a sad monument to the tendency of many critics to regard Coleridge's work as little more than a mosaic drawn from his extraordinarily wide reading. The danger is, then, that he becomes merely a channel for the work and ideas of others – David Hartley, Kant, the German transcendentalist philosophers, or the English seventeenth-century divines. The present study will attempt to focus solely upon the immediate subject, Samuel Taylor Coleridge, as a unique genius who was yet highly sensitive and original in his reading.

J. S. Mill's article of 1840, comparing Coleridge with Bentham, perceptively identifies why Coleridge is such a difficult writer (and why, therefore, it might be easier simply to dismiss him as a plagiarist):

> By Bentham, beyond all others, men have been led to ask themselves in regard to any ancient or received opinion, Is it true? and by Coleridge, What is the meaning of it? The one took his stand *outside* the received opinion, and surveyed it as an entire stranger to it, the other looked at it from within, and endeavoured to see it with the eyes of a believer in it; to discover by what apparent facts it was at first suggested, and by what appearances it has ever since been rendered continually credible – has seemed, to a succession of persons, to be a faithful interpretation of their experience.[1]

Coleridge is entirely involved in his material. His enquiries and poems matter deeply to him as a sinning, loving and creative being. He worries at the meaning of things and endeavours (a significant word) to see. Here is no cold observer or analyst.

The following pages set Coleridge in the context of European Romanticism. Many of the writers Coleridge did not know, and they are not intended to illustrate influences on him. The purpose, very briefly, is to indicate that the major themes of this book are to be found across a wide spectrum of English, German and French writers more or less contemporary with Coleridge. They have in common the characteristic of being literary critics or creative literary writers using religious forms and attending to ultimately religious or theological issues. In them, literature cannot be understood apart from theology, while theology begins to find a new language in literature. Poetry and divine revelation; the poet as prophet; the creative role of the imagination; the task of irony; these are some of the themes of Romanticism to which Coleridge was peculiarly sensitive. As poet, theologian, philosopher and literary critic his contribution was profoundly significant for English literature and theology in the nineteenth century. Internationally, he was a key figure in the aesthetic, theological and philosophical aftermath of the eighteenth-century Enlightenment and the work of Immanuel Kant.

I POETRY AND RELIGION

In the 'Essay, Supplementary to the Preface to *Lyrical Ballads*' (1815), Wordsworth writes of the affinity between poetry and religion:

> between religion – making up for the deficiencies of reason by faith; and poetry – passionate for the instruction of reason; between religion – whose element is infinitude, and whose ultimate trust is the supreme of things submitting herself to circumspection, and reconciled to substitutions; and poetry – ethereal and transcendent, yet incapable to sustain her existence without sensuous incarnation.[2]

It is the classic English statement of a relationship which is explored repeatedly in European Romanticism, recognizing both the illumination which the spiritual casts on the physical and that the spiritual only has sense in relation to the physical. The elusive qualities of poetry are described by Novalis in terms of religious mysticism and in its feeling for the arcane and the revelatory (Offenbarende).

> Er stellt das Undarstellbare dar. Er sieht das Unsichtbare, fühlt das Unfühlbare.

> (It represents that which cannot be represented. It sees the invisible, is aware of the imperceptible.)[3]

This mystical tendency in Romanticism – present also in Coleridge – finds its fullest expression in France in the work of the Vicomte de Chateaubriand (1768–1848) and his friend Pierre-Simon Ballanche, whose prose-poem *Orphée* (1827) celebrates the transcendental powers of the artist.

Le poète ne fait que traduire en paroles humaines ce que lui a été révélé sur le plan spirituel. . . . C'est toujours une vérité religieuse que le poète est chargé de transmettre. Religion et poésie ne font qu'une seule et même chose.

(The poet only translates into human words that which has been revealed to him on the spiritual plane. . . . It is always a religious truth which the poet is entrusted to transmit. Religion and poetry are merely one and the same thing.)[4]

A recurring theme of Romantic criticism is poetry as a channel for divine revelation. According to Wilhelm Heinrich Wackenroder (1773–97), a close friend of Ludwig Tieck (with whom Coleridge corresponded), God speaks to us through two languages, those of Nature and Art. In the latter he communicates through artists whom 'He has anointed as His favourites'. Combining the spiritual and the sensuous, the work of art sharpens human perception in a manner approaching the divine.

Ist es aber erlaubt, also von dergleichen Dingen zu reden, so möchte man vielleicht sagen, dass Gott wohl die ganze Natur oder die ganze Welt auf ähnliche Art, wie wir ein Kunstwerk, ansehen möge.

(If it is permissible to speak of such things in this way, one might perhaps say that God may indeed regard the whole of nature or the entire world in such a way as we regard a work of art.)[5]

Wackenroder's writings are characterized by a sense of art as a sacred and numinous object and of the artist as a quasi-divine creator. In a similar way Shelley describes poetry as 'something divine' in *A Defence of Poetry* (1821). Poetry ascends 'to bring light and fire from those eternal regions where the owl-winged faculty of calculation dare not even soar'. It is, indeed, a revealer, that which lifts the veil from things hidden; and a creator, for it 'creates anew the universe' as 'it purges from our inward sight the film of familiarity which obscures from us the wonder of our being'. Jesus Christ, above all, was a poet since, in the tradition of Plato and the ancients, he

divulged the sacred and eternal truths contained in these views to mankind, and Christianity, in its abstract purity, became the exoteric expression of the esoteric doctrines of the poetry and wisdom of antiquity.[6]

II THE ROLE OF THE POET

The role of art in the revelation of things hidden and divine went hand in hand in Romantic criticism with the sense of the poet as priest.

> Dichter und Priester waren im Anfang *eins*, und nur spätere Zeiten haben sie getrennt. Der echte Dichter ist aber immer Priester, so wie der echte Priester immer Dichter geblieben. Und soltte nicht die Zukunft den alten Zustand der Dinge wieder herbeiführen?

> (In the beginning poet and priest were *one*, and only later times have separated them. But the true poet is always a priest, just as the true priest has always remained a poet. And should not the future bring back anew the old state of things?)[7]

When Novalis wrote this in 1798, Coleridge had already delivered his *Six Lectures on Revealed Religion* (1795) in which he expressed a profound awareness of the defects of the established Church and its clergy. Contemptuous of the 'Toad of Priesthood',[8] Coleridge was discovering the poet's power, in purifying and recreating his own mind, to awaken spiritually a church and people sunk in 'Paleyite' apologetic and clerical abuse. Ballanche put it in a nutshell – 'Le poète est prêtre.'[9]

The poet was one inspired with a mission to communicate to mankind the workings of divinity. After his short and tragic life, Thomas Chatterton (1752–70) became a cult figure representative of the original mind crushed by authority, his suicide symbolic of youthful genius destroyed by materialism and philistinism. As the poet–martyr, Coleridge pictures him beside the 'eternal Throne' glowing with a 'fire divine' which illuminates the 'sad and gloomy hour'.[10] Among Coleridge's associates, Robert Southey and Joseph Cottle edited the authoritative edition of Chatterton's works in 1803. In 'Resolution and Independence' (1802), Wordsworth invokes the memory of 'the marvellous boy', while Keats – often compared with Chatterton in his own untimely death – dedicated his *Endymion* (1818) to his memory. In France no less than England Chatterton was venerated, most notably in Alfred de Vigny's highly successful play *Chatterton* (1835) and the subsequent translation of Chatterton's works into French in 1839. In his Preface to the play, de Vigny affirms that his concern is solely with the poet: 'Le poète était tout pour moi; Chatterton n'était qu'un nom d'homme' (The poet was everything for me; Chatterton was only a man's name).[11] In *Stello* (1832), de Vigny attributes to Chatterton a definition of the inspired task of the poet.

Chatterton resta dans sa première immobilité; c'était celle d'un homme absorbé par un travail intérieur qui ne cesse jamais et qui lui fait voir des ombres sur ses pas. Il leva seulement les yeux au plafond, et dit:

> Le poète cherche aux étoiles quelle route nous montre le doigt du Seigneur.

(Chatterton remained in his initial stillness; it was the stillness of a man absorbed by an inner labour which never ends and which makes him aware that ghosts are shadowing him. He merely raised his eyes to the ceiling, and said:

> The poet searches in the stars the route which God's finger shows to us.)[12]

Friedrich Schlegel in his *Athenäum Fragmente* (1798–1800) developed the idea of the poet as the mediator of the divine. We cannot see God, but the divine is evident everywhere and particularly 'in der Mitte eines sinnvollen Menschen' (in the midst of a man of sense). The poet, whose task is to create and think in a divine way, and 'mit Religion leben' (to live with religion), mediates to the rest of mankind.

> Vermitteln und Vermitteldwerden ist das ganze höhere Leben des Menschen, und jeder Künstler is Mittler für alle übrigen.

(To mediate and to be mediated is the entire higher life of men and every artist is a mediator for all others.)[13]

Responsible in this way to his fellow-men, the poet becomes, in Wordsworth's deliberately religious expression, 'the rock of defence for human nature'.[14] The notion of the poet as prophet was deeply embedded in Romantic thought. The centrality of the Biblical tradition and the revelatory status of poetry in Romanticism were, to a large extent, the effect of Bishop Robert Lowth's *Lectures on the Sacred Poetry of the Hebrews*. They were first delivered as the Oxford Poetry Lectures in 1741, and published in Latin in 1753. Their influence spread to Germany when an annotated Latin edition was produced by the theologian Johann David Michaelis in 1758 (vol. 2, 1761). Coleridge used Michaelis's work extensively in the *Lectures on Revealed Religion*. Lowth's *Lectures* were finally translated into English in 1787.

At the heart of the bishop's study is the relationship between the prophecy and the poetry of the Bible and a new understanding of the 'poetic' quality of much of the Old Testament, born of his investigations into Hebrew prosody. It was a relationship repeatedly explored in Romantic writings. Shelley wrote in *A Defence of Poetry*:

> Poets, according to the circumstance of the age and nation in which they appeared, were called, in the earlier epochs of the world, legislators or prophets: a poet essentially comprises and unites both these characters. For he not only beholds intensively the present as it is, and discovers those laws according to which present things ought to be ordered, but he beholds the future in the present, and his thoughts are the germs of the flower and the fruit of latest time. Not that I assert poets to be prophets in the gross sense of the word, or that they can foretell the form as surely as they foreknow the spirit of events: such is the pretence of superstition, which could make poetry an attribute of prophecy, rather than prophecy an attribute of poetry. A poet participates in the eternal, the infinite, and the one.[15]

III THE CREATIVE IMAGINATION

Coleridge's classic distinction between the primary and secondary Imagination in *Biographia Literaria* draws directly upon Schelling's *Entwurf eines Systems der Naturphilosophie* (1799), and more generally is the culmination of a poetic tradition in eighteenth-century England in which the young Coleridge was immersed. His early poem 'Religious Musings' (*c*. 1794–6), on which, Coleridge claimed in 1796, 'I build all my poetic pretensions',[16] is prefaced by lines from Mark Akenside's didactic poem *The Pleasures of the Imagination* (1744). Coleridge had read deeply in Akenside's work. In his poem, Akenside divides the pleasures of the Imagination into two parts. The primary pleasures are connected broadly with the objective world of 'fixities and definites', the world of the Coleridgean faculty of Fancy. The secondary pleasures are linked more closely with the creative faculties of man, both sensual and intellectual. Akenside, it would be fair to say, would have found similar the idea of Imagination which

> dissolves, diffuses, dissipates, in order to recreate; or where this process is rendered impossible, yet still at all events it struggles to idealize and to unify. It is essentially *vital*.[17]

Thus Coleridge characterizes the secondary Imagination. In the writings of William Blake, the poet creates his world by the forming power of his imagination. 'As a man is, So he Sees.'[18] Blake claims that the Bible is both more entertaining and instructive than any other book because it is addressed to the Imagination (rather than the reason or the understanding), and the world of the Imagination which the poet realizes 'is the world of Eternity; it is the divine bosom into which we shall go after the death of the Vegetated body'. And so the poet Blake writes:

> I assert for My Self that I do not behold the outward Creation & that to me it is hindrance & not Action; it is as the Dirt upon my feet, No part of Me. 'What', it will be Question'd, 'When the Sun rises, do you not see a round disk of fire somewhat like a Guinea?' O no, no, I see an Innumerable company of the Heavenly host crying 'Holy, Holy, Holy is the Lord God Almighty.' I question not my Corporeal or Vegetative Eye any more than I would Question a Window concerning a Sight. I look thro' it & not with it.[19]

In the matter of the creative Imagination, recurring themes in Coleridge's poetry and criticism are common currency in the writings of the Romantics. His discussion of the eighteenth-century distinction between Fancy and Imagination in *Biographia* was pre-dated by two years by Wordsworth's extensive examination of it in the 'Preface' to the 1815 edition of *Lyrical Ballads*. The form of the dream which Coleridge employed in 'Kubla Khan', one of his greatest meditations on the nature of poetry and poetic creation, apart from his endless prose discussions on the phenomena of dreams in his letters, was used repeatedly by Keats in his critical letters. On 22 November 1817 Keats wrote to Benjamin Bailey:

> The Imagination may be compared to Adam's dream – he awoke and found it truth – Adam's dream ... seems to be a conviction that Imagination and its empyreal reflection is the same as human Life and its spiritual repetition.[20]

In France, Victor Hugo was writing of 'ideas' in a manner similar to that of Coleridge in *On the Constitution of the Church and State* (1830). No doubt both were writing in the philosophical tradition which was profoundly affected by the 'noumena' of Kant. But, while Coleridge was writing a political tract, Hugo in his 1822 Preface to *Odes* was writing of poetry.

Les beaux ouvrages de poésie en tout genre, soit en vers, soit en prose, qui ont honoré notre siècle, ont révélé cette vérité à peine soupçonnée auparavant, que la poésie n'est pas dans la forme des idées, mais dans les idées elle-mêmes. La poésie c'est tout ce qu'il y a d'intime dans tout.

(The lovely works of poetry of every kind, whether verse or prose, which have brought honour to our century, have revealed this truth scarcely before suspected, that the poetry is not in the form of the ideas, but in the ideas themselves. Poetry is the intimate essence of everything.)[21]

Another important Romantic theme, central to Coleridge's writings, is the principle of progression. A. W. Schlegel, whose work on Shakespeare in particular was so influential on Coleridge, sums it up thus:

Die tote und empirische Ansicht von der Welt is, dass die Dinge sind, die philosophische, dass alles im ewigen Werden, in einer unaufhörlichen Schöpfung begriffen ist, worauf uns schon eine Menge Erscheinungen im gemeinen Leben gleichsam hinstossen.

(The dead and empirical view of the world is that things are, but the philosophical view is that all is in perpetual 'becoming', is engaged in a continual creation, as indeed is, as it were, demonstrated to us by a multitude of phenomena in ordinary life.)[22]

It was this sense that progression and change were always to be preferred to mere dead arrangement which makes so much Romantic writing elusive and difficult to grasp. It further linked in with the notion of the poet as a quasi-divine creator, adopting almost the role of the divine creator. In England, certainly, it was something of a reaction against the eighteenth-century notion of the divine watchmaker, that view of creation and the world which states 'that things are'. On the other hand, there is no doubt that Coleridge encountered the idea of 'progressiveness' in his early heroes Priestley and Hartley, for it is one of the central ideas in their systems of necessitarian optimism. In particular it is prominent in Priestley's *Essay on the First Principles of Government* (1768) and *Discourses on the Evidence of Revealed Religion* (1794), both of which were used extensively by Coleridge in his 1795 lectures. Thus, as well as being part of a wider climate of Romantic theory, the emphasis upon 'progression' and 'organic' in Coleridge's later writings is a significant development from his ideas of 1795.

IV SYMBOL AND ORGANIC FORM

Friedrich Schlegel remarked in his *Athenäum Fragmente* that as Nature is organic ('organisch'), so what is most beautiful must also be organic. The same is true of morality and love. But it was his brother A. W. Schlegel who made the distinction between mechanical and organic form which was so important for Coleridge.

Mechanism ist die Form, wenn sie durch äussre Einwirkung irgendeinen Stoffe bloss als zufällige Zutat, ohne Beziehung auf dessen Beschaffenheit erteilt wird, wie man z.b. einer weichen Masse eine beliebige Gestalt gibt, damit sie solche nach der Erhärtung beibehalte. Die organische Form hingegen ist eingeboren, sie bildet von innen heraus und erreicht ihre Bestimmtheit zugleich mit der vollständigen Entwicklung des Keimes.

(Form is mechanical when, through external force, it is imparted to any material merely as an accidental addition without reference to its quality; as, for example, when we give a particular shape to a soft mass that it may retain the same after its induration. Organic form, again, is innate; it unfolds itself from within, and acquires its determination contemporaneously with the perfect development of the germ.)[23]

Schlegel's *Vorlesungen über dramatische Kunst und Literatur* (1809–11), delivered in Vienna in the spring of 1808, became widely known in England after their translation into English by John Black, the editor of the *Morning Chronicle*, in 1815. There is little doubt, however, that Coleridge knew them in German, since the passage quoted appears in a literal translation forming part of a lecture on Shakespeare, probably dating from 1808.[24] A further Romantic commonplace found in both Schlegel and Coleridge on Shakespeare and dramatic art, is the distinction between classical and Romantic or Gothic forms. Victor Hugo in his Preface to *Odes et Ballades* (1826), making the same distinction, criticizes the mechanical regularity of contemporary French architecture.

Une cathédrale gothique présente un ordre admirable dans sa naïve irrégularité; nos édifices français modernes, auxquels on a si gauchement appliqué l'architecture grecque ou romaine, n'offrent qu'un désordre régulier. Un homme ordinaire pourra toujours faire un ouvrage régulier; il n'y a que les grands esprits qui sachent ordonner une composition. Le créateur, qui voit de haut, ordonne; l'imitateur, qui regarde de près, régularise.

(A gothic cathedral presents a wonderful order in its naïve irregularity; our modern French buildings, to which Greek and Roman architecture has been so clumsily applied, offer merely a regular disorder. Anyone will always be able to make a regular work; it is only great spirits who know how to order a composition. The creator, with elevated vision, shapes; the imitator, who observes from close up, systematizes.)[25]

The artist, then, whether architect or poet, is inspired, a quasi-divine creator bringing life and illumination, revealing the secrets of divinity. In his essay 'On the Principles of Genial Criticism concerning the Fine Arts' (1814), Coleridge, linking art with what is beautiful, defines beauty as 'the reduction of many to one'.[26] It is, as he points out, an ancient formulation, and it links the Romantic notion of organic form with the development of the idea of the symbol, which, in contrast to the eighteenth century, focused on the individual and the particular rather than the general. Thus Novalis wrote:

Wie die Philosophie durch System und Staat die Kräfte des Individuums mit den Kräften der Menschheit und des Weltalls verstärkt, das Ganze zum Organ des Individuums und das Individuum zum Organ des Ganzen macht – so die Poesie in Ansehung des Lebens. Das Individuum lebt im Ganzen und das Ganze im Individuum. Durch Poesie entsteht die hochste Sympathie und Koaktivität, die innigste Gemeinschaft des Endlichen und Unendlichen.

(Just as philosophy through system and state reinforces the energies of the individual with the energies of mankind and the universe, making the whole to be the organ of the individual and the individual to be the organ of the whole – so does poetry with respect to life. The individual lives in the whole and the whole in the individual. Through poetry arises the highest congeniality and interactivity, the closest association between the finite and the infinite.)[27]

Coleridge, in his definition of symbol in *The Statesman's Manual* (1816) regards it as that which draws the whole out of attention to the particular. The poet, reducing the unmanageable many into one, sees in the individual, whether person or flower, mountain or natural phenomenon, something of eternity and the infinite. In the symbol, the poet fans the flame of faith, which otherwise is in danger of being 'buried in the dead letter, or its name and honors usurped by a counterfeit product of the mechanical understanding'.[28]

V RELIGION AND IRONY

Coleridge summed up his speculations about the one and the many in the familiar phrase, 'multeity in unity',[29] which is an example of irony, according to a definition of the term which would include any sharp or seeming contrast. What is unified cannot be multiple. But the dialect of irony, both as disintegrative of old relationships and perceptive of new relationships in apparently incongruous situations, of opposition and reconciliation, was a base factor in the Romantic definition of the essence of reality as 'becoming'. Such perception Friedrich Schlegel called 'Witz' (wit), and Coleridge the secondary Imagination. Caught in the creative dialectic of ideal and real, infinite and finite, Schlegel characterizes the 'Transzendentalpoesie' of Romanticism:

> Die romantische Dichtart ist noch im Werden; ja das ist ihr eigentliches Wesen, dass sie ewig nur werden, nie vollendet sein kann. Sie kann durch keine Theorie erschöpft werden, und nur eine divinatorische kritik dürfte es wagen, ihr Ideal charakterisieren zu wollen. Sie allein ist unendlich, wie sie allein frei ist, und das als ihr erstes Gesetz anerkennt, dass die Willkür des Dichters kein Gesetz über sich leide.

> (Romantic poetry is still becoming; that is indeed its true essence, that it is perpetually becoming, it can never be finished. It can never be exhausted by any theory, and only a divinatory criticism could dare to risk characterizing its ideal. It alone is endless, it alone is free, and it acknowledges as its first statute that the poet's free will submits to no law.)[30]

Schlegel's 'wit' is a willed act of perception, a process towards consciousness which epistemologically parallels the ontological process of change in the universe. It reflects the emotional longing for 'Fülle' (abundance), the boundless life which resides in the infinitely becoming heart of reality. Irony criticizes the misplaced emphasis on the fictions of the finite mind, and releases the imagination to link finitude with infinitude. Irony then becomes, in Tieck's phrase, 'Das Göttlich–Menschliche in der Poesie' (the divine–human in poetry).[31]

The force of irony residing in the tension of opposites, the Romantics developed the concept to convey their sense that the spiritual can only be perceived in relation to the physical, while the physical can only be understood in the light of the spiritual. And so, for Coleridge, while 'all our forms of comprehension are confined to Phaenomena, or objects of Sense',[32] human existence becomes barren and absurd when taken literally and without the illumination of the divine, 'the translucence of the Eternal through and in the Temporal'.[33] Yet it is through irony, also, as it unsettles and undercuts, that the fragment becomes a Romantic literary form of such importance, nowhere more so than in 'Kubla Khan'. For the fragment embodies the Romantic sense of incompleteness and restless progress; more than that it invites an active, imaginative response to pursue and reconstruct the lost whole. In the poetic fragment, the divine mysteries dimly beheld by the poet are revealed in a symbolic indication of wholeness.

The poet's task is a religious one. Poetic inspiration lays upon him the prophetic burden of mediating divine revelations to mankind. Coleridge's vocations as poet and theologian are therefore inseparable, and each is regulated by the discipline of the critic and the philosopher.

3 The Early Writings and 'The Eolian Harp'

On 14 October 1797, Coleridge wrote to John Thelwall.

> – I can *at times* feel strongly the beauties, you describe, in themselves, & for themselves – but more frequently *all things* appear little – all the knowledge, that can be acquired, child's play – the universe itself – what but an immense heap of *little* things? – I can contemplate nothing but parts, & parts are all *little* – ! – My mind feels as if it ached to behold & know something *great* – something *one & indivisible* – and it is only in the faith of this that rocks or waterfalls, mountains or caverns give me the sense of sublimity or majesty! – But in this faith *all things* counterfeit infinity! – [1]

The last phrase is found also in a notebook entry of late 1796.

> inward desolations –
> an horror of great darkness
>   great things that on the ocean
>   counterfeit infinity.[2]

It can be traced back to Coleridge's reading of Ralph Cudworth's *The True Intellectual System of the Universe* (1678), which he borrowed from the Bristol Library from 9 November to 13 December 1796,[3] having already referred to it briefly in the previous year. Cudworth writes of 'Number, Corporeal Magnitude, and Successive Duration', that they may only '*Counterfeit and Imitate Infinity*'; that 'there is nothing *truly Infinite*, neither in *knowledge*, nor in *Power*, nor in *Duration*, but only One *Absolutely Perfect Being* or *The Holy Trinity*'.[4] In his letter to Thelwall, Coleridge describes the 'unregenerate mind' of 'The Eolian Harp' (l. 55); which aspires to the one absolutely perfect Being, and which, for the Cambridge Platonists, meant the Holy Trinity or the first hypostasis of the Divine Triad of Plotinus.

Later, Coleridge was to conclude that in the counterfeiting of infinity, the particular and the individual provided intimations of the infinite and the absolute. He draws upon Schelling in the *Biographia Literaria* to demonstrate that within the flux of time and space, 'time *per se*' is compresent and the 'absolute self' supratemporal.[5] Moreover, his developing theory of symbol recognized that the eternal and universal is glimpsed through the particular and individual, and God in man, made in God's image.

During his early years he developed the habits of reflection and self-reflection whereby he learnt that 'in the component faculties of the human mind itself'[6] is the key to truth about man, the world and God. Such self-reflection is a necessary prelude to theology. It is closely linked also with what Coleridge later called his 'Polar Logic', which is already apparent in the early poetry, most particularly 'The Eolian Harp' (1795). This was initially drawn, quite possibly, from Jacob Boehme's earliest work, *Aurora oder Morgenröte im Aufgang* (1612), which, Coleridge claimed, 'I had *conjured over* at School'.[7] According to Boehme, the essential condition for all progression and creativity is the tension between opposed forces.

The notorious difficulty of drawing into coherence the wide diversity of Coleridge's thought and writings resides partly in his constant desire to bind all together and to aspire to the One, the absolute. Yet it does account for the linking of all his forms of thought to an underlying religious concern, for it may be said that the purpose of religion is 're-ligere', to bind together or rebind.

I EARLY RELIGIOUS WRITINGS AND *THE WATCHMAN* (1796)

Between February 1797 and February 1798, Coleridge wrote a series of five autobiographical letters to his friend Thomas Poole, outlining his family history and his own childhood to his schooldays at Christ's Hospital. The letters do not always agree factually with other later childhood reminiscences, notably in *Biographia Literaria* (1817) and in the notes which Coleridge provided for James Gillman's *The Life of Samuel Taylor Coleridge* (London, 1838). They do, however, provide an early reflection on his childhood which suggests how Coleridge regarded himself during the period of his greatest poems and shortly before his 1798–9 tour of Germany.

In the first letter, dated 6 February 1797, Coleridge refers with some amusement to the Methodist ' "Experience" in the Gospel Magazine',[8] by which he means the tradition of spiritual autobiography taken up by the Methodists in the eighteenth century, which includes John Bunyan's *Grace Abounding to the Chief of Sinners* (1666). Despite his amusement, the techniques of such autobiography contributed in no small way to Coleridge's own religious profession through self-reflection in both poetry and prose. Indeed, as his point of departure in his metaphysical and religious explorations is the fact of personal weakness, guilt and suffering, so Coleridge admits that the task of autobiography 'will be a useful one; it will renew and deepen *my* reflections on the past; and it will perhaps make you behold with no unforgiving or impatient eye those weaknesses and defects in my character, which so many untoward circumstances have concurred to plant there'.[9]

It was through such self-reflection that Coleridge came to recognize that the process of inspiration which the poet experiences shares much in common with the mystery of divine inspiration, that both are projected in images 'which cannot be decoded, but must be allowed to signify what they signify of the reality beyond them'.[10]

The second letter to Poole, of March 1797, reveals, in some detail, Coleridge's admiration for his father, a clergyman of sound and broad learning – 'not a first-rate Genius – he was however a first-rate Christian'.[11] Indeed, such was Coleridge's up-bringing that at the age of three, he claims, he was already capable of reading a chapter of the Bible, and in the next letter, dealing with the years 1775–8, his expanding reading of 'tales of Tom Hickathrift, Jack the Giant-killer, &&&&', was terminated by his father, who burnt such books.[12] They haunted the young boy's mind and induced day-dreaming. Coleridge concludes this third letter with some remarks on his childhood prayers.

– I suppose you know the old prayer –

> Matthew! Mark! Luke! & John!
> God bless the bed which I lie on.
> Four Angels round me spread,
> Two at my foot & two at my bed [head] –

This prayer I said nightly – & most firmly believed the truth of it. – Frequently have I, half-awake & half-asleep, my body diseased & fevered by my imagination, seen armies of ugly Things bursting in upon me, & these four angels keeping them off.

There is evidence to suggest that by 1794, Coleridge had ceased to say his prayers. Yet the nightmares continued, as his poems and letters bear witness, and would continue until the imagination itself recognized afresh the controlling patterns and images of faith in the prophetic role of the poet.

Despite his disapproval of the boy's reading habit, it seems that his father was particularly fond of his youngest son, and intended that he should be a clergyman. Samuel, however, continued to read of 'Faery Tales, & Genii', and reflected to Poole that it was this which established him in his life-long habit of endeavouring to see all things as a harmony, to see the One in the many, and to perceive the infinite through the finite and the particular. His mind 'habituated *to the Vast*' by his reading, Coleridge imperiously dismissed empirical evidences: 'I never regarded *my senses* in any way as the criteria of my belief.' He concludes:

> Those who have been led to the same truths step by step thro' the constant testimony of their senses, seem to me to want a sense which I possess – They contemplate nothing but *parts* – and all *parts* are necessarily little – and the Universe to them is but a mass of *little things*.[13]

The last of the five letters is chiefly concerned with Coleridge's experiences as a school-boy at Christ's Hospital. It is a prosaic and dry account, reflecting the misery of the lonely child, 'pent 'mid cloisters dim'.[14] Yet during these years, according to Charles Lamb, on evidence supplied by Coleridge himself, he was becoming fluent in Greek and unfolding 'the mysteries of Jamblichus, or Plotinus (for even in those years thou waxedst not pale at such philosophic draughts)'.[15]

In *Biographia Literaria* Coleridge claims that before he was fifteen he had bewildered himself with metaphysics and theological controversy.[16] Lucyle Werkmeister, in her article 'The Early Coleridge: His "Rage for Metaphysics"', argues that Coleridge's studies were prompted at an early age by his recognition of guilt and its resultant suffering. Certainly his sense of failure and inadequacy throughout his life was to initiate much self-reflection and established in him a deep yearning for strength, support and forgiveness. The end-products were to be the discussions of original sin in *Aids to Reflection* (1825) and the endless Trinitarian musings in the 'trichotomous logic' of the last notebooks. Werkmeister's explanation of Coleridge's early response to this recognition of guilt in his 'rage for metaphysics' (a phrase taken from Gillman's *Life*, p. 23) is less than satisfactory. Gillman records that this rage was 'occasioned by the essays on Liberty and Necessity in Cato's Letters, and more by theology'. 'Cato' is a pseudonym for John Trenchard and Thomas Gordon, and their Letters were part of a controversy between the

Newtonian apologist and correspondent of Leibniz, Samuel Clarke (1675–1729) and the Deist Anthony Collins (1676–1729). Cato's argument, in brief, is that human suffering is caused by vice, and that, of himself, man is unable to overcome vice. Coleridge, suggests Werkmeister, discovered the proof of 'Cato's' contention in himself.[17]

The problem was met, she continues, in his reading in Neoplatonism and particularly Plotinus' *Enneads*. In such juvenile poems as 'Easter Holidays' and 'Quae Nocent Docent', both composed while Coleridge was a school-boy, he is supposed to be following the Plotinian purging of the soul by 'virtue' through which it reasserts its original goodness. For according to Plotinus:

'Αρεταὶ μὲν διὰ τὸ ἀρχαῖον τῆς ψυχῆς, κακίαι δε συντυχίᾳ ψυχῆς πρὸς τὰ ἔξω.

(Virtues are due to the ancient state of our soul, vices to its chance encounter with things outside it.)[18]

Although Coleridge claimed to have pondered on Plotinus at Christ's Hospital, it is difficult to derive from his earliest poems more than immature platitudes such as might be expected from an unhappy yet undeniably talented boy.

> Yet he who Wisdom's paths shall keep
> And Virtue firm that scorns to weep
>   At ills in Fortune's power,
> Through this life's variegated scene
> In raging storms or calm serene
>   Shall cheerful spend the hour.[19]

If any consistent theme can be derived from these earliest poems it is of the helpless children of Christ's Hospital, worn by 'wan Resignation struggling with despair'.[20] Even at this stage, in one sense, Coleridge longs for a saviour, for the Lord who 'beholds with pitying eye' to rescue him from his misery and inadequacy. Yet, concurrent with this he believed in an extreme form of Necessitarianism which led to the abandonment of prayers and the presupposition that God has literally predetermined every detail of life.

> He knows (the Spirit that in secret sees,
> Of whose omniscient and all-spreading Love
> Aught to *implore* were impotence of mind)[21]

Between 1794 and 1796, Coleridge's poems proclaim, in an abstract manner, the principles of harmony, unity and optimism, governed by the law of Necessity.[22] Underlying the abstractions, however, is the experience of human weakness, so that the study of David Hartley and Joseph Priestley was never quite separate from a watchfulness of the life within himself. 'I do not *like* History. Metaphysics, & Poetry, & 'Facts of mind'... are my darling Studies', wrote Coleridge in 1796.[23] By 1797 he 'utterly recanted' the sentiment contained in the line 'aught to implore were impotence of mind'.[24] It was true to human nature and experience to offer *'petitions* ... to Deity'.

Coleridge's relationship with the thought of David Hartley was never easy, nor on the other hand was it an aberration which he later shed. Elements in the thought of Hartley were consistent with his long-term objectives and with what finally emerged from his life-long experience as a poet, a man and a philosopher. He was attracted initially to Hartley's model of human growth as the first clue to what in the 'Essays on the Principles of Method' was later explored as the 'principle of progression'.[25] For the model did suggest a crude vegetable analogy to human growth which hinted at a view of organic mental development answering to Coleridge's experience of himself and his own mind. It is possible also, as Stephen Prickett has pointed out,[26] to see the threefold characteristics of human nature – Prudence, Morality and Religion – as set out in the Preface to *Aids to Reflection*,[27] as a revised Hartleianism, reducing to three Hartley's seven stages of human development from Sense to Theopathy.

The paradox in Coleridge's relationship with Hartley between the system which does not precisely fit the individual experience finds a parallel in his uneasy response to the French Revolution. In May 1793 he attended the trial in Cambridge of the Unitarian William Frend which resulted in Frend's expulsion from his Fellowship at Jesus College. Frend had profoundly influenced Coleridge's religious and intellectual development during his undergraduate days, and the trial was part of the reaction against suspected radicalism by 1793, after the events of the French Revolution. On 21 January Louis XVI had been executed and on 1 February France declared war on England and Holland. Coleridge's political radicalism had been ignited by Frend and fanned by Robert Southey whom he met in June 1794. By September of the same year the two poets had collaborated in a drama in three acts, *The Fall of Robespierre*, wherein Southey reaffirmed the nobility of Revolutionary principles.

<blockquote>
never, never
Shall this regenerated country wear
The despot yoke ...
Sublime amid the storm shall France arise,
... she shall blast
The despot's pride, and liberate the world!
(Act III)[28]
</blockquote>

For Coleridge, however, the Revolution was the public expression of what was, in the end, a private vision. Kelvin Everest, in his book *Coleridge's Secret Ministry* (1979) has well expressed the relationship between private and public in Coleridge's radicalism. It

> starts with Southey, not the intellect, but the strong, sympathetic man. And much of his best poetry will grow out of an essentially private mode of vision, the deep self-absorption of complete domestic security; but it is poetry about belief, about value, and in this aspect its vision transcends the narrow limits of a basis in domesticity. We cannot understand the conversation poems in particular unless we realize the special resonance for Coleridge of the public in the private.[29]

By the early 1790s, public reaction against the enormities of the French Revolution brought suspicion upon Unitarians and any who seemed to share their dangerous intellectual and radical views. Coleridge's radical activities became ever more self-isolating. For his public pronouncements were generated by his individual experience and the intellectual attempt to come to terms with it, until the inevitable disillusionment led to a division between the stance of radicalism and the domestic, pastoral tone of the conversation poems, dedicated to 'Peace, and this Cot, and thee, heart-honour'd Maid!'[30]

Nevertheless, this ought not to be seen simply as a retreat from public life to domesticity.[31] Rather, it establishes the distinction and relationship between public life and the private life of the individual in which social experience and political theory begins; discovering the general in the particular or the infinite in the finite. It lies at the heart of Coleridge's theory of symbol and, in the later writings, of the discussions about Christ as both universal and the particular man in history.[32] The 1795 *Lectures on Revealed Religion* are his first sustained attempt to relate the nature of man as an individual and as a social being in the context of his views on religion, politics and morality. The *Lectures*, it seems, were written in haste and, in places, are only in the form of rough notes. They do however reveal the breadth of Coleridge's reading at this early stage, and that some of his later diverse developments in literature, philosophy and theology are implicit in this early material.

It is not easy to fix Coleridge in any single intellectual tradition in the *Lectures*. Of overriding importance in them is the psychological evidence offered in support of the truth of Christianity by David Hartley (1705–57) in his *Observations on Man, His Frame, His Duty, and His Expectations* (1st edn 1749; 1791). But he also used Cudworth's *The True Intellectual System* extensively, revealing his early respect for seventeenth-century English Platonism. The tone which characterizes the *Lectures* is well described by Coleridge in a letter to Southey as 'the pious confidence of Optimism',[33] drawing upon the Hartleian notion of 'benevolence' which, by the theory of association, changes love of self into love for family and, ultimately, all mankind. The manner of the enquiry is entirely characteristic of Coleridge throughout his life. In the Prospectus he describes one of the purposes of the first lecture as the establishment of the 'Necessity of Revelation deduced from the Nature of Man'.[34] The truths of religion must always be tested by experience, and mankind is discovered in the undertaking of his proper activity when reflecting Divine revelation or enlightenment. In the fourth lecture Coleridge writes: 'though I had never seen the Old or New Testament, I should become a Christian, if only I sought for Truth with a simple Heart'.[35] Christianity answers the deepest needs of human nature and is continually being adjusted to the capacity of its recipients,[36] for revelation is an 'optic glass' which assists 'without contradicting our natural vision' and enables us 'to see far beyond the Valley' of our present world.[37]

In one of his earliest notebook entries, entitled 'Sermon on Faith' (1794),[38] Coleridge insists that scripture nowhere contradicts 'Reason', and that Faith and Reason 'are all operations of one faculty'. Writing to Southey in October of the same year, he quotes Mary Evans, his first love, that '*Faith* be only Reason applied to a particular Subject'.[39] These remarks are entirely consistent with the 'Confessio Fidei' (1810), *Aids to Reflection* and *Confessions of an Inquiring Spirit*, subtitled 'Letters on the Inspiration of the Scriptures' (1840).

Another of Coleridge's concerns in the *Lectures* is the problem of sin and how it is to be dealt with,[40] raising the question of the nature of Jesus Christ.

That in the most corrupt Times of the Jewish state there should arise the Son of a Carpenter who in his own conduct presented a perfect example of all human excellence and exhibited a system of morality, not only superior to the ethics of any single Philosopher of antiquity but to the concentrated Wisdom of every Philosopher of every age and nation, and this unspotted by one single error, untinged with one prejudice of that most prejudiced people among whom he was educated is a fact that carries with it an irresistible force of conviction, and is of itself in the most philosophical sense of the word a Miracle.[41]

Again, and in a remarkable way, this draws together a number of themes which preoccupied Coleridge throughout his life, yet within the context of Hartley's 'system of necessity'. Human sin and failure, the need for redemption, Christ's identification with human nature, are addressed under an attempt to call up the theory of association in defence of Christian apologetics. For Christ's freedom from the characteristics of his age and its philosophical limitations breaks the law of association which would tie the individual to his period and its customs, and is therefore a 'psychological miracle'.[42]

Also from Hartley, but more from Joseph Priestley and from the intellectual Unitarians of Bristol, Coleridge learnt the notion of 'gradual progressiveness'[43] in the religious life. The sense of continual process, development and restlessness became a keystone of his notion of art as perpetually creative and de-creative, of irony as contradicting the temptation to settle upon finite conclusions, and of faith as a yearning in the finite being to reach out to the infinite where all coheres in the Absolute and the One, of which we now perceive but the many parts. In 1795, however, the notion learnt from Priestley was an important element in his 'optimist' philosophy, and in the writings of Unitarian acquaintances like the Revd John Prior Estlin of Bristol,[44] which Coleridge was soon to question and reject, as early as *The Watchman* (1796).

On 16 June 1795, Coleridge delivered a 'Lecture on the Slave Trade' at the Assembly Coffee-house on the Quay, Bristol, which was later reworked as the essay 'On the Slave Trade' in the fourth number of his short-lived periodical, *The Watchman*.[45] The Lecture contains Coleridge's first reference to the faculty of the Imagination.

To develope the powers of the Creator is our proper employment – and to imitate Creativeness by combination our most exalted and self-satisfying Delight. But we are progressive and must not rest content with present Blessings. Our Almighty Parent hath therefore given to us Imagination that stimulates to the attainment of *real* excellence by the contemplation of splendid Possibilities that still revivifies the dying motive within us, and fixing our eye on the glittering Summits that rise one above the other in Alpine endlessness still urges us up the ascent of Being, amusing the ruggedness of the road with the beauty and grandeur of the ever-widening Prospect. Such and so noble are the ends for which this restless faculty was given us[46]

In many respects this foreshadows the definition of Imagination in *Biographia Literaria*, Chapter 12. There Coleridge draws upon his later reading in German philosophy and develops what is here suggested in a more original way – the repetition in man of the divine creative activity, the combining of disparate elements and the ascent of knowledge by the exercise of the Imagination.[47] But in the 'Lecture on the Slave Trade' and throughout *The Watchman* it would appear that Coleridge's doctrine of progressiveness and 'the contemplation of splendid Possibilities' are secondarily derived from his early reading in Priestley and Hartley.

When he reworked the Lecture for *The Watchman*, Coleridge developed his discussion of 'Benevolence' as an element in creativeness, drawing directly on David Hartley.[48] Politically, he still believes in the progression towards perfection of revolutionary France, and that 'the juvenile ardour of a nascent Republic would carry her on, by a rapid progression, in a splendid career of various improvement'.[49] The language of 'perfectibility' (a word first used in 1794 according to the *Shorter Oxford Dictionary*) was in the air. It derived from Rousseau, Jean Condorcet (1743–94) and the French Philosophes, and had been already used in England by William Godwin in an earlier reference in 1793, in *Political Justice*. In *The Watchman*, Coleridge refers to the English translation of Condorcet's *Equisse d'un tableau historique des progrès de l'esprit humain* (1794).

> Let us (says Condorcet) be cautious not to despair of the human race. Let us dare to foresee in the ages that will succeed us, a knowledge and a happiness of which *we* can only form a vague and undetermined idea. Let us count on the *perfectibility* with which nature has endowed us.[50]

Indeed, 'optimism' seems to have been much under discussion in Coleridge's circle during 1795–6, and for Coleridge himself it was a religious subject. In *The Watchman* he wrote that 'they therefore who struggle for freedom fight beneath the banners of omnipotence![51] The image of calling in the Omnipotent to fight the inevitably successful battle is also found in the notebooks of 1795–6, and the poem 'Religious Musings' (1794–6), on which, wrote Coleridge in a letter of 11 April 1796, 'I pin all my poetical credit'.[52] This preoccupation might well account, in part, for his early attraction to the philosophy of Leibniz (1646–1716), of whom he wrote from Germany in 1799 that he was 'almost more than a man in the wonderful capacious of his Judgement & Imagination!'[53] In 1801 he still felt that it was worth his while to search out Leibniz's works in the Dean and Chapter Library of Durham. For in the *Essais de Théodicée* (1710), Leibnitz taught the basic agreement between the realms of nature and grace and the admission of the best possible world for the kingdom of God and for human happiness. He also recognized the principle of individuality proper to the concept of God and for man's freedom, which was threatened by the mechanistic pantheism of Spinoza.[54] This latter principle remained with Coleridge as a vital element in his rejection of the pantheist tradition, but in *Biographia Literaria* (Chapter 8) he renounces Liebniz's best possible world as 'repugnant to our *common sense*'.[55]

While Coleridge, despite his assertions to the contrary, never completely overthrew the doctrines of association, the seeds of doubt concerning an 'optimist' philosophy are sown in *The Watchman* itself, and their origins are in the literature and poetry of the eighteenth century. In the issue for 2 April 1796, Coleridge printed a lengthy extract from William Crowe's poem 'Lewesdon Hill' (Oxford, 1788). He had borrowed a copy of the work in a collection of recent poetry entitled *Poetical Tracts Vol. 3* from the Bristol Library between 2 and 10 March 1795,[56] and there are other evidences of Coleridge's attraction to and use of 'Lewesdon Hill' before April 1796.[57] Crowe, the public orator at Oxford, was known for his radical and pro-republican sympathies and his public support at least for the initial stages of the French Revolution. His radicalism was accompanied, however, by a dislike of mechanist psychology and Hartleian necessitarianism, whose advocates are denounced in 'Lewesdon Hill'. They set out:

> to prove that what must be must be,
> and shew how thoughts are jogg'd out of the brain
> By a mechanical impulse; pushing on
> The minds of us, poor unaccountables,
> To fatal resolution.[58]

Coleridge's references to Imagination in the 'Lecture on the Slave Trade', as progressive and moving towards perfection, may have been derived equally from Crowe's poem or from the poetry of Akenside, with which he was also well acquainted, rather than the 'optimism' of Hartley and Priestley. While the subject of the lecture is political, Coleridge's terms are drawn from the language of aesthetics and poetry, his description of beauty in relation to the Imagination recalling Addison's qualities of greatness, novelty and beauty. In Mark Akenside's poem *The Pleasures of Imagination* (1757), which commends these Addisonian qualities, Imagination enlarges the prospect until 'infinite perfection close the scene',[59] while in 'Lewesdon Hill' it leads 'by soft graduations of ascent' to increased knowledge and wisdom. There is another reference to the Imagination by Coleridge in a fragment of a theological lecture of 1795, which, again, rests heavily on the poets. Imagination is given to us by 'our Almighty Parent' as that which

stimulates to the attainment of real excellence, by the contemplation of splendid possibilities, that still revivifies the dying motives within us, and fixing our eyes on the glittering Summits that rise one above the other in Alpine endlessness, still urges us up the ascent of Being, amusing the ruggedness of the road by the beauty and wonder of the ever-widening Prospect. The noblest gift of Imagination is the power of discerning the *Cause* in the *Effect*.[60]

Once again, in a tentative way and like the very similar references in the 'Lecture on the Slave Trade', this account of the functions of the Imagination looks forward to *Biographia Literaria* in its description of an active power, related to the activities of reason ('discerning the *Cause* in the *Effect*'), and penetrating to the limits of human potential with endless persistence. It has a vitality which owes little to Hartley and Priestley, but is well represented in 'Lewesdon Hill' and *The Pleasures of Imagination*, embracing concerns moral, religious, intellectual and aesthetic.

It seems, therefore, that in 1795–6, Coleridge was alert to contemporary political and philosophical discussions of optimism, perfectibility and progress. Certainly he found much that was attractive in the writings of Hartley and Priestley, establishing patterns of thought that were to remain with him. Nevertheless, he was also learning from a tradition of English poetry whose concerns were similar. William Crowe was a political radical, but also a poet who questioned profoundly doctrines of necessity and mechanist psychology. In the prose of *The Watchman* Coleridge was beginning to recognize the importance of such questioning,[61] and, despite having declared himself to be 'a compleat

Necessitarian' in December 1794,[62] increasingly in his poetry of 1795 he was beginning to question the moral implications of Hartley's teachings even while Hartley remained as an important influence on his methods of reading and composition.[63] This is most evident in 'The Eolian Harp' (Aug–Oct 1795). Generally, by 1796 it is clear that the leading concerns of Coleridge's thinking throughout his later life are becoming apparent. A youthful concern for radical politics led to self-questioning and the examination of certain philosophical principles. This involved the realization of the importance of his vocation as a poet and of the perspectives of religion. Poetry and theology become increasingly interdependent and his writing is of a man who is trying to come to terms with the workings and complexities of his own mind. The habit of self-reflection is becoming established, and the religious life is more and more perceived as something 'felt'.

In a letter to John Prior Estlin of 26 July 1802, Coleridge states that his religious concerns focus upon 'the original corruption of our Nature, the doctrines of Redemption, Regeneration, Grace, & Justification by Faith' and that Joseph Priestley has become quite inadequate as a guide in these matters.[64] Christianity must deal with the practical problem of human sin and corruption, and the imagination, taught by poetry, can begin to furnish mankind with an insight into revealed religion. Already in *The Watchman*, Coleridge is beginning to recognize this,[65] and further to perceive the dangers of a dogmatic religion,[66] and, perhaps most important of all, to wrestle with the relationship of the individual and particular to the whole.[67] From this stems the central problem of the unity of the many in the One, the theory of symbol wherein the particular is necessary to render intelligible the general and universal, the ambition of the finite for the infinite, and the balance of opposites in the Polar Logic which became the preoccupation of Coleridge's last years. In the explicit Unitarian radicalism of 1794–6 is much unease and speculation which foreshadows his later religious and literary thinking.[68]

II   THE EARLY PREFACES TO POEMS AND EARLY CRITICS

Coleridge's first collection of poems to come before the public was published in 1796 under the title *Poems on Various Subjects*. Included in it were 'Religious Musings', 'Monody on the Death of Chatterton' and 'Songs of the Pixies'. The Preface to the collection is perhaps his earliest substantial reflection on the nature and purposes of his poetry, making two points which were later to be developed in his more mature verse and criticism.

First, poetry is the expression of a process of self-reflection which is preserved from 'egotism' and self-regard by a rigorous exercise of the intellect.

> The communicativeness of our nature leads us to decribe our own sorrows; in the endeavor to describe them intellectual activity is exerted; and by a benevolent law of our nature from intellectual activity a pleasure results which is gradually associated and mingles as a corrective with the painful subject of the description.[69]

This process was most comprehensively explored in *Biographia Literaria* and linked with a theology which recognized man in his true nature as made in the image of God. Second, Coleridge regards his public not in general but as 'a number of scattered individuals', every one unique and responsive in his own way. When addressing a whole, the poet must be conscious of the particular individuals within it, just as later a symbol was the necessary particular by means of which the whole and the general might be perceived and addressed. The One is only to be seen in the many.

Also in 1796, Coleridge wrote an Introduction to a privately printed 'sheet of Sonnets collected by me for the use of a few friends',[70] in which he describes the composition of the sonnet. He refers particularly to the writings of William Bowles whose 'Fourteen Sonnets' had been published in 1789, and the characteristic of the sonnet of self-reflection or the expression of 'some lonely feeling'. The brevity of the sonnet form enables the poem to 'acquire, as it were, a *Totality*, – in plainer phrase, may become a *Whole*'. Coleridge continues:

> but those Sonnets appear to me the most exquisite, in which moral Sentiments, Affections, or Feelings, are deduced from, and associated with, the scenery of Nature. Such compositions generate a habit of thought highly favourable to delicacy of character. They create a sweet and indissoluble union between the intellectual and the material world.[71]

In atmosphere so eighteenth century, these remarks do begin to intimate a unifying activity, and an interaction between the mind and the natural world which suggests an early approach to the later formulation of the secondary Imagination in *Biographia Literaria*, Chapter 13.[72] Finally, in this Introduction, Coleridge reiterates that the sonnet, inasmuch as it 'domesticates with the heart', becomes a part of the reader's identity and forces him to reflect upon himself and to perceive in himself the infinite possibilities glimpsed in the 'union between the intellectual and the material'.

In 1797, Coleridge published a second edition of his *Poems*, an abbreviated form of the *Poems on Various Subjects*, and with his 1796 Preface reprinted, largely unchanged. Poems of Charles Lamb and Charles Lloyd were added to his own. The Preface to the Second Edition is his first formal response to public criticism, and he is prepared to admit his faults. 'My poems have been rightly charged with a profusion of double-epithets, and a general turgidness', he confessed.[73] Much of this he has pruned away. Nevertheless, he denies the charge of obscurity, since an author is only obscure 'when his conceptions are dim and imperfect, and his language incorrect, or unappropriate, or involved'. Coleridge, looking back to Milton, Gray and Collins, claims that the difficulty of reading lies not so much in the verse itself as in the 'high and abstract truths' to which it attends by the exercise of a 'warm and rapid' imagination. To his contemporaries a poet may seem to be obscure, while future generations come to appreciate his genius. Coleridge was certainly not insensitive to his public, this criticism or disregard, but there is much truth in his identification of the purpose of his poetry for him.

> Poetry has been to me its own 'exceeding great reward': it has soothed my afflictions: it has multiplied and refined my enjoyments; it has endeared solitude; and it has given me the habit of wishing to discover the Good and the Beautiful in all that meets and surrounds me.[74]

Much in these early Prefaces of 1796–7 is suggestive of later developments in Coleridge's poetry and criticism. Further, these hints link his literary work and reflections to his increasing concern for theology. Poetry is a means of self-examination, of discovering the nature of the relationships between the self and the material world, and of glimpsing thereby a wholeness and an ideal which the aesthetic mind of the poet identifies with the God and the Beautiful, and which the later Coleridge regarded in a more theological light, as the infinite or the transcendent perceived in the secret places of the heart and mind of man.

All this, however, as Coleridge rightly recognized in 1797, was beyond the powers of contemporary critics to discern. Inevitably they saw him in eighteenth-century terms and provide a timely reminder that Coleridge learnt his trade as a poet in the traditions of the English eighteenth century. In those terms, a reviewer in the *Monthly Mirror* for June 1796 could write that 'Mr. Coleridge is a poet of the first class'.[75] An article in the *Monthly Review*, attributed to John Aikin (1747–1822), lavishes praise on 'Religious Musings',[76] which Coleridge himself felt to be something of an embarrassment by 1797, a poem merely derivative of the thoughts of others and turgid in expression. Reviewers do indeed criticize Coleridge for his 'bombast', his 'compound epithets' and his 'affectation'.[77] But their main suspicion is reserved for Coleridge's reputation as a political radical, and, whatever his poetic merits, he is, in the end, generally regarded as a young man led astray in politics and potentially dangerous if taken too seriously.

> It is not to be disguised [wrote the *Monthly Mirror*] . . . that he is one of those young men, who, seduced into a blind and intemperate admiration of theoretic politics, forget the necessary discrimination between liberty and licentiousness.[78]

Contemporary reviewers rarely perceived the real import of Coleridge's work, not least because it cut across so many of their assumptions and critical presuppositions. Inasmuch as he wrote in the traditions of the eighteenth century, they recognized his talent as a poet, but the great and original poems of 1798 left them bewildered. (There is some attention given to criticism of 'The Rime of the Ancient Mariner' in Chapter 4.[79]) It was left to friends like Charles Lamb to discern initially the significance of his writing. Increasingly in the nineteenth century the nature of his poetic sensibility and literary criticism was discovered in the context of contemporary theological concerns. Thus, the Conclusion of the present study will give some brief attention to Coleridge's place in the literary and theological concerns of the nineteenth century, and then, at more length, to a modern debate which involves theologians and literary scholars.

III 'AT ONCE THE SOUL OF EACH, AND GOD OF ALL': JACOB BOEHME AND 'THE EOLIAN HARP'

Much has been written about Coleridge's 'Conversation Poems' of 1795–8, and not least 'The Eolian Harp', first published in 1796. The remarks made here, therefore, will be limited to the specific purposes of the present discussion. In the 'Conversation Poems', principally 'The Eolian Harp', 'Reflections on having left a Place of Retirement', 'This Lime-Tree Bower my Prison', 'Frost at Midnight' and 'Fears in Solitude', Coleridge explores thoroughly the tensions between his public

and his private life, the community and the individual, and what 'is' and
what 'might be'. In 'The Eolian Harp' this exploration is made in the
context of a growing uneasiness about Hartleian necessitarianism and
mechanism.

It should, of course, be recognized that lines 26–33 were no part of the
original poem, and appeared only in the version of 1817 in *Sibylline
Leaves*. In many ways they now form the heart of the poem, illustrating
both that Coleridge's mature thought was a direct development from his
earliest work, and that there is an undoubted immaturity about the rest
of the poem.

> O! the one Life within us and abroad,
> Which meets all motion and becomes its soul,
> A light in sound, a sound-like power in light,
> Rhythm in all thought, and joyance every where -
> Methinks, it should have been impossible
> Not to love all things in a world so fill'd;
> Where the breeze warbles, and the mute still air
> Is Music slumbering on her instrument.[80]

The connection between these lines and those which link the music of the
wind-harp with experience of the universal, lines 44-8, is clear, but
equally clear, as Humphrey House has indicated,[81] is the lack in the
earlier lines of any close integration with the perception of the human
senses.

> And what if all of animated nature
> Be but organic Harps diversely fram'd,
> That tremble into thought, as o'er them sweeps
> Plastic and vast, one intellectual breeze,
> At once the Soul of each, and God of all?

Nevertheless, the outline of Coleridge's mature thinking is clearly
present in the earlier lines. The possible relationship between the 1795
version of 'The Eolian Harp' and Coleridge's school-boy reading of
Boehme's *Aurora* has already been noted.[82] In a letter to Ludwig Tieck
of 4 July 1817, he wrote:

Before my visit to Germany in September, 1798, I had adopted
(probably from Behmen's Aurora, which I had *conjured over* at
School) the idea, that Sound was = Light under the praepotence of

Gravitation, and Color = Gravitation under the praepotence of Light: and I have never seen reason to change my faith in this respect.[83]

There is one line in the 1817 version of 'The Eolian Harp' which clearly links in with this idea, 'A light in sound, a sound-like power in light', and specific passages in *Aurora* have been suggested as sources. Duane Schneider proposes *Aurora* X:11 and 15 as the original of Coleridge's 'sound–light theory', while J. B. Beer prefers *Aurora* IV:29 and X:1.[84] Despite Coleridge's claim of early reading in Boehme, there is no specific evidence of such precise references before 1817. Nevertheless, it seems highly likely that the earlier version of the poem was influenced by the writings of the German shoemaker. For in *Aurora* is revived the old alchemical sense of the mutual illumination of man and nature, and the correspondence between man and nature in Boehme provided for Coleridge a means of reuniting in his poetry human felings and intellectual processes, which were always in danger of dissociation in eighteenth-century poetry. In *Aurora* also, the heart, its energy likened to the rays of the sun, is the source of warmth, linked with the idea of the Son as the 'light' in the Father, and the Holy Spirit as the sense of outgoing motion.[85]

But it is to the reworking of the 'The Eolian Harp' and to the later marginalia on Boehme that we must look for the specific linking of such early hints to Coleridge's mature literary, philosophical and religious concerns. There is a detailed reference to the 'sound–light theory' in a letter of 12 January 1818.

Thus – I Prothesis
Chaos

2 & 3 Thesis and Antithesis = Light, and Gravity – or Matter, that is, phaenomenon imponderabile, and Body, phaenom. ponderabile et fixum: each necessarily supposing the other as co-existent and *in*existent or co-inherent. 4. Synthesis, in two forms, namely, Indifference, and (I want a *proper* term; but in the absence of a better, let me say) Combination. – For instance, Sound is to Light what Color is to Gravity – viz. Sound = Light under the predominance of Gravity: Color = Gravity under the pre-dominance or, as it were, the Dynasty of Light.[86]

Coleridge continues by defining the law of Polarity or 'the Manifestation of unity by opposites'. This, and the elaborate system of natural philosophy which Coleridge was developing by 1818, was heavily dependent upon his reading in Schelling and Heinrich Steffens,[87] although its articulate beginnings can be traced back to February 1808, the date of the earliest marginalia made in the four-volume 'Law' edition of Boehme's *Works* which Coleridge acquired from De Quincey in 1807 or 1808. The annotations continue as late as March 1826.

A note on *Aurora*, probably dating from 1808, defends the orthodoxy of Boehme on the Trinity. The 'actuality of reality' in the infinite Trinity lies beyond the power of language to articulate, and mankind, therefore, must recognize the inadequacy of its intellect.[88] Indeed the 'eternal and creative Mind' of God may be glimpsed by the finite, human spirit only in the discontinuity of the opposition of thesis and antithesis or 'the Ipseity, which in all eternity God realizes in the Alterity . . . co-inherently the reality of each other'.[89] Coleridge argues from Boehme that the fixing of the 'act of adhesion' to God in the will rather than in the intellect lies at the heart of the idea of God's 'personeity' and the denial of pantheism.

In these marginalia, however, he insists that he is merely recognizing in Boehme what had been his 'own original Conception' of Polar Logic.[90] Certainly he continued to develop the conception throughout his life, and it remained as the sheet-anchor of his mature Trinitarian theology. In the early poems, it seems, Boehme assisted Coleridge in the articulation of his reaction against the eighteenth-century poetry of 'sensibility', and in *Aurora* also he would find expressed his own experience of the fallenness of man and his desire to regain Paradise. The correlation between Coleridge's later poetry and his reading in Boehme will be examined in some detail below, in Chapter 6,[91] and in the very late marginalia in the 'Law' edition, probably dating from 1825–6, he continues to discuss at length Boehme's Polar Logic, the 'necessity of a Negative or re-introductive Principle in the infinite Nature', and to suggest that from Boehme may be elicited the 'true Joanno-Pauline doctrine of the Eucharist'.[92] Nevertheless, as a theologian he was not uncritical of Boehme, aware that his final Christian resolution must rest rather on a 'detailed commentary on the Gospel of St. John' – the planned climax of his never-completed *Opus Maximum*.[93] Boehme, indeed, paved the way, as Coleridge demonstrates in a note on *Aurora* in which he comments on the treatment of light in the creation and Incarnation:

That not Heat but Light is the Heart of Nature is one of those truly profound and pregnant Thoughts that even and anon astonish me in

Boehme's writings. ... The affinity ... of the Flesh and Blood generally to Light I trust that I shall make clear in my commentaries on the first and sixth chapters of the Gospel of John. Hence in the Logos (distinctive energy) is *Light*, and the *Light* became the *Life* of Man.[94]

In the end, however, the Fourth Gospel alone might prove that 'Christianity is the true Philosophy', while Boehme, along with Giordano Bruno and Spinoza, was to be considered among the 'Mystics and Pantheists'.[95]

In the marginalia to Boehme's *Works*, it must yet be admitted, are some of Coleridge's earliest extended meditations on the Trinity or 'Truinity' of God drawn from the principles of Polar Logic, and that in the earlier version of 'The Eolian Harp' the clear influence of *Aurora* can be traced. In a very private way, the poem is an example of Coleridge's early poetic ambition to provide a frame of reference which was theological and moral for a nation and world beset by upheaval and strife, and in which the politics of revolution needed the prophetic guidance of the poet, since 'the Bard and the Prophet were one and the same character'.[96] The tone of 'The Eolian Harp' is intimate and conversational, beginning with the description of a scene in nature to which the senses – sight, smell and hearing – respond. Via the image of the wind-harp, the description moves to the inward play of the poet's consciousness. The outer and the inner mingle in a delicate interaction of the physical and the interior, until a moment of vision is achieved, balanced between the finite particular and the infinite – 'at once the Soul of each, and God of all'. The poet finally returns to the nature scene, shared with his wife, with which he began. Coleridge made various changes in the published versions of the poem before the final form of 1817, when it was first entitled 'The Eolian Harp', but apart from the addition of lines already referred to, they have little bearing on the present discussion.

The term 'plastic', used in the climactic lines 44–8, was widely used in the 1790s, and was almost certainly derived from Ralph Cudworth and seventeenth-century English Neoplatonism, describing a formative and organizing principle within nature. In 'The Eolian Harp' and other poems of this period, this principle threatens to merge the personal, transcendent Creator of the Christian tradition with the 'Anima Mundi' of the Stoics and Neoplatonists which indwells the material world and all consciousness. Coleridge recognized that he was moving in the direction of pantheism. Thus, the final lines of the poem return to the domestic Christian piety of his wife Sara, an aspect, indeed, of his own mind. He turns from 'These shapings of the unregenerate mind' (l. 55), and to a religion which attends to man's need for salvation.

> I praise him, and with Faith that inly *feels*;
> Who with his saving mercies healéd me,
> A sinful and most miserable man.
>
> (ll. 60–2)

The Christian piety, however, cannot wholly deny or overcome the visionary moment, and, in some ways, Coleridge's life can be characterized as a continuing effort to achieve a reconciliation between the two. The struggle culminated in his mature meditations on the Trinity and in the attempt in the projected *Opus Maximum* to reconcile what Thomas McFarland describes as the 'I am' and the 'it is'.[97] 'The Eolian Harp' provides early evidence of the perception of a universal wholeness, 'the One Life within us and abroad', in the reflective act of consciousness, by which, through 'the universal Law of Polarity' reconciling the outer world of 'object' and inner world of 'subject', it re-creates the natural world within which it is itself created and of which it is still a part.[98] In the poem, the human and non-human world meet at the point of visionary consciousness, and by the imaginative act of the poet, the finite is opened momentarily to the infinite.[99]

IV   GIORDANO BRUNO AND THE *DE UMBRIS IDEARUM* (1582)

The Italian Giordano Bruno (1548–1600) was, together with Boehme, one of the 'Mystics and Pantheists' which Coleridge was to consider in the fifth Treatise of the *Opus Maximum*. He is referred to at this point, not because he was particularly significant in Coleridge's early writings, but because Coleridge's use of his work in the early years of the nineteenth century is a logical development from his earlier use of Boehme, and his transformation of Bruno points to his later Trinitarianism.

Coleridge first refers to Giordano Bruno in a notebook entry of March–April 1801, quoting from two works, the *De monade* (1591) and the *De innumerabilibus immenso* (1591).[100] In another entry of November 1804, he lists eleven works of Bruno, while in a footnote to *The Friend*, no. 6, 21 September 1809, he wrote that 'out of eleven works, the titles of which are preserved to us, I have had an opportunity of perusing six'.[101] It seems certain that one of these six works was the *De umbris idearum*, which is mentioned in the 1804 notebook entry, and quoted from in the Preliminary Essay 'On the Principles of Genial Criticism Concerning the Fine Arts' (*Felix Farley's Bristol Journal*, Aug 1814).[102]

Coleridge was well read in the Renaissance and Hermetic tradition of which Bruno was a representative, and aware also of its degeneracy and its pure origins.[103] Not least he was suspicious of its mysticism when separated from the Judaeo-Christian tradition, without which it was intellectually vacuous and spiritually distorted. In *Aids to Reflection* (1825), Coleridge categorically denounces any such private inspiration which is not linked to universal experience by the bonds of reason and scholarly humility.

> When a man refers to *inward feelings and experiences*, of which mankind at large are not conscious, as evidences of the truth of any opinion – such a man I call a Mystic: and the grounding of any theory or belief on accidents and anomalies of individual sensations or fancies, and the use of peculiar terms invented, or perverted from their ordinary significations, for the purposing of expressing these *idiosyncrasies* and pretended facts of interior consciousness, I name Mysticism.[104]

The *De umbris idearum* was Bruno's first published work on the art of memory, the purpose of which was to impress on the psyche particular images, organized in such a way as to promote the return of the mind and intellect to unity and a perception of the unity of the All in the One.[105] In the *De umbris* the universe is reflected in the mind as a religious experience, being grasped in its unity through an art of memory which arranges significant images and symbols. Thus the mind begins to perceive a coherence in all things, and through this unifying activity to experience a divinity at the heart of and beyond the particulars of nature. Bruno, an ex-Dominican friar, is ardently religious, but in the pagan traditions of the Egyptian mysteries, and in the opening dialogue of the *De umbris*, the book is presented by Hermes as a rising sun of Egyptian revelation.

Clearly Bruno's vision of diversity enlightened by unity, and of the One encountered in the All, was attractive to Coleridge. Yet he diverges from Bruno in that he retains that Judaeo-Christian tradition, to abandon which is to fall into the delusions of empty mysticism and pantheism. For where Bruno seeks the One, Coleridge seeks the Tri-unity, and where Bruno searches within the world for his principle of unity, Coleridge seeks beyond and above. Nevertheless, Coleridge's debt to Bruno is a further instance of his readiness to draw upon a wide diversity of material in the development of his thinking and practice in literature, philosophy and theology which may be traced from his earliest writings through to his most mature meditations on poetic practice and Christian belief.[106]

4 'Kubla Khan', 'The Rime of the Ancient Mariner' and 'Dejection'

It is not the purpose of this study to try and establish with any precision the historical origins of these three poems. 'Kubla Khan' was probably written in the autumn of 1797, rather than the summer as Coleridge claims in his prose Preface to the poem. Yet the Preface itself, which has so profoundly influenced the way in which the poem has been understood, is much later, and it was published only in 1816. According to a note which Wordsworth dictated to Isabella Fenwick in 1843, 'The Rime of the Ancient Mariner' was planned by Coleridge and himself during a walk on the Quantock Hills in the spring of 1798. On 23 March, Wordsworth records, 'Coleridge ... brought his ballad finished.'[1] A month previously, on 18 February 1798, Coleridge had written to Joseph Cottle, 'I have finished my ballad – it is 340 lines.'[2] In the *Lyrical Ballads* of 1798 it was 658 lines and was to undergo extensive revisions and the important addition of prose marginal glosses in 1815–16, published in *Sibylline Leaves* (1817). The earliest draft of 'Dejection' was addressed as a letter to Sara Hutchinson, and dated 4 April 1802. The subsequent drastic revisions of the poem have been examined by Herbert Read in his essay 'The Creative Experience in Poetry',[3] as the process of using control and order to enable the poet to regard his own confession; to adopt the perspective of spectator and artist. As Coleridge himself wrote in 1808, 'the spirit of poetry ... must of necessity circumscribe itself by rules. ... It must embody in order to reveal itself.'[4]

In brief, 'Kubla Khan' and 'Dejection' might both be described as fragments, while 'The Ancient Mariner' was completed only by a prose gloss which has the effect of unsettling the text of the poem itself. In all three poems there is a sense of a wholeness, vast beyond human comprehension, which the poet momentarily intimates in his imagination. The revisions tend to create new narrative levels which force poet and reader to become spectators of themselves as the poetry is experienced, and which open the way for a pattern of reflections pointing to an infinity, and to the glimpsed completeness and unity.

43

I 'KUBLA KHAN' AND THE TOMORROW YET TO COME

On the morning of Saturday, 14 October 1797, Coleridge wrote a letter to John Thelwell. It tends to confirm a note on an autograph copy of the poem in the relatively recently discovered Crewe MS[5] which contradicts in a number of ways the factual claims of the published Preface. The note merely records:

> This fragment with a good deal more, not recoverable, composed, in a sort of Reverie brought on by two grains of Opium, taken to cheat a dysentery, at a Farm House between Porlock & Linton, a quarter of a mile from Culbone Church, in the fall of the year 1797.[6]

In the first sentence of his letter Coleridge mentions having been absent for a day or two – the stay near Porlock – while the preoccupations and even language of the letter are strongly suggestive of 'Kubla Khan'. 'My mind feels as if it ached to behold & know something *great*' wrote Coleridge,

> something *one & indivisible* – and it is only in the faith of this that rocks or waterfalls, mountains or caverns give me the sense of sublimity or majesty! – But in this faith *all things* counterfeit infinity!

He concludes with some lines from 'This Lime-Tree Bower my Prison' (1797), beginning with line 38, misquoted as 'Struck with the deepest calm of Joy'.[7] The prose Preface is an expansion of the brief Crewe MS note with a lax concern for facts which suggests that its purpose might be other than simply conveying to the reader a sequence of past events. Rather, it prepares the reader for the experience of reading the poem which conveys sublimity through the images of caverns and exotic scenery, and then anchors sublimity in the more domestic setting of Porlock, for all things, indeed, counterfeit infinity.

The reader, drawn into the creative processes of reading, glimpses in his imagination on infinite unity, 'a distinct recollection of the whole'.[8] Yet it remains an intimation, for 'a person on business from Porlock' (ll. 26–7) will always arrive as finitude puts bounds upon the infinite vision. For all that a 'dim recollection' remains (l. 30), and that is enough to draw the reader back to the fragment of poetry with its mysterious indications of a vision that can never be fully recovered. The process is uncomfortably asymptotic, and the tomorrow is always yet to come.

D. F. Rauber has described the person from Porlock as 'necessary to create the illusion of the cut short rather than the stopped'.[9] That 'Kubla Khan' is a fragment may be a deliberate exercise of the Imagination; of the primary Imagination which repeats in the finite mind the infinite act of divine creation, and of the secondary Imagination whose re-creative potential must necessarily be incomplete and fragmentary.[10] If, as Rauber suggests, there is here the familiar Platonic or Neoplatonic conception of progressively more shadowy images or reflections of the full reality, there is also in 'Kubla Khan' and *Biographia Literaria* a clear link betweem Coleridge's poetic concerns and his later theological and philosophical interests which they both prompt and illuminate.

'Kubla Khan' begins with a paradise garden decreed by an emperor who is threatened by the past of his 'ancestral voices'. But the paradise which is threatened by Original Sin is found again by the poet and his vision which he has but to remember in order to re-create an image of the harmony and wholeness of the Paradise with which the poem concludes. In 1815, Coleridge wrote to Wordsworth that he hoped his poetry would have 'affirmed a Fall in some sense, as a fact, the possibility of which cannot be understood from the nature of the Will, but the reality of which is attested by Experience & Conscience'.[11] While, as will be discussed, one of the themes of 'The Ancient Mariner' is the problem of the origin of evil, in 'Kubla Khan' it is not the ontology of evil, but the theological task of the poetic imagination which is explored, as it 'revives' the symphonic vision and rebuilds Kubla's dome; paradise lost and regained.

Despite the oriental barbarism of 'Kubla Khan', it remains within the structural plot of the JudaeoChristian tradition,[12] and it is within this context that the echo of Plato's *Ion* in the poem must be placed.[13] In the *Ion* the connection is made between the poet and the divine, and the poem is understood as a gift from beyond the poet himself. Literally possessed by the divine, the poet embodies a mystery which must remain within the encircled sanctuary. Plato's Socrates says to Ion that:

ὅτι οὐκ ἀνθρώπινά ἐστι τὰ καλὰ ταῦτα ποιήματα οὐδὲ 'ανθρώπων, ἀλλὰ θεῖα καὶ θεῶν, οἱ δὲ ποιηταὶ οὐδὲν ἀλλ' ἢ ἑρμηνῆς εἰσὶ τῶν θεῶν, κατεχόμενοι ἐξ ὅτου ἂν ἕκαστος κατέχηται.

(beautiful poems are not human, not made by man, but divine and made by God; and the poets are nothing but the gods' interpreters, possessed each by whatever god it may be.)[14]

Kathleen Raine has looked in some detail into Coleridge's use of Plato's images of the poet who draws milk and honey from rivers in paradisial gardens as their souls fly from flower to sweet flower.[15] In two ways, therefore, Wilson Knight's interpretation of Coleridge's poetry in *The Starlit Dome* (1941) is to be distrusted. First, Coleridge does not distrust his 'secular inspiration' (p. 125), since inspiration is never actually 'secular', but linked with the divine. Second, his 'orthodox belief' (p. 99) cannot be said to clog his imaginative faith, since if Coleridge can be regarded as reaching an orthodox profession of Christianity it is through the experience of the poetic imagination upon which he reflected. Furthermore the structure of 'Kubla Khan' lies firmly within the traditional plot upon which Christian theology is set.

But we must be careful to distinguish between the poet who is possessed by a divine frenzy which is not his own, and the self who reflects and recollects. For as Coleridge deliberately establishes a number of narrative levels in 'The Ancient Mariner', so in 'Kubla Khan' he prompts reflection by an interplay between a number of perspectives or visonary centres. In the last stanza, for example, he switches from first person to third person narrative; the poet with flashing eyes and floating hair, mysteriously and divinely inspired, is distanced from the visionary (in the first person) who deliberately recollects and re-creates what once he saw. Different again is the dry and, one suspects, ironic third person narrative of the Preface. The effect of these parallel levels of perspective is to prompt the reader to reflect creatively upon his own reading, to perceive that his own limited vision and reductive rationality will supply a person from Porlock to cut short the 'dream' which is released and completed only when, in the third stanza, the imagination and creative powers assume command and the poet is received in holy fear and reverence, and the vision becomes a religious experience.

It is not precisely accurate to describe 'Kubla Khan' as being about the act of poetic creation.[16] Rather, as a deliberate fragment, it has as its subject the poet's consciousness of his process of creation. He is looking at his language, what it is doing to him and what he is doing to it. The perceptual process is obviously not a response to an observed, external landscape. The lush descriptions are rather the transformation of subjective, internal experiences into public objects. But neither is the poem simply an example of the desire of the human psyche to create objects. For as the language becomes active in the processes of reading, its metaphor of mental process is drawn back in a new, creative and imaginative experience. That which the poem describes would not be were it not for the poem-as-it-is-read.

By the Khan's decree, almost a divine fiat, is the pleasure-dome brought into being. The poet's dream or vision, conducting that act of creation through language, repeats the eternal act of creation in the infinite I AM, an act of the Imagination in its primary aspect. But the vision ends in a 'lifeless ocean' (l. 28) and the threat of the ancestral voices. It is picked up in a Coleridgean reconciliation of opposites, the 'sunny pleasure-dome with caves of ice' (l. 36), in an exercise of the conscious will of the poet: the Imagination in its secondary aspect, progressively de-creative and creative, revives the vision. The waking mind of the poet, both artist and spectator, turns the poem's subject into object, even to himself. The vision itself is extinguished - 'close your eyes with holy dread' (l. 52) – as the poet embodies an imaginative fulfilment of paradise where reconciled opposites are discovered to be one from the first. Thus Coleridge describes the poet in *Biographia*:

> The poet, described in *ideal* perfection, brings the whole soul of man into activity, with the subordination of its faculties to each other, according to their relative worth and dignity. He diffuses a tone and spirit of unity, that blends, and (as it were) *fuses*, each into each, by that synthetic and magical power, to which we have exclusively appropriated the name of imagination.[17]

The creative poet is no dreamer without will. He sets about reviving the vision of the Abyssinian maid in the third stanza of the poem. Later, in *Biographia*, Coleridge clearly criticized Hartley's associationalism as defective in the controlling powers of will, reason and judgement.[18] In 'Kubla Khan', ll. 37–47, the poet in the first person speaks in the conditional. His conscious will reaches out to a revival of his vision and the 'deep delight' which would result from it. Then at l. 48 comes the switch to the third person. By his own prophecy, as it were, the poet is made visible, distanced from himself. The creator becomes the spectator and self-reflection has resulted in a self-transcendence which points beyond the poetic fragment to a mysterious infinity. The blindness of the audience and the inward gaze of the poet's 'flashing eyes' looks forward to the blind old man of 'Limbo', whose 'eyeless Face all Eye' gazes within to a transcendent mystery, the divine illumination no longer a vision - for the dream is broken - but an inward experience.[19]

The preface to 'Kubla Khan', with gentle irony, shakes the reader out of a literal reading which fails to perceive that the dream and the fragment are metaphors for what is happening to him.[20] Like the prose gloss of 'The Ancient Mariner', it draws the reader into a participatory role which takes him ultimately beyond the prison of language and image, for language can trap things in its finitude. Its capacity to project an image of what is there may act like a person from Porlock, while the heightened consciousness of the poet may find, paradoxically, in his poetic creativity a release by language from language, so that it may begin to intimate what is not there, a glimpse of Paradise or the tomorrow yet to come.[21]

In his essay 'On Poesy or Art' (?1818), Coleridge describes artistic creativity in the man of genius as both an 'unconscious activity' and also 'according to the severe laws of the intellect'.[22] It is the 'co-ordination of freedom and law'. Mary Rahme concludes that:

> the symbols created by the artist are not representations merely of objective outer nature, nor are they representations of the artist's own subjective feelings. Rather they are forms created by the human mind *in the same way* that the forms of nature are created by the Divine Mind. The implication is that the artist is peculiarly fitted by his genius to achieve an insight into this process and re-create it in his art. Thus a symbol is both a result of, and, in a sense, a representation of, the artistic insight which inspires and guides its own creation.[23]

This dual nature of poetic activity settles it firmly in the central preoccupation of all Coleridge's thinking, that polar logic whereby one becomes two while yet remaining one. Without imagining polarity, the nature of reason is not to be understood, and nor is the nature of God, since 'God is reason'.[24] The apparent dislocations of 'Kubla Khan' – the person from Porlock, the Preface from the poem, the sunny dome and icy caves, the third stanza from the first two stanzas – reflect the two worlds of the poet, the conscious and the unconscious, or perhaps the conscious and the self-conscious. The fragment which is the conscious intellect creates the impulse to move beyond the broken form to an infinity, so that, in a sense, the poem never really ends.

II   THE TWO WORLDS OF 'THE ANCIENT MARINER'

It is recorded that Coleridge described 'the Rime of the Ancient Mariner' as a work of 'pure imagination'.[25] He dismissed 'the obtrusion of the moral sentiment so openly on the reader as a principle or cause of action'. The artistic freedom of the poem must be preserved both from a theory of the imagination encountered by Coleridge in his reading of

Kant[26] and from those interpreters who seek to impose an arbitrary pattern on the poem on the basis of preconceived philosophical or theological structures. Leaving aside any moral or interpretative imperatives, the narrative must be allowed to do its own work on its own terms, while the reader needs to become aware of the delicate interaction between the various levels of narration and the way in which this sustains two ontological bases of form, here described as the two worlds of the poem. Briefly, on the one hand, there is the assumption that society and the self, through art, are encompassed by an ultimate transcendent. Second, there is the contrasting assumption that, by structuring its life upon simple 'orthodox' religious formulations, society and the self appear to be self-creating and self-sustaining, paying lip-service to an imagined deity by a suitably respectable code of conduct. The ambiguous co-existence of these two worlds will be the subject of the conclusion to this section.

Although the close observation of natural phenomena and powerful physical detail of 'The Ancient Mariner' encourage one to agree with David Jones that 'the imagination takes-off best from the flight-deck of the known, from the experimental and the contactual', nevertheless, as 'pure imagination', the poem is a willed creation of the poet drawing little upon what has actually been seen or experienced in the world.[27] Furthermore, it eludes critics who would roughly clamp preformed philosophical or theological systems onto its narrative structure, systems in which it can more or less be proved that Coleridge was well read.[28] However, if such arbitrarily imposed patterns serve only to distort a reading of the poem, it is equally unacceptable to follow critics like John Livingston Lowes in *The Road to Xanadu* (1927) or Maud Bodkin in *Archetypal Patterns in Poetry* (1934), who argue that there must not be a meaning in the poem because any meaning we can guess at would be too petty. It is fantasy without meaning – the despairing conclusion of most of Coleridge's contemporaries.

However, it will not do to fight shy of 'meaning' in this way since, as a literary critic, Coleridge was well aware that narrative flows according to particular rules, and 'as rules are nothing but means to an end previously ascertained . . . we must first ascertain what the immediate end or object of the [narrative] is'.[29] During the course of the narrative its rules and object may indeed be hidden from our comprehension, since it could be said that more important than any predictable relation between events is rather the opposite – not that some earlier event leads necessarily to a later one, but that a later event requires, as its necessary condition, some earlier one.[30] This very hiddenness of the rules of the game can encourage the unwary reader into a grateful adherence to landmarks of meaning which lie temptingly on the surface of the narrative. Coleridge himself warns us against taking the simple rule – 'He prayeth well who loveth well' – too much at face value in his reply to the redoubtable Mrs Barbauld, who had complained that the poem 'was impossible, and had no moral':

> as to the want of a moral, I told her that in my own judgement the poem had too much; and that the only, or chief fault, if I might say so, was the obtrusion of the moral sentiment so openly on the reader as a principle or cause of action in a work of such pure imagination. It ought to have had no more moral than the Arabian Night's tale of the merchant's sitting down to eat dates by the side of a well, and throwing the shells aside, and lo! a genie starts up, and says he *must* kill the aforesaid merchant, *because* one of the date shells had, it seems, put out the eye of the genie's son.[31]

If 'The Ancient Mariner' *ought* to have had no more moral than this, the fact remains that it has, and that the Mariner's moralizing is, to say the least, uncomfortable in the context of the poem. Secondly, within its own confines, the sequence of the Arabian Nights' tale is unexceptional. Any interpreter – and therefore any reader – of a narrative will tend to impose constraints on it, structures of explanation drawn from the theoretical presuppositions of a culture or institution with their morality or religion, and which come between the reader and the text. Interpretation is therefore almost inevitable, but a 'pure narrative' in a work of 'pure imagination' will also play its own game against the interpreters, its art, triumphant in deceit, transferring the ground for hope in a sceptical and mysterious universe from structural orthodoxies to ambiguity and holy dread.[32]

One of the themes of 'The Ancient Mariner' is the problem of the origin of evil. In a letter of 10 March 1798 (two weeks before he completed the poem) to his brother George, Coleridge declares his belief in the doctrine of Original Sin and demonstrates his knowledge of Augustine's theology.[33] In a letter from Charles Lamb, written early in 1797, we learn that Coleridge was contemplating a long poem on the Origin of Evil.[34] Much later, on 3 November 1810, he wrote in the 'Confessio Fidei': 'I believe, and hold it as the fundamental article of Christianity, that I am a fallen creature';[35] and in a manuscript note on *Richard II*, of about 1810, he suggests that both dramatic and epic poetry (like 'The Ancient Mariner') 'are founded on the relation of providence to the human will. ... In the drama, the will is exhibited as struggling with fate ... and the deepest effect is produced when fate is represented as a higher and intelligent will, and the opposition of the individual as springing from a defect.'[36] This mystery, explored in the poetry, finds a different expression in the poet's post-Kantian phase of Christian philosophy and theology, and such writings as the 'Confessio Fidei' provide probably the best theoretical commentary on 'The Ancient Mariner'. It will be examined later in some detail. However, as Maud Bodkin has said, 'it is hard to force the meaning conveyed by imaginative speech into terms more precise than that speech itself'.[37] To the poem, therefore, we turn for enlightenment.

It has been remarked that, if read apart from the distorting critical effects of outside sources, a narrative will perform its own work on its own terms. Further, Coleridge asserted that narrative follows particular rules dedicated to an immediate end or object. In the note on *Richard II* he makes the important point that the narrative must have a narrator 'from whom the objects represented receive a colouring and a manner'. The narrative of 'The Ancient Mariner' operates on three distinct levels, over all of which Coleridge himself hovers ultimately and invisibly. These levels – of narrator, the Mariner and the reader – between them sustain the two ontological bases of form, the two worlds of the poem, one inhabited by the Wedding-Guest and finally embraced by the Mariner in his concluding moral of love for all things, and the other quite arbitrary and beyond his understanding or control.

The first level is maintained by the narrator, who, controlled by Coleridge as part of the complex narrative pattern, establishes the self-generating and self-sustaining world of the poem: 'It is an ancient Mariner'; 'There was a ship'. The narrator, by selectively choosing what we see, gives the poem its colour and ethos. More important, he controls the pace and even the sequence of events, in the basic fictional dimension of time, creating what Coleridge describes in *Biographia Literaria* as the peculiar logic of poetry. As compared with the logic of science this is 'more difficult, because more subtle, more complex, and dependent on more and more fugitive causes'.[38] Such logic can often be mistaken for arbitrariness, dangerous to the reader because its rules are hidden.

The second narrative level is represented by the Mariner himself who, with a particular and limited degree of self-knowledge, relates, as he tells his story, in a complex and often ambiguous way to the other two levels – the narrator and the representative of the third level, that is the reader. For, come what may, the reader, by making judgements and an imaginative response, is there in the poem as much as any of the characters. Like the Wedding-Guest he adheres to the Mariner as he tells his tale, while he drifts in and out of a relationship of trust with the narrator, who has a treacherous habit of misleading the too-trusting reader. Thus, the reader may ask, is it not naïve to accept the final moral that 'he prayeth well who loveth well' at its face value? Whatever the Mariner may say, it is surely not self-evident that God loves everyone. And yet the suspicion remains – perhaps it is right to be naïve.

It is both important to understand that the narrative is composed of words and therefore imaginary insofar as the words are divorced from any observable reality, and to perceive that its theme sustains a pattern of interpersonal relations in which the reader is inextricably involved. The machinery of the poem involves albatrosses, ships and lighthouses, but the machinery is not the same thing as the theme. Because the narrative is unreal and imaginary it is therefore a logically independent and self-sustaining world requiring the reader to indulge in the 'willing suspension of disbelief ... which constitutes poetic faith'[39] and to recognize the sometimes paradoxical and puzzling elements in a coherent whole. Everything – each consequential action in an ambivalent world – must be accounted for in the logic of the narrative. From the multiple perspective of such a world the reader may return to the apparent logic of his own, enlightened maybe, a sadder and wiser man, perhaps 'a little nearer Hagia Sophia'.[40]

The earliest critics of 'The Ancient Mariner' were almost uniformly hostile precisely because they were not prepared to undertake the necessary willing suspension of disbelief, and wished to grasp the poem in the familiar mould of their understanding and within their reassuring critical orthodoxies. A review of *Lyrical Ballads* in the *Critical Review* for October 1798, attributed to Robert Southey, complains that 'Many of the stanzas are laboriously beautiful; but in connection they are absurd or unintelligible.... We do not sufficiently understand the story to analyse it.'[41] In the same vein, there appeared in the *Monthly Review* for June 1799:

['The Ancient Mariner'] is the strangest story of a cock and a bull that we ever saw on paper: yet, though it seems a rhapsody of unintelligible wildness and incoherence, (of which we do not perceive the drift, unless the joke lies in depriving the wedding guest of his share of the feast) there are in it poetical touches of an exquisite kind.[42]

Finally, in the *British Critic*, the poem was condemned for 'a kind of confusion of images, which loses all effect, from not being quite intelligible'.[43]

The repeated demand is for the poem to be clear to the understanding and to carry a definable message. However, the tone changes with the criticism of Coleridge's friend Charles Lamb, and an essay attributed to John Gibson Lockhart (the biographer of Scott) in *Blackwood's Magazine* for October 1819.[44] Instead of wishing to control the poem by their understanding of its 'meaning', Lamb and Lockhart are content to be controlled by it. Neither try to make sense of the poem, as such, being not so concerned with what it means, rather with what it does. They describe their own responses to the narrative: 'I never so deeply felt' (Lamb); 'it is a poem to be felt, cherished, mused upon, not to be talked about, not capable of being described, analyzed or criticized' (Lockhart). But Lamb and Lockhart were aware that their approach was in danger of robbing them of any language at all with which to talk about the poem. Their experience of the devices of storytelling crossed the limits of understanding as they remained open to the affective power of the narrative. As Coleridge himself was to confess concerning the Christian scheme of things, Lamb and Lockhart might admit of the power of 'The Ancient Mariner' that it is a 'fearful Mystery I pretend not to understand – I cannot even conceive of the possibility of it – but I know that it is so!'[45]

Professor Frank Kermode in his book *The Sense of an Ending* suggests that the Bible and the theologians who seek to interpret it are attempting to give some coherence and shape, even a literary form, to the 'endless successiveness' of world history. The literary artist follows the theologians. Fictions, Kermode would say, meet a need, summed up in what Bacon said of poetry which may 'give some show of satisfaction to the mind, wherein the nature of things doth seem to deny it'.[46] The artist, in other words, plays a dual role, creative of a finite, ordered world wherein, simultaneously, an infinity of endless successiveness demands an acknowledgement of human limitation; demands of the artist a de-creation of his ordered world. Friedrich Schlegel, whose concept of Romantic irony will be discussed in Chapter 5, balances the artist between 'Selbstschöpfung' (self-creation) and 'Selbstvernichtung' (Self-destruction).

This duality is sustained by Coleridge in the fiction of 'The Ancient Mariner', identifiable in the two ontological bases of its form, the one resting upon an ultimate transcendent directing human life and society and the other concealing behind religious platitudes a belief in the self-supporting and sufficient nature of society and the individuals who compose it. A study of this duality is, in the end, a religious exercise, an exploration into poetry which is 'neither simply theological, nor simply aesthetic, but ... an indivisible union of the two'.[47] What is required in reading Coleridge's poetry is an awareness of his belief that poetry and all artistic narrative exists in movement and openness. It never reaches the poise of perfection, and points beyond itself to an infinity beyond the range of literary or aesthetic criticism. More precisely, a special type of attention to language is demanded in reading such poetry – to the ambivalences of the interrelationship of the images which are presented by a variety of narrators, and to the life inhering in a particular order of words. An attitude of faith is demanded of the reader, since, as John Coulson has suggested of Coleridge:

> For him the primary response to language is not analytic, but fiduciary. In religion, as in poetry, we are required to make a complex act of inference and assent, and we begin by taking *on trust* expressions which are usually in analogical, metaphorical, or symbolic form, and by acting out the claims they make: understanding religious language is a function of understanding poetic language.[48]

On examining in detail the sequence of events and images in 'The Ancient Mariner', it becomes plain that no simple chain of cause-and-effect is operative. Unless we are prepared to isolate sections of, and elements in, the narrative, the poem as a whole proceeds on the basis of an arbitrary and apparently discontinuous series of incidents. The dramatic context is established abruptly – 'it is an ancient Mariner'. A gulf is fixed between the merry world of the wedding and the haunted, dream-like world of the Mariner. As an isolated problem the contrast provides nourishment for critics who would wrench its 'symbolism' out of the context of the whole narrative. What could be more arbitrary than that? As the unfortunate Wedding-Guest, one of three, asks, why does the Mariner single him out? What has all this to do with me? The retiring reader may ask the same question, and yet be no less involved in the complex narrative structure of the poem. 'He cannot choose but hear.'[49]

Why does the Mariner shoot the albatross? Is it through sheer pathological misery or the wanton destruction of the possibility of affection?[50] Is it an example of Coleridge's belief in the Augustinian concept of original sin, by which 'an evil ground exists in my will, previously to any given act, or assignable moment of time in my consciousness'.[51] Perhaps that may be so, but it cannot therefore be linked into any identifiable sequence, since the result of the crime in good weather or bad produces a correspondent reaction among the sailors of approval or disapproval as it affects them for good or ill. One could describe the sailors as theologians and moralists in the mould of

Archdeacon Paley, in whose *Natural Theology* (1804) attention is given to the question of external evidences, to the almost total neglect of the content of religion. Paley's motive is to establish man's happiness. Consequently self-interest threatens to demolish morality.

After the killing of the albatross, the weather is, as always, unpredictable, open to any interpretation the Mariner, the narrator or the reader may wish to supply. Coleridge supplies none, respecting the weather for what it is. The Mariner's recovery from the worst of his depression in the blessing of the water-snakes is partial, a recognizable psychological and aesthetic necessity wherein the failure which is required for individual spiritual growth engenders a childlike sense of weakness and distress. Nevertheless, the recognition of love and blessing of the snakes is no great affirmation or example of the gratuitous operation of divine grace. It is not so much a step forward in a linear moral progression, but the necessary recognition of the irreparable damage which has been done and the first intimation of a platitudinous religious affirmation which is a statement of loss rather than gain.

But, apart from what can be recognized as a perfectly acceptable psychological drama operative in the Mariner himself, the poem is increasingly strewn with supernatural and gothic horrors which have their own logic in the drama of crime and punishment: phantom-ships with wraiths dicing for men's souls; the ship's miraculous propulsion; seraph-bands; earthquakes; and insanity in the Pilot's boy. On the one hand, the origin of these horrors may lie in Coleridge's contemporary reviewing of Gothic literature for the *Critical Review*.[52] In particular he had been reading J. G. Lewis's *The Monk* (1796) in which features a vivid 'flesh-and-blood ghost', a 'Spectre-woman ... who thicks man's blood with cold'.[53] He was not, however, one to be taken in by the 'perpetual moonshine of ... the literary brood of the *Castle of Otranto*'.[54] What, therefore, was his purpose in including derivatives of such nonsense in a serious poem, and how far do they relate to the psychological and spiritual crisis of the Mariner and his ambiguous recovery which meets so inadequately the vision of horrifying potential which has been glimpsed in human nature?

According to J. H. Green, Coleridge's admirer and literary executor, the 'great Coleridgean position' can be summed up thus:

Christianity, rightly understood, is identical with the highest philosophy, and apart from all question of historical evidence, the essential doctrines of Christianity are necessary and eternal truths of reason – truths which man, by the vouchsafed light of Nature and without aid from documents or tradition, may always and anywhere discover for himself.[55]

Although this was to be the basis for many critical pronouncements on Coleridge,[56] it will not do if the literary communication of 'The Ancient Mariner' is to be taken seriously. The ostensible faith finally declared by the Mariner that:

> He prayeth best, who loveth best
> All things both great and small;
> For the dear God who loveth us,
> He made and loveth all –
>
> (ll. 614–17)

may certainly imply that traditional Christian doctrine and morality may be made manageable within the reasonable confines and constitution of human experience and the human mind. It was taken into Victorian hymnody and the Victorian sense of a Christian dispensation undergirding a well-structured society in which God confirms the rich man in his castle and the poor man at his gate. Of 'all things bright and beautiful', Mrs C. F. Alexander (1818–95) would say, in words very reminiscent of the Mariner:

> He gave us eyes to see them,
> And lips that we might tell
> How great is God Almighty,
> Who has made all things well.

In the Mariner's experience, however, the world is indubitably unfair and hostile. It has been suggested that the inconsequential nature of the Mariner's progression from abject misery and grief in guilt to a partial recovery which carries with it a need for periodic confession, is psychologically perfectly comprehensible. Some device is required to enable us to cope with a world so full of menace and threat. The sense in the Wedding-Guest and the Mariner himself of being unfairly singled out was well known to Coleridge in his unfortunate life. At the end of his poem 'The Pains of Sleep' (1803), he wrote pathetically and childishly:

> Such griefs with such men well agree.
> But wherefore, wherefore fall on me?
> To be beloved is all I need,
> And whom I love, I love indeed.[57]

Petulant this may seem, yet do we not convince ourselves of the genuinesness of our love for others, and the purity of our motives? Like the Mariner, do we not enfold our self-justification in the guarantee of religious respectability? Such a process of self-questioning is important for each reader since each partakes of the narrative structure of the poem. As Coleridge wrote in 'Dejection':

> we receive but what we give
> And in our life alone does Nature live.[58]

The change in the Mariner stems from a changed attitude to himself: the response of the reader will be conditioned by the reader's attitude to himself. Yet odd forces are at work in the narrative, obscuring the familiar landscape of experience from which that attitude draws its customary shape and logic.

For whatever the Mariner says, and quite possibly believes, it is quite clear that the 'dear God who loveth us' is, in the context of the poem, a deity with an independent mind and will whose expression of love for his creation is, to say the least, ambivalent. Why should the sailors all die while the Mariner suffers only – after the throw of a dice – Life-in-Death? Why, indeed, should God have allowed the albatross to suffer such a fate? What relation does this trusted and loving God have with the Polar Spirit and his fellow daemons who grimly threaten the Mariner, but lately relieved of the albatross about his neck, with 'penance more' (1. 409)? What is the objective correlative of the phantoms which people the poem and which do, undeniably, have a physical effect on the narrative, providing, if nothing more, physical propulsion for the ship's homeward journey. No theory of psychological discontinuity is sufficient to embrace this world of spirit effects which, however hard we may try to account for them, lie outside the concluding psychological package conveyed in the Mariner's closing words. Nor is it sufficient to claim that, after all, man cannot bear very much reality, for the experience of the Mariner is more than he is prepared to admit in his own narrative, an experience under the domination of a metaphysic more profound than the concluding 'Christian' affirmation. What doctrine of the Fall and Redemption through Grace there is in the poem, is mysterious and laden with paradox, bearing within it an agony of repetition 'at an uncertain hour', and if wisdom yet also sadness.

But if this pattern of Fall and Redemption in 'The Ancient Mariner' bears no simple religious affirmation, yet neither is it irretrievably fractured because it cannot sustain Green's 'great Coleridgean position' of poetry regarded as deducible from the constitution of the human mind. It should not be regarded simply as an exploration into the psychological origins of guilt and suffering,[59] but as a literary exercise illustrative of the poet's power to convey the paradoxes and dualism of the religious experience which is balanced between the transcendent and the imminent and lies at the heart of other pairs of words which Coleridge took and developed from his eighteenth-century inheritance or reading of Kant – fancy/imagination; understanding/reason. His approach to words and language is profoundly significant for his sense of the religious experience, and thus it behoves the critic to attend to the literary and narrative techniques of 'The Ancient Mariner' which contribute to its total effect and sense, and which link it with the whole corpus of Coleridge's writings on religion.

The interwoven and interdependent three narrative levels of narrator, Mariner and the internal contribution of the reader, constitute a rhetoric, a 'unity in multeity' which represents in poetic terms an all-pervading moral – religious – philosophical preoccupation in Coleridge's writings. A symbol, for Coleridge, focuses two separate levels of existence – eternal and temporal, universal and individual[60] – corresponding to the two ontological bases of form of 'The Ancient Mariner'. It achieves this through the exercise of the Imagination, which makes a coherent whole of what appears to be disparate, or, as Coleridge described the secondary Imagination, 'dissolves, diffuses, dissipates in order to recreate'.[61] Second, in his theory of the Imagination, Coleridge extended Kant's discussion of what is primarily a representational faculty to one which is creative, shaping the world as it is experienced. The wholly created world of 'The Ancient Mariner' takes its power and authority from its independence as a poetic structure which is purely of the imagination, standing over against the outside world and society of the reader. Professor Nicholas Lash in his book *Theology on Dover Beach* (1979) provides another model which illuminates the distinction between Kant and Coleridge on the imagination. Giving two dimensions to the human quest for meaning and truth, explanation and control (equivalent to the Kantian bondage to the world of things, which Coleridge called 'It is') are replaced by understanding – though not in Coleridge's limited sense of the word – and interpretation (which Coleridge called 'I am'). Such knowledge involves the commitment, openness and risk of poetic creativity. Professor Lash concludes:

And it is not only in respect of our relationship with other human individuals that the model of loving attention, of contemplative wonder, is more appropriate than the model of explanation and control. Something similar is the case where those forms of the quest for truth characteristic of, for example, the poet, the artist or the novelist are concerned.[62]

This creative energy which is released in the poetry remained an important element in every aspect of Coleridge's later religious writings, related closely to his thoughts on the nature of divine creativity and revelation. As, at one level, the narrative of 'The Ancient Mariner' is propelled mysteriously and beyond the comprehension or control of the protagonists, so in a letter of late April 1814, Coleridge accepts the Christian faith 'not as deduced from human reason, in its grovelling capacity for comprehending spiritual things, but as the clear revelation of Scripture'.[63] This limitation of human reason and understanding in the mysteries of religion is dealt with at some length in the 'Confessio Fidei', which is largely concerned with a matter central to the theme of 'The Ancient Mariner' – the problem of sin and moral guilt. The Mariner cannot comprehend the mystery in which he plays a central part. 'I am born', writes Coleridge in the 'Confessio', 'a child of Wrath. This fearful Mystery I pretend not to understand.'

Nevertheless, the Mariner's conclusion, inadequate though it may be, is important as a constructed means of coming to terms with a forbidding, incomprehensible pattern of events. Nor can this latter 'religious' level be altogether endured without some psychological explanation. Neither world of the poem seems satisfactory within its own terms without the other. As Coleridge wrote in *Confessions of an Inquiring Spirit* (1840): 'all Power manifests itself in the harmony of correspondent Opposites, each supposing and supporting the other'.[64]

In 1843, Wordsworth dictated a series of comments on his poetry to Isabella Fenwick, and in remarks attached to 'We are Seven' reveals how extensive his part was in the initial stages of the composition of 'The Ancient Mariner'. It was Wordsworth who had been reading George Shelvocke's *A Voyage Round the World by Way of the Great South Sea* (London, 1726), which suggested to him the incident of the albatross. No doubt elaborated from Coleridge's reading in contemporary Gothic literature, the 'skeleton ship, with figures in it' was first hinted at in a dream of his friend John Cruikshank.[65] Perhaps more important than a survey of such immediate literary and personal sources, many of which lie obscurely in Coleridge's vast reading of seventeenth- and eighteenth-century books of travel, however, would be an attempt to reconstruct the secret purposes of the poem, and its place in a tradition of creative writing and philosophy. Contemporary events also played their part in its creation and development.

In a notebook entry of late 1796, Coleridge revealed that the mutiny

on board *HMS Bounty* in 1789 had not passed him unnoticed. The guilt
of the mutineer Fletcher Christian and his subsequent wanderings,
coupled with the terrible voyage of Captain Bligh, cast adrift on the
South Seas in an open boat, find mention in notebook, letters and finally
'The Ancient Mariner'. The 1796 note is no. 22 of a list of projected
works, and reads 'Adventures of CHRISTIAN, the mutineer.[66] Coupled
with it, as no. 16, is a plan to write 'a dissection of Atheism', which is
described as 'an outcast of blind Nature ruled by a fatal Necessity – Slave
of an ideot Nature!' In a letter almost exactly contemporary with the
notebook entry, Coleridge laments upon his lack of domestic stability:
'What am I to do then? – I shall be again afloat on the wide sea unpiloted
and unprovisioned.[67] Such was exactly the plight of Captain Bligh. The
letter links these references to the later poem ('Alone on a wide wide
sea!') and suggest, through the name of Fletcher Christian, that it may be
read as something of a pilgrim's progress, the story of a Christian soul
who rebels, becomes an 'outcast of blind Nature' and eventually
struggles back to a form of Christian affirmation. The clearest evidence
for this reading, which provides not a theme but only matter for a theme,
is supplied by the marginal glosses first published in *Sibylline Leaves*
(1817). They do not form part of the narrative itself, for its autonomy as
a work of pure imagination is always to be respected, but are Coleridge's
later contributions to providing a consciously religious framework.
Indeed, they could be regarded as Coleridge adding another layer to the
fabric of the work, to be seen not as a commentary on it so much as a
further interwoven strand balanced within its existing texture. Other
references in the marginal glosses link the poem to certain learned
traditions, perhaps most significantly that of 'the Platonic Constanti-
nopolitan, Michael Psellus'.[68]

A direct link was established between Coleridge's extensive knowledge of the work of the Cambridge Platonists and his poem with the
addition in 1817 as an epigraph, of an adapted quotation from Thomas
Burnet's *Archaeologicae Philosophicae sive Doctrina Antiqua De Rerum
Originibus* (London, 1692). Burnet was an admiring pupil of Ralph
Cudworth (1617–88), whose *True Intellectual System* (1678) was well
known to Coleridge. A translation of the Latin reads:

> I can readily believe that there are more invisible than visible natures
> in the universe of things. But who shall explain their family, their
> orders, relationships, the stations and functions of each? What do
> they do? Where do they live? Human nature has always sought after
> knowledge of these things, but has never attained it. Meanwhile, I do

not deny the pleasure it is to contemplate in thought, as though in a picture, the image of a better and greater world: lest the mind, habituating itself to the trivia of life, should become too narrow, and subside completely into trivial thoughts only. But, at the same time we must be vigilant for truth, and set a limit, so that we can distinguish the certain from the uncertain and night from day.[69]

Coleridge echoed Burnet in a profound belief in a world beyond human observation and conception, and in an approach to it through the 'shaping spirit of Imagination'. Despite the well-established tradition of the imagination as a representational and reproductive faculty upon which Kant drew, Coleridge's creative imagination has a place in English eighteenth-century poetry. Apart from Joseph Addison's ode 'The Spacious Firmament on high', inspired by Newton and the Nineteenth Psalm,[70] James Thomson (1700–48) in *The Castle of Indolence* (1748) portrays the fate of those whoses senses have quite overcome the creative will.

> Each sound too here, to languishment inclin'd,
> Lull'd the weak bosom, and induced ease ...
> ... Entangled deep in its enchanting snares,
> The listening heart forgot all duties and all cares.[71]

The Nightmare Life-in-Death whom the Mariner encounters, and by whom he is won as she dices with Death, brings with her an enslavement of the will to act and all freedom of creative, emotional response. The equivalent in 'Dejection' is the drying up of the poet's creative responses, a death-in-life 'which finds no natural outlet, no relief' (l. 23). In that Ode, things take life from 'the eddying of [the] living soul', the creative imagination enduing them with joy and freedom. To experience its drying up is to experience a living death.

This doctrine of creative 'joy', which the Mariner faintly begins to rediscover in the beauty and happiness of the water-snakes, lay embedded in the tradition of Christian Neoplatonism from which the epigraph by Thomas Burnet is drawn, and in which Milton played a major poetic role. In Milton's 'At a Solemn Music' (?1633) the World Music which was heard in Eden before the Fall is even now occasionally audible and can lead us to glimpse the prelapsarian state of paradise. The doctrine, conserved by the Cambridge Platonists, found echoes in eighteenth-century literature in Addison, Thomson and Akenside, who each subscribed to the intellectual tradition which believed that man has, or ought to have, a responsive 'music in himself'. Their heirs were Coleridge and Wordsworth who developed their own doctrine of creative 'joy', in which the 'pure imagination' of Coleridge achieved the most radical expression of the self as primary in creative activity. In Mark Akenside's poem *The Pleasures of the Imagination* (1744) and in Addison, on whom Akenside drew heavily, the Neoplatonist tradition, combined with a reconciliation of modern thought and classical-Christian values, was formative in establishing a relationship between 'joy' and creativity which Coleridge employed extensively.

This linking of 'The Ancient Mariner' as a poem of 'pure imagination' with a tradition of Christian Neoplatonism is of crucial importance for the theme of the two worlds of the poem. Professor McFarland in his book *Romanticism and the Forms of Ruin* (1981) establishes the distinction between Kant and Coleridge. McFarland links the Imagination which can almost be equated with memory with art in the mimetic mode, of which the godfather is Aristotle. The mimetic mode reproduces and to some extent focuses experienced reality.[72] Coleridge's creative imagination, however, produces what McFarland calls meontic art, of which the ontological basis is veiled in origins deeper than perception or observed experience. To describe this, he employs a phrase of Plato, the godfather of meontic art, in the *Theaetetus*, which speaks of the philosopher as investigating 'the being of everything that is', in the process searching 'below the earth' and 'beyond the heavens (οὐρανοῦ τε ὑπερ)'.[73] It is from the basis of such statements that Plato issues his denials that mimetic poets are really concerned with the truth. McFarland quotes Karl Jaspers' book *Plato and Augustine* (1962) to summarize the nature of meontic art.

'Thus Plato knows two worlds: the world of Ideas and that of the senses, the world of being and that of becoming, the noetic (intelligible) world and the world of appearances.'

The cognizance of 'two worlds', with the second one as the dwelling place of 'true being', generates the meontic mode in art. The 'places beyond the heavens' relates to our concerns here and at the same time transcends them. But it must be understood as no less real than the things that surround us; otherwise, the realm of meontic art becomes a pure fiction.[74]

These two worlds are present in 'The Rime of the Ancient Mariner', the one partially grasped in the Mariner's psychological affirmation of unity and community which falls short of the other, a mystery of religion which escapes any theoretical formulation or control by doctrine. In the resulting dualism, only the poetic imagination in the context of the narrative and literary structures of the poem can begin to focus and bring coherence to the different levels. For theory cannot embrace the two worlds which do not simply coexist, one a shadow above the other. Since finite human beings, infinitely ironic and self-questioning, can never fully comprehend that infinite becoming, between aspiration and realization there must be a radical break. For now the Mariner's formulations of community remain a psychological necessity, while yet in the imagination 'the exalted Christ must be seen as an ideal symbol of hope'.[75]

The problem of historicity in the Christian context of Coleridgean 'symbol' will be examined in Chapter 7. Among his notes on Shakespeare, Coleridge comments on the need for 'poetic faith' in reading dramatic narrative, before which 'our common notions of philosophy give way ...: this feeling may be said to be much stronger than historic faith'.[76] The effect of the Weird Sisters on Macbeth and their limiting of the freedom of his moral will by encouraging him to limit and attempt to control an equivocal future, create a double perspective similar to that in 'The Ancient Mariner'.

> That I have assigned the true reason for the first appearance of the Weird Sisters as the key-note of the character of the whole play is proved by the re-entrance of the sisters, after such an order of the king's as establishes their supernatural powers of information. Yet still it was information: 'king hereafter' was still contingent, still in Macbeth's moral will, though if he yielded to the temptation and thus forfeited his free-agency, then the link of cause and effect 'more physico' would commence; and thus likewise the prophetic visions afterwards in the fourth act. I surely need not say that the *general* idea is all that can be required from the poet, not a scholastic logical consistency in all the parts so as to meet metaphysical objections.[77]

Coleridge succinctly expresses the interrelatedness of levels which preserve in the dramatic narrative the freedom from the necessitarian chain of cause and effect, the delicate network of supernatural powers and moral will – albeit tainted – which preserves its apparently arbitrary and inconsequential pattern. Macbeth, like the Mariner, exists under the shadow of a disturbing dualism, in the realm of the noetic and the world of appearances. The Weird Sisters, like the supernatural agencies in Coleridge's poem, impose themselves upon Macbeth's moral will in a highly ambiguous way: the supernatural world continually leads us back to the moral, while the moral repeatedly acknowledges the power of the supernatural. Macbeth, of course, unlike the Mariner, never finally comes to rest in a psychological compromise which enables him at least to endure a relationship with the world 'beyond the heavens'. He does, however, experience the tragic conflict between the two worlds of supernatural agencies and his defiant moral will which, in Coleridge, despite the final apparently placid words of the Mariner, leaves the Wedding-Guest forlorn, and establishes the language of revelation and religious experience as stretched between two ultimately irreconcilable spheres, vibrant, numinous and free from platitude or sterile doctrine.

III 'A NEW EARTH AND NEW HEAVEN': 'DEJECTION: AN ODE'

In his marginalia on John Petvin's _Letters Concerning Mind: To which is added a sketch of universal arithmetic_ (London, 1750), Coleridge enlists the aid of Kant in rectifying the slovenly use of language. His notes on Petvin, a student of John Locke, are dated 14 October 1820. On Petvin's remarks concerning God's happiness, Coleridge remarks:

> The very word 'happy' as applied to the Being above Fate & Chance, that is strangely lax and slovenly. But we will suppose the proper word – viz. blest or blissful – this at least implies mind, self-comprehension – not merely an infinita cogitatio sine centro, but a Self as the Copula or proper _Oneness_ of all Positives.[78]

Exact use of language makes 'Dejection: An Ode' (1802) a demanding poem to read. 'Joy', 'genial', 'eddying' – such words require careful attention and precise placement in tradition and in Coleridge's writings as a whole.

The history of the composition of 'Dejection' is complex and not altogether clear. Its details need not detain us here, and they are fully considered by George Dekker in his book _Coleridge and the Literature of Sensibility_ (1978).[79] Suffice it to say that, while its genesis may be as early as the summer of 1800, the first complete draft was in the form of a letter to Sara Hutchinson, dated 4 April 1802. A mutilated version, described as an ode, was published in the _Morning Post_ on 4 October 1802, and dedicated to Wordsworth under the pseudonym 'Edmund'. The final version was published in _Sibylline Leaves_ (1817), much shorter and tighter than the original verse letter. Like 'Kubla Khan' and 'The Ancient Mariner', therefore, the final version of the poem is the result of years of reflection, although Coleridge provides no ironic commentary equivalent to the prose Preface and glosses of the earlier poems.

Part of Coleridge's purpose is to contradict Wordsworth's teaching that a man may be healed by exposure to nature and its forces,[80] and it is no doubt a bitter comment on the wreck of Coleridge's marriage and his hopeless passion for Sara Hutchinson that 4 October 1802 was Wordsworth's wedding-day. Coleridge, in a state of depression, has been out of doors on a 'long eve, so balmy and serene'.[81] Rationally he has grasped its beauty, but his emotions remain unaffected. What is required, and missing, is a joy in the poet which will respond to the beauty of the scene:

> ... is the spirit and the power,
> Which wedding Nature to us gives in dower
> A new Earth and new Heaven.
>
> (ll. 67–9)

Coleridge, and indeed Wordsworth, would have known the emphasis which David Hartley placed on the terms 'Pleasure' and 'Joy' as the consummation of love necessitating the presence of the beloved object. But for both poets there was a more ancient, Christian ancestry for the word which is found in eighteenth-century poetry. Apart from the reference to Revelation 21:1 in line 69 of 'Dejection', more important is the use of Acts 17:24–8. Wordsworth quotes the passage in his enlargement of 1802 to the Preface to *Lyrical Ballads*, in reference to the poet's art.

It is an acknowledgement of the beauty of the universe ... it is a task light and easy to him who looks at the world in the spirit of love: further, it is a homage paid to the native and naked dignity of man, to the grand elementary principle of pleasure, *by which he knows, and feels, and lives, and moves.*[82]

Verse 28 of the passage from Acts reads: 'for in him we live, and move, and have our being' (Authorized Version). For Wordsworth and Coleridge these verses are seen as expressive of the divine presence of the Holy Spirit in nature, and it is through the 'elementary principle of pleasure' that the Spirit operates. Thus, 'men and especially poets are most like, and interact with, the Holy Spirit when they rejoice'.[83]

Joy is that state of mind which is necessary for the poet's creative power. The much-quoted lines:

> O Lady! we receive but what we give
> And in our life alone does Nature live:
> (ll. 47–8)

might suggest simply an Idealist philosophy in which nature is an expression of the creative mind. In fact, there seems to be a more specifically theological substance behind Coleridge's word 'joy' which recognizes the actuality of an independent, external world. Its beauty is perceived only by joy:

> This light, this glory, this fair luminous mist,
> This beautiful and beauty-making power.
> (ll. 62–3)

For John and Charles Wesley in the eighteenth century, 'joy' was an important emotion, but primarily an attribute of God rather than man. The influence of the Methodist revival upon English Romanticism, and particularly upon Wordsworth and Coleridge, has been traced by Frederick C. Gill in his book *The Romantic Movement and Methodism* (1937).[84] The overflowing of Divine joy, according to the Wesleys resulted in the great act of creation, 'when the morning stars sang together, and all the sons of God shouted for joy' (Job 38:7). This creative joy finds its echo in man. Charles Wesley paraphrased Zephaniah 3:17,

> Thy gracious Lord shall soon for thee
> His whole omnipotence employ,
> Delight in thy prosperity,
> And condescend to sing for joy;
> They God well pleas'd and satisfied
> Shall view his image in thy breast,
> Shall glory o'er his spotless bride,
> And in his love for ever rest.[85]

As creation comes about through God's joy, so also there is Divine joy in his contemplation of man, his own image. For Wesley the contemplation is of the Church, the 'spotless bride'. Coleridge in 'Dejection' repeats the wedding image (l. 68), but the joy is now as *man* contemplates man, made in God's image – 'we in ourselves rejoice!' (l. 72).

A slightly different perspective is found in Mark Akenside's poem *The Pleasures of Imagination* (1757), which was well known to Coleridge. Here, as in the Wesleys' hymns, creation is seen as an overflowing of Divine joy, but now the joy comes from the contemplation of uncreated forms.

> Then liv'd the almighty One: then, deep-retir'd
> In his unfathom'd essence, viewed at large
> The forms eternal of created things;
> The radiant sun, the moon's nocturnal lamp,
> The mountains, woods, and streams, the rolling globe,
> And wisdom's mien celestial. From the first
> Of days, on them his love divine he fix'd,
> His admiration; till in time complete,
> What he admir'd and lov'd, his vital smile
> Unfolded into being.[86]

In 'Dejection', the attribute of God is found in man, whose experience of joy is an essentially divine activity which relates, like the primary Imagination, the creative act of the poet to the mysteries of God's creation. For God and man, made in his image, creativity finds its genesis in emotion. Coleridge is concerned with neither simply a realist contemplation of what is there, nor with a 'subjectivist' reading of nature as merely a projection of our minds. Rather he is seeking to make the 'external internal, the internal external',[87] entering into a loving relationship with what is outside us so that its mystery may be glimpsed in the creative, symbol-making activity of the Imagination. It is perhaps this sense of the revelation of the Divine in human 'joy' which lies behind Coleridge's endless 'disquisitions' on subject and object, which Carlyle was to ridicule in his *Life of John Sterling* (1851).[88]

As Coleridge contemplates the beauties of the evening, he complains 'I see, not feel, how beautiful they are!' (l. 38). His loss is described in the following line, 'My genial spirits fail'. What, precisely, does 'genial' mean in this context? According to Dr Johnson, it is 'festive' or 'that gives cheerfulness',[89] linked therefore with the concept of joy. In its earliest sense, however, as given in the *Shorter Oxford Dictionary*, genial is a sexual term 'pertaining to marriage', possibly then linked with the image in 'Dejection', 'Ours is her wedding garment' (l. 49, also l. 68). Johnson, also, gives as a secondary sense, 'contributing to propagation'. It would be reasonable to find both these meanings in Coleridge – that of joy and of creativity. In both senses his spirits had failed him. However, in the *Shorter Oxford* there is a further suggestion which hardly seems to to be adequately covered by Johnson's third sense of 'natural'. This suggestion is dated 1827, as 'pertaining to genius', deriving from the German 'genial'. The reference is to the publication of Carlyle's translation of *Wilhelm Meister's Travels* in *German Romance* (1827).

This line of 'Dejection', there seems little doubt, echoes Milton's 'So much I feel my genial spirits droop' (*Samson Agonistes*, l. 594), and, with some bitterness, Wordsworth's buoyant reworking of Milton in *Tintern Abbey* (1798):

> If I were not thus taught, should I the more
> Suffer my genial spirits to decay:
> For thou art with me here . . .[90]

Equally however, for Coleridge, who knew the German language well by 1802, the failure of his *genial* spirits would suggest, on the one hand, a loss of that joyful creativity and productiveness which the poet shared with God, and, on the other, the decay of his 'genius', that gift which makes him a poet among men. He is robbed of inspiration and revelation.

In the final stanza of 'Dejection', however, the poet wishes that the joy which he has lost may be discovered in his Lady.

> Joy lift her spirit, joy attune her voice;
> To her may all things live, from pole to pole,
> Their life the eddying of her living soul!
> O simple spirit, guided from above,
> Dear Lady! friend devoutest of my choice,
> Thus mayest thou ever, evermore rejoice.
>
> (ll. 134–9)

Here joy is the great unifying and animating principle of the world, from pole to pole. In his *Philosophical Lectures* Coleridge stated that

> in joy individuality is lost. . . . To have a genius is to live in the universal, to know no self but that which is reflected not only from the faces of all around us, our fellow creatures, but reflected from the flowers, the trees, the beasts, yea from the very surface of the [waters and the] sands of the desert. A man of genius finds a reflex to himself, were it only in the mystery of being.[91]

But perhaps the most important word of these final lines of the poem is 'eddying', and its metaphorical implications require careful elucidation.

It occurs a number of times in Coleridge's writings before 1802. An early poem of 1794, 'On Bala Hill', contains the line 'That eddy in the wild gust moaning by'.[92] More significant is a note of 1797–8 which describes his children at play:

> the elder whirling for joy, the one in petticoats, a fat Baby, eddying half willingly, half by the force of the Gust – driven backward, struggling forward – both drunk with the pleasure, both shouting their hymn of Joy.[93]

It is a marvellous description of excited children. But more than that, it is placed in the context of 'Joy', which is given religious overtones with the word 'hymn'. The younger child both controls and is controlled in his movements, a balance of opposing forces, one his own energy and the other from the elements beyond him. The joy makes him drunk – again, the suggestion is of possession combined with conscious energy. There is an exercise of the will, which is necessary to be seized by joy. One is reminded of the poet in the final stanza of 'Kubla Khan'. Finally there is a note of October 1799 which describes the fall of the River Greta. Edward Kessler in his book *Coleridge's Metaphors of Being* (1979) prints it as verse.[94] Here is Coleridge's original prose.

> River Greta near its fall into the Trees – Shootings of water threads over down the slope of the huge green stone – The white Eddy-rose that blossom'd up against the stream in the scollop, by fits & starts, obstinate in resurrection – It *is the life* that we live.[95]

The Eddy-rose is the foam caused by the water which is thrown up against the downward current of the stream. Like the child's 'eddying' in the gusting wind, it is a metaphor of the human spirit which ever struggles and falls back, creative and decreative. It is, perhaps, an image of the poet ever reflecting upon himself, the ironic processes of *Biographia Literaria* whereby our awareness of life becomes the life we live. Like 'Kubla Khan', the eddy reconciles opposites which 'like magnetic forces, suppose and require each other'.[96] The magnet is implied in 'Dejection' by the words 'from pole to pole'. But first, a problem is presented in the image of the Eddy-rose. Here are two further examples of Coleridge's use of the 'eddy'.

1. in Lear's [ravings], there is only the brooding of the one anguish, an eddy without progression.[97]

2. one of those brief sabbaths of the soul, when the activity and discursiveness of the thoughts are suspended, and the mind quietly *eddies* round, instead of flowing onward[98]

In the words of 'Dejection', there seems 'no natural outlet' (l. 23), the eddy being without progression and without that openness to infinity which is implied in, for example, the fragmentary nature of 'Kubla Khan', or the deliberate uneasiness of the final compromise of 'The Ancient Mariner'. But what, then, of that phrase in the River Greta note, 'obstinate in resurrection'? The language is deliberately Christian, and the resurrection is *willed*. The will to force against the stream, to create counter to the flowing river, enables a resurrection to take place. Or, at least, the will reaches for the possibility of a resurrection and the creative spirit, the 'shaping spirit of Imagination' ('Dejection', l. 86), orients the being of man in a balance beyond the mutable current of life. In *Biographia Literaria* there is an image of a water-insect which wills its way against the current, as a metaphor of 'the mind's self-experience in the act of thinking'.[99] Its propulsion depends upon the momentary 'fulcrum' which is established in the balance of the current and the insect's own energy. The passage is discussed in detail in Chapter 5.[100]

The image of the Eddy-rose suggests no vague or mystical search for transcendence or abandonment of the world. As was to be clearly stated in the 'Confessio Fidei' of 1810, the will is an essential element both in faith and in the inspiriting of objects and the things of nature which are otherwise 'essentially fixed and dead'. [101] As Edward Kessler suggests, the final lines of 'Dejection' anticipate the possible collaboration of 'natura naturata (nature made)' and 'natura naturans (nature making)'.[102] Here may be picked up the double-meaning of 'pole to pole'. On the one hand it refers to the whole world of nature which is enlivened by 'the eddying of her living soul'. On the other hand, the image is of the magnet.

John Beer in his book *Coleridge's Poetic Intelligence* (1977), and his paper 'A Stream by Glimpses: Coleridge's later Imagination',[103] examines in some detail various references in Coleridge's writings to the terms 'single touch' and 'double touch'. They were used in his time to describe the operation of the magnet. A magnetic effect cannot properly be achieved by 'single touch', or rubbing only one pole of the lodestone. However, 'double touch', rubbing both poles, will result in a sustained magnetism, apparently through the creation of a 'vortex'. In the *Philosophical Lectures* is recorded Coleridge's 'long long ago theory of Volition as a mode of *double Touch*'.[104] The vortex of the magnet, the balance of the eddy, in Sara Hutchinson is the creative power which Coleridge feels he has lost. Such a reconciliation of opposites is the bringing of things into a unity, the creation of a new Earth and new Heaven. In 'Dejection', the theological and biblical background which has here been suggested, in the history of the word 'joy' and the references to Acts and Revelation, combine with the secular imagery of the poem to suggest a further 'double touch' – the sacred and the secular which, as 'polar forces' in the poetry 'are necessarily *unius generis*, homogeneous'.[105] This seems to be a happier reading of Coleridge's poem than that suggested by M. H. Abrams who would drive too deep a wedge between traditional Christian truths and Romantic secular metaphysics, and for whom the 'characteristic concepts and patterns of Romantic philosophy and literature are a displaced and reconstituted theology, or else a secularized form of devotional experience'.[106]

As 'Kubla Khan' ends with the word 'Paradise', so 'Dejection' ends with the word 'rejoice'. But the vision of the poet was to remain clouded by 'Reality's dark dream!' ('Dejection', l. 95). Between March and November 1802, Coleridge's relationship with his wife became increasingly strained. A period of desultory wandering and ill health culminated in the departure, on 9 April 1804, for Malta. Coleridge did not return to England until 17 August 1806. Prior to his departure from Portsmouth, he wrote to the Wordsworths:

> I seem to grow weaker & weaker in my moral feelings/and every thing, that forcibly awakes me to Person & Contingency, strikes fear into me, sinkings and misgivings, alienation from the Spirit of Hope, obscure withdrawings out of Life. . . .[107]

In his notebook for 3 May 1804, he records that the sea at Gibraltar was 'swarming with insect life, *all* busy-swarming in the path'.[108] He lived in the voyage the fate of his own Ancient Mariner.

In the years to come the poet was to reflect upon his creative experience in critical prose – literary criticism, philosophical and theological reflections. There is, indeed, a continuity of thought and theme through his writings, so that what has been discussed regarding three of his greatest poems was not lost in the wreckage of his life after 1802, but emerges, reworked in his prose and again in his later poetry and the highly theological, and as yet unpublished, notebooks of his last years. The deliberate and sometimes highly complex prose writings which are to be discussed in the next chapter, with all their heavy dependence on Coleridge's vast reading in German and English, are none the less shot through with a belief in the radiant moment of vision in the earlier poems, that joy which glimpses in a 'state of consciousness'

> A light, a glory, a fair luminous cloud
> Enveloping the Earth.
>
> ('Dejection', ll. 54–5)

The 'glory' is taken into a later poem, 'Constancy to an Ideal Object' (?1825), as the halo or ring of light around the head of the Broken Spectre.[109] It is both phantasmal and yet perceived to be there, partaking of both human and divine – a 'glory' dependent upon both, and

the generation of the Sense of Reality & Life out of us, from the Impersonation effected by a certain phantasm of double Touch.[110]

5 The Critical Prose

The second decade of the nineteenth century saw an extremely complex and much neglected series of changes in Coleridge's poetic and intellectual development. The miseries and creative decline recorded in 'Dejection: An Ode' hang over the early years of the period, reaching a climax with the demise of *The Friend* and the break with Sara Hutchinson in the winter of 1810–11. On the other hand, it was the period of his most developed literary criticism, including the Shakespeare Lectures of 1811–12 and concluding with the publication of *Biographia Literaria* in 1817. His study of literature, against the background of contemporary German philosophy and criticism, led him into discussions of aesthetics, history and Christian theology, and are a necessary study as a prelude to considering both his later theological and philosophical writings, and his later poetry.

1 COLERIDGE AND KANT: IMAGINATION AND 'ANSCHAUUNG'

Biographia Literaria has been described as a book largely about poetry, in its definition of the secondary Imagination giving emphasis and honour to poetic creation. Yet, rather than being simply a programme for the writing of poetry, its deepest concern is to link the poetic with the theological and philosophical concerns of its author.[1] Thomas McFarland concludes that:

> the lineage of the secondary imagination extends not only backward beyond Kant to Tetens, but also beyond Tetens to Leibniz, and finally beyond Leibniz to Plato. With antecedents of this kind, it is inevitable that Coleridge's threefold theory of imagination actually bears less on poetry than it does on those things that always mattered most to him – as they did to Leibniz and to Kant – that is, 'the freedom of the will, the immortality of the soul, and the existence of God'.[2]

McFarland argues at length, and somewhat restrictively, for the direct influence of Tetens on Coleridge's definition of the secondary Imagina-

73

tion (*BL*, vol. 1, p. 202), to the neglect indeed of other sources, primarily the stimulation of reading Kant and Coleridge's eighteenth-century heritage, not least of his early reading in Hartleian associationalism.

Johann Nikolaus Tetens (1736?–1807) was a psychologist of some distinction, a professional man of science whose vast two-volume work *Philosophische Versuche über die menschliche Natur und ihre Entwick-elung* (Leipzig, 1777) was read and extensively annotated by Coleridge. Certainly Chapters 14 and 15 – entitled 'Von der bildenden Dichtkraft' (On the shaping poetic power) – of Tetens's first essay are highly suggestive of Coleridge's description of the secondary Imagination. Tetens describes 'Dichtkraft' as 'Auflösen (dissolving), 'Wiederverein-igen' (reuniting) and 'Vermischen' (blending).[3] Tetens, however, was also extremely important for Kant in the *Kritik der reinen Vernunft* (1781), and more specifically *The Inaugural Dissertation, De mundi sensibilis et intelligibilis forma et principiis* (1770). This latter work had a profound influence on Coleridge, and it seems more likely that he learnt more from Tetens filtered through Kant, than from a direct reading of the dry original. Furthermore, and despite Coleridge's protestations to the contrary,[4] Tetens's scientific destruction of the theories of Hartley and Priestley[5] runs quite counter to the persistence of Hartley in Coleridge's poetry and thought in the form of his own idiosyncratic presentation of the law of association. This will be dealt with in more detail later in the chapter.[6]

Before considering Coleridge's enormous debt to Kant, it would be well to establish some fundamental differences between them in their treatments of Imagination and 'Einbildungskraft'. The deficiencies which Coleridge perceived in the eighteenth-century 'laws of association of ideas' might be summed up in his distinction in *Biographia Literaria* between Imagination and Fancy. For Fancy is 'indeed no other than a mode of Memory emancipated from the order of time and space'.[7] Yet even while this is felt to be subordinate to the creative Imagination, Coleridge maintained a respect for those 'items of awareness which force upon the subject the task of coming to terms with elements in his past that have made him what he is'.[8] Such respect may explain not only the ambivalence of his attitude towards associationalism in his later years, but also his debt to Kant, despite, or even perhaps because of, their differences in the matter of the Imagination.

In comparing Coleridge and Kant here, it is useful to draw upon the images of the mirror and the lamp, which were established in critical discussion by M. H. Abrams.[9] Kant would explain the Imagination as fundamentally an act of the memory, as reproductive, and art as an imitation of aspects of the universe. Coleridge, on the other hand, employs an expressive approach. His debt to Kant is enormous, but his differences are noted in his practical emphasis on poetry and his active concern for religion.

In Kant's *Kritik der reinen Vernunft*, 'Einbildungskraft' is regarded primarily as the capacity to reproduce that which has been experienced or observed, and this is consonant with the notion of art in the *Kritik der Urtheilskraft* (1790), in which art is beautiful and great to the extent to which it follows or copies nature. In his discussion of the 'Synthesis of Reproduction in Imagination' in the earlier *Critique* (A 100–2),[10] Kant portrays the Imagination as finding opportunity for the excercise of its powers in the reproduction and ordering of external objects. Without such exercise it 'would remain concealed within the mind as a dead and to us unknown faculty'. The passage is well summarized by Kwang-Sae Lee:

> The subjective state of the empirical imagination here seems to be conceived by the 'Lockean' Kant as being 'conditioned' by the transcendental synthesis of imagination, which, in the present context, might well be taken as our scientific conception of the primary qualities of physical objects.[11]

Later in the *Critique*, in the Refutation of Idealism, Kant notes that 'determination of my existence in time' (B 275) is possible only if it presupposes knowledge of external objects. Further, *The Critique of Judgement* emphasizes the power of the Imagination as memory which 'is able on occasion, even after a long lapse of time, not only to recall the signs for concept, but also to reproduce the image and shape of an object'.[12] Nevertheless, aesthetic judgements demand an ordering and the establishment of laws by the Imagination which is determined by the visible forms before it.[13] In aesthetic judgements, the Beautiful is the ✓ imitation of the beautiful in nature. This ordering is achieved by an agreement between the Imagination and the law of the understanding – which Kant calls 'finality apart from an end'. Moreover, a particularly Kantian note is struck in that such ordering is directed towards a moral end which is in conformity with regulative ideas of 'God', 'Self', 'Freedom', 'Immortality' and 'Moral Duty'. Regulative ideas by definition exclude the 'subjects' of the ideas from cognition. This form of agreement between Understanding and Imagination epitomizes the ✓ inescapable element of subjectivity upon which Kant's entire philosophical system is based. There can be no scientific laws valid for all experience unless we ourselves, by our own understanding and imagination, impose these laws on the appearance of things.

However, as Austin Farrer has pointed out, 'there is nothing like a common orthodoxy as to which the practical attitudes or activities are, that anchor floating metaphysical theses to the rock of solid experience'.[14] Any extended analysis of Coleridge's theory of the Imagination would probably only succeed in echoing the numerous books already written on that subject, and yet there are important differences to be observed in a comparison with Kant, not least because of the poetic activity already explored in such works as 'The Ancient Mariner'. This is so despite Coleridge's profound reverence for Kant whom, after fifteen years, according to *Biographia Literaria*, he can still read 'with undiminished delight and increasing admiration'.[15]

Kant's 'Eidbildungskraft' had a long history in philosophy, beginning with Aristotle. Descartes' 'imaginatio' is an inferior faculty to 'intellectio' (which needs no images). In *Leviathan* (1651), Hobbes describes imagination as 'decaying sense . . . so that Imagination and Memory, are but one thing'.[16] Indeed, the greatest poetry of Wordsworth 'still takes its origin in the memory of given experiences to which he is often pedantically faithful'.[17] Yet for Coleridge it is 'Fancy', mirror-like, which recollects and reproduces like Kant's 'Einbildungskraft', while 'Imagination' is a shaping spirit. The artist, trusting more to the imagination than to the memory,[18] abandons the minimal role of holding up a mirror to nature and shapes the world as he experiences it, in metaphor and symbol, his art a self-expression, illuminating and not merely reflecting. The Imagination, dissolving, diffusing, dissipating and then re-creating, is a symbolizing activity, the symbol focusing and shaping through the very particularity of an event or object the eternal 'ideas' which underlie it and of which it is a part.

For Coleridge art was not a copy of the phenomenal world but an imitation of it, offering a glimpse into the noumenal, and linking the ideal and the real, subject and object. For this reason his criticism of the *Kritik der praktischen Vernunft* (1788) is very similar to his misgivings about Hartley. In both, he felt, religious aspiration was not matched by an adequate sensitivity to the psychology of human insight and imagination. According to Kant, the role of the practical reason is the realization of a law rather than an intuition.[19] The phenomenal and the noumenal were bridged only by an exercise of our moral duty which provided experiential knowledge of a supersensible order. So far Coleridge follows Kant in the exercise of a practical reason, but then moves beyond the merely moral contact with the noumenal. At this stage the ideas of 'God', 'Freedom', and so on, are regulative, evidence indeed that 'God created man in His own image' yet furnishing the clue to his 'moral self-determination'.[20] So far, the Imagination, restricted to the realm of the ethical and productive merely of a copy of the phenomenal world, is well characterized by Benedetto Croce as 'the sensible and imaginative vesture of an intellectual concept'.[21]

Coleridge's extension of the practical reason beyond the merely ethical, however, begins in his question in Appendix E of *The Statesman's Manual* as to 'whether Ideas are regulative only, according to Aristotle or Kant; or likewise CONSTITUTIVE, and one with the power and Life of Nature'.[22] In effect he transformed the role of Kant's practical reason from ethical theory to the intuition of ideas as real. Imagination is now productive of art which is the expression of an intuitively known reality, constitutive, and no longer, as in Kant's view, only subjectively valid. As regulative ideas now become constitutive, religion is seen as the parent of the fine arts:

> in all the ages and countries of civilisation Religion has been the parent and fosterer of the Fine Arts, as of Poetry, Music, Painting, &c. the common essence of which consists in a similar union of the Universal and the Individual.[23]

As art deals with the objects of the senses *in re*, as symbols, there is, therefore, 'a metaphysical ground for a special religious aim and vision for highest poetry'.[24] The importance of this poetic aim and vision is stressed by Wordsworth as 'the commerce between Man and his Maker [which] cannot be carried on but by a process where much is represented in little, and the Infinite Being accommodates himself to a finite capacity'.[25] Imagination and poetry, while perhaps seeming to be secular, are essentially spiritual.

If Coleridge's misgivings about Kant's regulative ideas and the *Kritik der praktischen Vernunft* bear comparison with hs criticism of Hartley's doctrine of association, it is not surprising if his transformation of practical reason resembles his pre-Kantian struggle with associationalism and his reshaping of Hartleianism.[26] As far as Kant was concerned, Coleridge approached him as a poet. In *The Inaugural Dissertation*, Kant proposes a doctrine of time and space (later developed in the *Kritik der reinen Vernunft*) in which, contradicting Leibniz, their objectivity is denied. Time is 'a pure intuition', and space 'a schema for co-ordinating'.[27] This subjective status of time and space has the effect of devaluing, ontologically, the world revealed to us by the senses. For Coleridge this provided the basis for the notion of a creative Imagination, or, following his definition of the primary Imagination, of 'a repetition in the finite mind of the eternal act of creation in the infinite I AM'.[28] Kant had written:

> The human mind is not affected by external things and the world is not open to inspection by it to infinity, except in as much as the mind itself together with all other things is sustained by the same infinite force of one being.[29]

Embraced by infinity, the Imagination is creative in perception and able to overcome the 'conditions of sensibility',[30] and is capable of seeing a unity in the fragmented and temporally distracted world. In *Biographia* Coleridge writes of 'time *per se*' in distinction from our notion of time, and drawing also upon his reading of Schelling's *System des transzendentalen Idealismus* (1800), concludes that the true 'self' of the individual, released from the material body which is conditioned by spatiality, experiences everything not separately and consecutively but simultaneously.[31] In *The Inaugural Dissertation*, Kant had affirmed that such perceptiveness suggests that 'this world, although existing contingently, is sempiternal, that is, simultaneous with every time, so that it is therefore wrong to assert that there has been some time at which it did not exist'.[32]

However, while for Kant the glimpses of infinity which are given by the Imagination are purely intellectual – ideas are regulative only – for Coleridge they intimate something ultimately more substantial and speak to poetry and theology. The poet took *The Inaugural Dissertation* gratefully, not least Kant's dynamic definition of God as 'the principle of the coming into being of all perfection'.[33] It reflects the open-endedness of Coleridge's poetry with its participation in the limitless process of life which alone expresses the truly infinite and inexhaustible divine. Apart from poetry, it was the starting point also for philosophical irony, which was so important for Coleridge.

Kant's intellectualism, however, excluded 'intuition', since intuition, he says, is passive and bound to forms. Coleridge gives a great deal of attention to Kant's term 'Anschauung' (intuition) in his later prose and particularly in the MS *Logic* (?1822–3), reinstating intuition into the process of the creative Imagination. Its ultimate place in the poet's divine task is represented by a notebook entry of May 1830.

The mind can form no higher conception of blessedness in employment, than to have a spiritual intuition of the union of the personality
of God with his infinity and omnipresence.[34]

In God, Coleridge says, we see all things, and God therefore represents
that unity and harmony which the Imagination perceives in the
particulars which constitute the universal: and the spring of inherent
activity in the imaginative mind is intuition. In a slightly earlier
notebook, dated 27 November 1827, Coleridge wrote a 'corollary' to the
statement that all things are seen in God:

> The simplification of the definition of *Mind*, as a pure *active* and
> proper *Perceptivity*: thus cleansing my system from the last adhesion
> of the Berkleian *Passivity*.[35]

Coleridge repeatedly affirms that, far from being bound to forms, the
'insight or intuitive possession of the true philosophy' is not to be
achieved by that man 'whose imaginative powers have been *ossified* by
the continual reaction and assimilating influences of mere *objects* on his
mind'.[36]

It is, however, through objects – whether palace domes, albatrosses or
embers in the grate – in their symbolic role of particulars which
enunciate the whole, that the imagination works by drawing upon the
'inward experience' of man made as a creative soul in God's image.
Coleridge's most extended discussion of intuition in the *Logic* is as a
preface to a long reference to the conceptions of time and space which he
had learnt from the *Kritik der reinen Vernunft* and *The Inaugural
Dissertation*. Initially he follows Kant's use of 'Anschauung' closely.
'Intuition' is a term 'of prime necessity in all philosophical enquiries',
hitherto neglected by English in technical use, and employed periphras-
tically by Hooker as 'equivalent to instinctive, natural or innate', as
'"immediate beholding"'.[37] Quite simply, intuition is merely looking at
an object, and is indistinguishably both the act of beholding and 'the
simple product thence resulting'. There is nothing conscious or reflective
in it, although intuitive knowledge may feed the reflective faculty. Thus
far, Coleridge follows Kant closely in his definition 'Anschauung,
unmittelbare Offenbarung' (intuition, immediate disclosure).[38] Coleridge confesses the necessity for an object upon which the mind can
work.

It would be something worse than absurd to suppose in a finite mind the power of creating anything out of itself; but what I cannot create for myself I must have given to me if I am to have it at all.[39]

But, moving beyond Kant, he pursues ways in which the intuition, in its universal forms, might be antecedent to the presentation of the object. Already, echoing Kant in *The Inaugural Dissertation* (p. 79), he had dismissed 'the doctrine of Malebranche and of some other Cartesians [who] have taken refuge in the hypothesis of inspiration or immediate acts of divine agency',[40] which *may* represent a proper piety or even truth, but is suspect as impatient of philosophy logically deduced. Nevertheless, 'knowledge *a priori* is possible, but *possible* then only when the knowledge and the object known, the *scire* and the *scitum*, are one and the same'.[41] This doctrine of inspiration assumes the constitutive nature of Ideas and an answer to the highest problem of philosophy as set by Plato and Plotinus. Coleridge, in setting the problem in Appendix E of *The Statesman's Manual*, concludes by quoting a variant version of John 1:4, 'ἐν λόγῳ ζωὴ ἦν , καὶ ἡ ζωὴ ἦν τὸ φῶς τῶν ἀνθρώπων' (In the Word was life, and the life was the light of men).[42]

Given the nature of space (outward) and time (inward) as universal forms in the *Logic*, Coleridge can appeal to the 'productive imagination', variously combining the two, to reflect upon particular objects as symbols of the eternal and the universal. Imagination balances, or at least holds in tension, the finite and the infinite, since it stands also at the intersection of the object 'out there', and the mind which shapes what it intuits in symbol and metaphor. The artist shapes his world, but in accordance with an infinitely regressive yet constitutive Idea of the divine.

Coleridge borrowed from Schelling's *Entwurf eines Systems der Naturphilosophie* (1799) the distinction between the primary (unconscious) Imagination and the secondary (conscious) Imagination.[43] The discussion here has focused upon his use of and difference from Kant in his understanding of the nature of imagination and intuition in art. Certainly he found in Kant a toughness of thought which he required to free himself from Schelling's romanticism. While there was an element of mysticism in Coleridge, his avowed purpose was to propound a system 'that of all Systems that have ever been presented, ... has the least of *Mysticism*, the very Object throughout from the first page to the last being to reconcile the dictates of common Sense with the conclusions of scientific Reasoning'.[44] Yet important though Kant was for him intellectually, Coleridge was too much of a poetic to be satisfied with a merely reproductive 'Einbildungskraft', and other sources contributed to his self-expressive imagination – for example, Schelling, not to mention much English writing of the eighteenth century. James Beattie, once much fêted as the great defender of those who feared the moral anarchy which might arise from David Hume's scepticism, wrote in 1762 that 'it is not memory, or the knowledge of rules, that can qualify a poet ... but a peculiar liveliness of fancy and sensibility of heart'.[45] Coleridge certainly read Beattie. Further, Joseph Addison's ode 'The Spacious Firmament on high', became a popular Protestant hymn. It concludes:

> What though, in solemn Silence, all
> Move round the dark terrestrial Ball?
> What tho' nor real Voice nor Sound
> Amid their radiant Orbs be found?
> In Reason's Ear they all rejoice,
> And utter forth a glorious Voice,
> For ever singing, as they shine,
> 'The Hand that made us is Divine'.

Such Reason, which has no place in the silent universe of Newton, is a creative faculty in man whose inspiration waxes as the glory and sounds of heaven wane.

Finally, the symbolic Imagination of Coleridge's post-Kantian writings is a developed expression of the shaping power of Imagination in 'Frost at Midnight', which reconciles ideas based in the opposed systems of Berkeley in *An Essay Towards a New Theory of Vision* (1709) and Hartley's *Observations on Man* (1749),[46] expressive on the one hand of an active Imagination, and on the other of a passive associationalism. The Imagination straddles the unresolvable tension between things – for Coleridge, the 'It is' – and intuition or 'inward experience', the 'I am'.

The limits which Kant set upon human knowledge, together with the moral necessity which he saw for proposing a noumenal realm with God as first cause and authority for the categorical imperative, resulted in an unsatisfied desire for the absolute in his followers.[47] Furthermore, from Kant stemmed an emphasis upon the phenomenal as against the noumenal world, which, in the case of Coleridge among others, developed into an enquiry concerning the mind's capacity to shape what it sees. How was this despair for the absolute to be overcome? How were finite and infinite to be reconciled? In the *Wissenschaftslehre* (1794), Fichte, having concluded the non-existence of Kant's noumenal world, denies the reality of an external, infinite world which is not created by the self. The Ego creates its antithesis, the Non-Ego (the finite world), in order to expand its own consciousness. But for Friedrich Schlegel, and for Coleridge – who continued to be attracted by, though sceptical of, Schlegel's pantheism – it was by the means of philosophical irony that the noumenal realm of the pure infinite could be glimpsed by our finite resources in a 'progressive transition' or process of becoming wherein is effected the 'union and interpenetration of the universal and the particular'.[48]

II COLERIDGE, THE SCHLEGELS AND ROMANTIC IRONY

The nature of Coleridge's dependence on German critics, confusing enough in itself, is continually muddied by his own insistence of his priority, or at least independence of them. He managed to persuade some of the truth of his claim, although in the case of A. W. Schlegel it was based on the erroneous statement that Coleridge's Shakespeare Lectures were delivered before the publication (admittedly in German) of Schlegel's *Vorlesungen über dramatische Kunst und Literatur* (1808– 11). J. C. Shairp in his *Studies in Poetry and Philosophy* (1868) praises Coleridge's originality, especially in his distinction between mechanical and organic form, drawn, in fact, straight from Schlegel's 22nd Lecture.[49] Shairp was followed by A. W. Ward in his *History of English Dramatic Literature* (1875). Others, however, perhaps in a better position to realize how closely Coleridge could follow a German text, and the priority of Schlegel's work, included John Black, the first translator of A. W. Schlegel into English, in the *Morning Chronicle* for 22 December 1818. Also J. S. Mill in his 1840 essay enlarges in a variety of ways on Coleridge's 'posteriority in date' to the Germans who influenced him, his position being therefore 'necessarily a subordinate one'.[50]

As opposed to either of these extremes, it may be suggested that Coleridge, who certainly used the Germans in his literary criticism, did so in an idiosyncratic way and guided by his own theory and literary practice dating back to his earliest days. Furthermore he stood at a crucial transition-point in the development of German literary theory, and, as an outsider, presented an ambivalent attitude equally towards an earlier generation in Herder and Schiller and the later writings of Friedrich and A. W. Schlegel. His presence at such a critical crossroads provides a powerful catalyst for his later theological and philosophical developments.

For example, in a note made in March 1819 (and expanded by H. N.

Coleridge in *The Literary Remains* as material for an 1818 lecture[51]), Coleridge compares the Spirit of Pagan Greece with that of Christianity. In the former, 'the Ideas must be turned into finites, and these into Finites anthropomorphic', while in the latter 'Finites, even the Human Form, must be brought into connection with the Infinite'.[52] In fact, he is paraphrasing and condensing from Schiller's 'Über naive und sentimentalische Dichtung':

> Jener ... ist mächtig durch die Kunst der Begrenzung; dieser ist es durch die Kunst des Unendlichen.

> (that [ancient poetry] is mighty through the art of limitation; this [modern] through the art of the infinite.)[53]

Schiller's poetic in his essay is chiefly psychological. The remark is made in the context of a discussion of the relationship between 'poetry' and 'doctrine'. Coleridge, however, further places it within the context of the advent of Christianity. Such a literary–historical approach to poetry plays no part in Schiller's literary scheme. It was something, however, which Coleridge shared with the Schlegels, who, although they derived much from Schiller, in their literary surveys were propounding primarily an historical typology. Thus in the first of his *Lectures on Dramatic Art and Literature*, A. W. Schlegel distinguishes between 'classic' and 'romantic', ascribing the change to the coming of Christianity. Like the Schlegels, and unlike Schiller, Coleridge similarly identifies the change of style with Christian beginnings.

In the lectures on Shakespeare delivered variously between 1811 and 1814, and the lectures on literature delivered in 1818, together with numerous notebook fragments,[54] Coleridge undoubtedly drew heavily on A. W. Schlegel's *Lectures on Dramatic Art and Literature* and Friedrich Schlegel's *Geschichte der alten und neuen Literatur* (1815), but diverged from them and combined their historical poetic with the earlier psychological criticism of Schiller. A further element in Coleridge's writing lay in the influence on him of Herder's *Briefe, das Studium der Theologie betreffend* (1790), which he carefully annotated,[55] and from which he perceived that to salvage Christianity was both a religious and a literary problem. Certainly Coleridge placed but small emphasis on the historical events of the life of Jesus. Indeed, Jesus' historical existence little more than confirmed the eternal truths which man may perceive in reflecting on his own nature. Nevertheless, the study of literature does involve an historical pespective which may enlighten the study of

Christian origins. For if the power of the Bible lies in its capacity to find the individual in the depths of his being,[56] then a consideration of its historical setting will begin to discover the particular milieu in which such power was originally generated. As the particular present is placed in the context of an historical particular then a more general and universal view of the conditions and nature of religious experience can be built up.[57] 'Revealed Religion' is, as Coleridge stated in *Confessions of an Inquiring Spirit* (1840), 'at once inward Life and Truth, and outward Fact and Luminary'.[58]

Clearly Coleridge was combining the thinking of a whole period of German criticism, both theological and literary, the result being not merely subordination to them (as Mill suggested) or total originality (as he himself claimed), but a positive contribution to the process of theoretical thinking in the philosophy of art and the German Romantic concept of irony. The result was of lasting significance for Coleridge as poet, critic, philosopher and theologian.

Much has been written of 'the disorientating instabilities of European romantic irony',[59] of its open-endedness and denial of an absolute order. Less, however, has been said about the *teaching* role of irony, which applies particularly to Coleridge who was, *par excellence*, a teacher. For, first of all, irony establishes a precise and peculiar relationship between author and reader, as, for example, in the manner already explored in 'The Ancient Mariner'. Then, the teacher is not one with knowledge which he seeks to impart to the ignorant. Rather:

> He is someone who attempts to re-create the subject in the student's mind, and his strategy in doing this is first of all to get the student to recognize what he already potentially knows, which includes breaking up the powers of repression in his mind that keep him from knowing what he knows.[60]

The teacher's task, then, is to ask questions rather than to answer them; to change rather than consolidate the mental level of enquiry. Irony demands that author and reader begin at a shared, common level, a move from the known (where the author pretends to be), to the unknown (where the author actually is). This advance is an act of reconstruction or re-creation which cannot really be said, but must be performed. From the author's point of view there is risk involved, since the performance may fail, but where it succeeds, the irony generates an energy out of conflict and disturbing ambiguity, and the energy carries the reader to the revelation of a new unknown.

In *Biographia Literaria*, Coleridge links his reading of A. W. Schlegel's lectures with the rest of his philosophical study. He begins with Schelling.

In Schelling's 'NATUR-PHILOSOPHIE', and the 'SYSTEM DES TRANS-CENDENTALEN IDEALISMUS', I first found a genial coincidence with much that I had toiled out for myself, and a powerful assistance in what I had yet to do.[61]

To Schlegel (to which he next alludes) as to Schelling, Coleridge claims priority. The reason for the 'genial coincidence' is not far to find.

We had studied in the same school; been disciplined by the same preparatory philosophy, namely the writings of Kant; we had both equal obligations to the polar logic and dynamic philosophy of Giordano Bruno; and Schelling has lately, and, as of recent acquisition, avowed that same affectionate reverence for the labours of Behmen, and other mystics, which I had formed at a much earlier period.[62]

The terms 'polar logic and dynamic philosophy' are of fundamental significance to Coleridge's Shakespearean criticism and its relation to the German Romantic concept of irony.

A summary of the substance of Coleridge's regard for Shakespeare as a poet may be found in an amalgamation of six fragments gathered into one by H. N. Coleridge in *The Literary Remains*, and published by T. M. Raysor under the title 'Shakespeare's Judgement Equal to his Genius'.[63] In a fragment entitled 'Lecture' in Egerton MS. 2800, f. 24, now in the British Library, Coleridge acknowledges a 'continental critic' – undoubtedly A. W. Schlegel – in making the distinction between mechanic and organic form. The acknowledgement was omitted by H. N. Coleridge. Its replacement from Coleridge's original manuscript establishes the basic contentions of his reading of Shakespeare in the context of Schlegel's work. Further, the solution to the critical conflict between genius and rules, together with the affirmation of Shakespeare's conscious artistic judgement, was discussed by Schlegel not only in his *Lectures*, but as early as his essay 'Romeo und Julia' written in 1797 and published in *Charakteristiken und Kritiken* (1801). There is a fragment on the subject written by Coleridge in October 1802 which Shawcross and Coburn use as evidence to substantiate Coleridge's claim to independence of the Germans.[64] However, the language of the Egerton

'Lecture' suggests that he was translating from Schlegel seven years before John Black published his English translation of the *Lectures* in 1815. G. N. G. Orsini, in his article 'Coleridge and Schlegel Reconsidered',[65] refers the whole discussion back to Kant's *Kritik der Urtheilskraft* (1790) Book II: 'Analytic of the Sublime', Section 46: 'Fine art is the art of Genius'.[66]

Also, the distinction between 'mechanical regularity' and 'organic form' was made by Schlegel whom Coleridge follows, sentence by sentence. Yet it would also be true to say that it was a Romantic commonplace,[67] and occurs frequently in Coleridge who would, no doubt, be anxious to establish the point against such eighteenth-century arguments as David Hume's *Dialogues Concerning Natural Religion* (1779) Part III.

Finally, in expansion of the notion of organic form, by which Coleridge defends the structure of Shakespeare's plays against the demands of the classical unities, he paraphrases Schlegel:

> The spirit of poetry, like all other living powers, must of necessity circumscribe itself by rules, were it only to unite power with beauty. It must embody in order to reveal itself; but a living body is of necessity an organized one – and what is organization but the connexion of parts to a whole, so that each part is at once end and means![68]

The question then is raised of the nature of revelation – here poetic, but taken up later by Coleridge in the context of the divine – expanding into a statement on what lies at the centre of Coleridge's thought, the interrelationship between all the parts of a whole, of which the unity is perceived in the structure of each part. It further points to the extended discussion of Shakespeare in 'Essays on the Principles of Method' in *The Friend* (1818).[69] Coleridge describes the form and unity of Shakespeare's plays not as 'mere dead arrangement' (p. 457) but as 'continuous transition'. Yet such transition or 'principle of progression' is an application of Method wherein 'everything is in its place' (p. 449). It is the very antithesis of generalization since, as its unity lies in the connection of parts to a whole, 'we find individuality everywhere' (p. 457). Of Shakespeare's plays, therefore

> we may define the excellence of *their* method as consisting in that just proportion, that union and interpenetration of the universal and particular, which must ever pervade all works of decided genius and true science.

This principle of Method in the construction of a Shakespearean drama involves antitheses between the individual and the universal, and in the relationship of organic form and unity with progression (p. 476), behind which lies Coleridge's belief that if the Invisible is denied 'the component parts can never be reduced into a harmonious whole', relating the invisible to the visible, the infinite to the finite (p. 441).

It is suggested, therefore, that Coleridge's relationship with contemporary German literary criticism, and in particular A. W. Schlegel's *Vorlesungen über dramatische Kunst und Literatur*, was neither slavish nor totally free but consisted in a careful use and adaptation of their work for his own purposes. A few more points made by Schlegel in his *Lectures* should be noted in the general context of Coleridge's writings. In his discussion of organic form, Schlegel develops at some length its quality of innateness and paradox. (The translation used is that of John Black, revised by A. J. W. Morrison in 1846.)

Organical form, again, is innate; it unfolds itself from within, and acquires its determination contemporaneously with the perfect development of the germ.

The ancient art and poetry rigorously separates things which are dissimilar; the romantic delights in indissoluble mixtures; all contrarieties: nature and art, poetry and prose, seriousness and mirth, recollection and anticipation, spirituality and sensuality, terrestial and celestial, life and death, are by it blended together in the most intimate combination.[70]

Romantic drama – and Schlegel refers particularly to Shakespeare and the Spanish writer Pedro Calderón de la Barca (1600–81) – perceives and combines the unity even of the apparently most disparate.

For Conception can only comprise each object separately, but nothing in truth can ever exist separately and by itself; Feeling perceives all in all at once and the same time.[71]

As his criticism of Shakespeare developed, Schlegel's comments can be seen more and more as illustrative of Coleridge's own earlier poetic practice, particularly of the narrative poems. Shakespeare's writings, says Schlegel, are a mixture of the 'natural activity of genius' and deep reflection with the exercise of judgement (p. 359). In structure they waive the claims of 'the logical connexion of causes and effects', asserting rather

the rights of poetry and the nature of the romantic drama, which, for
the very reason that it is and ought to be picturesque, requires richer
accompaniments and contrasts for its main groups.   (p. 361)

In abandoning a logical sequence of cause and effects, Shakespeare
adopts the ironic device of multiple levels of narration, different
characters providing a variety of perspectives on situations or other
characters in the drama. As has been seen, it is a device used by Coleridge
in 'The Rime of the Ancient Mariner' and 'Christabel' to uproot self-
deception.

> Nobody has ever painted so truthfully as Shakespeare has done the
> facility of self-deception, the half self-conscious hypocrisy towards
> ourselves, with which even noble minds attempt to disguise the most
> inevitable influence of selfish motives in human nature. This secret
> irony of the characterization commands admiration as the profound
> abyss of acuteness and sagacity. . . . In every case we are conscious that
> the subject itself is not immediately brought before us, but that we
> view it through the medium of a different way of thinking.   (p. 369)

What begins in criticism as an analysis of a narrative device whereby
quite new, revealing and often ironic perspectives can be brought to bear
on a single subject, was to become a matter of great importance in
Coleridge's later writings on imagination, aesthetics and theology.
     One result, according to Schlegel, is that a sequence of events, having a
hidden logic, may appear to be arbitrary and inconsequential. Concerning love in *Twelfth Night*, imagination (Einbildung) seems to control an
incoherent pattern of emotions of which the careful balance only
gradually becomes apparent. Schlegel, in a manner familiar to the reader
of Coleridge, contrasts 'imagination' and 'fancy'.

> Die Liebe des musikberauschten Herzogs zur Olivia ist nicht nur eine
> Phantasie, sondern eine Einbildung; Viola scheint sich anfangs
> willkürlich in den Herzog zu verlieben.[72]

> (The love of the music-enraptured Duke for Olivia is not merely a
> fancy, but an imagination; Viola appears at first to fall arbitrarily in
> love with the Duke.)   (p. 392)

It is precisely this contrast between the arbitrary appearance of things
and, in Shakespearean tragedy particularly, the conscious attempts to

exercise a moral will by a character, to which Coleridge returns repeatedly in his criticism. The classic instance, to which reference has already been made, is his discussion of the contingent nature of the Weird Sisters' information and its fulfilment in Macbeth's struggle within himself.[73]

Finally, and not unconnected with the inherently ironic contrast in Shakespeare's drama between the apparently incoherent and *de facto* order of events, Schlegel returns at the end of his course of *Lectures* to the question of organic form and method. Just as Coleridge rejects 'dead arrangement' as a principle of method, so Schlegel seeks to avoid 'festen Grundsätzen' or 'fixed principle'. Coleridge describes Shakespeare's unity as a 'principle of progression', while Schlegel suggests that 'everything good and excellent . . . arises more from transient ebullition than fixed principle'.[74]

The preceding discussion may serve to link Coleridge, initially via his Shakespearean criticism but also his own poetic practice, with a consideration of the German romantic concept of irony. In his own most substantial work of criticism, *Biographia Literaria*, Coleridge exemplifies how a metaphorical method and an ironic attitude may act as principles of unity in a work which – as he and Schlegel might claim of Shakespeare's plays – masks coherence with a surface incoherence and fragmentation. Dr Kathleen Wheeler in her recent study *Sources, Processes and Methods in Coleridge's 'Biographia Literaria'* (1980) has rightly emphasized the role of irony in the theory of art, creativity, and by implication, therefore, perception and knowledge. In establishing a relationship between author and reader, and distinguishing between the artist and his art, irony involves necessarily an appreciation of the distinction between thought and what is thought about; art and reality; the mind as self-conscious and creatively perceptive, inspired to reveal what is most truly there by the 'shaping spirit of Imagination'.

In a note entitled 'Heads of Lecture the third' of February 1818, Coleridge questions A. W. Schlegel's implicit assumption of the identity of poet and poem,[75] being himself always careful to distinguish between the man and his work. In this he was closer to Friedrich Schlegel, Ludwig Tieck and Karl Solger who, among others, were concerned to establish the principle of irony as a key factor in Romantic criticism. For a poet relates to his poem in an inescapably ambivalent way, both as creator and spectator, as controller and one who is controlled, as observer and observed. Thus the irony which works at the level of a multiple perspective upon a particular character or incident (one might cite Browning's *The Ring and the Book*, 1868–9), works also at a deeper level in the work of art in which both author and reader are subject to possibly a variety of critical attitudes. What is apparently happening and what is apparently seen may suffer discontinuity in the service of a greater continuity. The familiar and the finite may need to be shattered in order that the infinite may be glimpsed.

According to Friedrich Schlegel, higher irony in the Romantic sense is self-criticism (Selbstpolemik) transcended.[76] This leads directly back to the claim that Shakespeare's judgement is equal to his genius, to the claim that is, that Shakespeare could perceive his poetic genius at work, cultivate his own talent and adopt a critical posture towards his own creations which acquire, thereby, a dialectic and self-consciousness such as lies at the heart of Romantic irony. This higher irony, however, poses no questions about the artifact itself (unlike dramatic irony), but about the relationship between the artist and his material, or the material and its audience. Indeed it transcends the work allowing a perspective from which the roles of author and reader, artist and spectator, as apparent opposites are necessarily homogeneous, 'rivals ... who inhabit the opposite banks of *the same stream*'.[77] And so the artist–spectator, creating what he sees, glimpses an infinity in his creation through the simple contemplation of the finite.

The sense of the paradoxical and contradictory nature of existence is everywhere apparent in the critical writings of Friedrich Schlegel, and the 'tension of opposites' lies at the heart of his concept of irony. Beauty and perfection are to be found in the 'Fülle' of an ontological chaos from which an inexhaustible 'becoming' triggers a process in the individual consciousness towards an infinite self and a sense of an infinity of becoming.

> Aber die höchste Schönheit, ja die höchste Ordnung ist denn doch nur die des Chaos, nämlich eines solchen, welches nur auf die Berührung der Liebe wartet, um sich zu einer harmonischen Welt zu entfalten, ... alles greift in einander, und überall ist ein und derselbe Geist nur anders ausgedrückt.
>
> (But the greatest loveliness, indeed the greatest order, is then after all solely that of chaos, namely such as only awaits the touch of love to develop it into a harmonious world, ... everything is involved with everything else, and everywhere one and the same spirit is expressed only in different ways.)[78]

The progression of the inexhaustible abundance of this chaotic becoming is discussed in the *Lyceums-Fragmente* and the *Literary Notebooks* in philosophical terms as polarity which implies a dialectic as the necessary means of progression towards an ever-greater participation in the 'Fülle', or the achievement of – in the language of A. W. Schlegel and Coleridge – organic form. Furthermore, polarity is discussed in the *Lyceums-Fragmente* as the relationship between 'Bedingt und Unbedingt', the conditioned and the unconditioned,[79] leading straight back, once again to Coleridge's assessment of judgement (conditioned) and genius (unconditioned) in Shakespeare.[80]

It is the capacity of 'Witz' or imagination in Schlegel (as of the secondary Imagination in Coleridge) to strike up fertile relationships between seeming opposites. The result, however, is not a synthesis as in Hegel's dialectic, for the new relationship of perspective must, in turn, be subjected to irony and critical analysis – and so on, *ad infinitum*. So, Schlegel insists, 'Irony is analysis of thesis and antithesis.'[81] Similarly in Coleridge's 'Essays on the Principles of Method' is the notion of progression as being in the nature of art which hovers with self-critical irony between the finite and the infinite. Thesis and antithesis remain in contradiction, while philosophical irony examines the contradiction. Art, therefore, portrays neither infinity nor the absolute but rather perceives and reveals it in the human consciousness active in the spiritual longing of the process towards the infinite and the divine. The 'Unbedingt' – the absolute – embraces the finitude of human art.

What has been said concerning the Romantic concept of irony relates to Coleridge both as poet and literary critic. *Biographia Literaria* should be received not only in terms of its subject matter, art and imagination, but also as an exercise in the perception of the consciousness of the reading and creative processes. It is a practical experiment which attempts to gain and to grant insight into the activities of creation and perception, the writer and reader continually reflecting upon himself, reflecting upon himself, . . .: the finite pursues infinity. Just as here, and in the Shakespearean criticism, the 'Essays on the Principles of Method' are of fundamental importance, they pertain to the whole corpus of Coleridge's later religious and philosophical writings. In *Hints Towards the Formation of a more Comprehensive Theory of Life* (posthum. 1848), Coleridge refers to the 'polarity, or the essential dualism of Nature, arising out of its productive unity'.[82] The language employed to describe organic unity in terms of the 'principle of progression' or 'productive principle' is the same as in the earlier writings. Similarly, the relationship between parts and a whole which was discussed in 1808 in 'Shakespeare's Judgement equal to his Genius', is taken up at length in the *Theory of*

Life in an examination of the 'principle of individuation': 'I define life as the principle of individuation, or the power which unites a given all into a whole that is presupposed by all its parts.[83]

The central themes and processes of Coleridge's work reappear in this late, fragmentary writing, which convinced its editor, Seth B. Watson, that Coleridge was a 'pious Christian' for whom life was not a thing but 'an act or process', in which what are sought are not 'historical facts' but 'appropriate symbols of great fundamental truths'.[84] Such symbols are discovered in the paradoxical relationship between the parts and the whole, the finite and the infinite, or art and reality, the artist and his creation.

In *Table Talk*, Coleridge is reported to have described Shakespeare in terms of the creator God.

> In Shakespeare one sentence begets the next naturally; the meaning is all interwoven. He goes on kindling like a meteor through the dark atmosphere; yet when the creation in its outline is once perfect, then he seems to rest from his labour, and to smile upon his work, and tell himself that it is very good.[85]

The Shakespearean divinity was endlessly fascinating inasmuch as he may be said to represent that final transcendence in which 'polar forces' are found to be *unius generis*; the eternal oppositions and paradoxes of Romantic irony to be bound in a magnetic unity. For Coleridge, the existence of pairs of opposites is a necessary condition of life. In *Aids to Reflection* he proposes, 'for the purposes of the universal *Noetic*', his Noetic Pentad.

	Prothesis	
Thesis	Mesothesis	Antithesis
	Synthesis[86]	

The mesothesis he explains as follows:

> When two objects, that stand to each other in the relation of antithesis or contradistinction, are connected by a middle term common to both, the sense of this middle term is indifferently determinable by either; the preferability of the one or the other in any given case being divided by the circumstance of our more frequent experience of, or greater familiarity with, the term in this connexion.[87]

The synthesis, as follows:

> Synthesis is a putting together of the two [thesis and antithesis], so that a third something is generated. Thus the *synthesis* of hydrogen and oxygen is water, a third something, neither hydrogen nor oxygen.[88]

And finally, prothesis:

> or the Identity of T[hesis] and A[ntithesis], which is neither, because in it, as the transcendent of both, both are contained and exist as one.[89]

The prothesis, therefore, in its absolute meaning is the Infinite, the One of which the Many are the parts, that totality in which 'polar forces' are found to be one from the first.

Romantic irony, from a mortal viewpoint, preserves the ability to function and gaze upon eternity by forever examining the intrinsic contradictions of those finite landing-places, 'doctrinal adhesions' I. A. Richards called them, which bind and limit.[90] It would be a mistake to see irony, so often deplored by moralists, as serving only the voice of eternal denial. In the *Opus Maximum* MS[91] Coleridge suggests that human personality should not be defined in terms of limitation, for it is developed through an expanding consciousness and organic growth in continuing struggle to transcend the ironies of the suffering Mariner. Yet the ironies keep hope alive and make the struggle worthwhile. Art thus approaches the divine. Coleridge, in tune with much German criticism, explored through the levels of metaphor and the concept of irony, the relationship between art, religion and philosophy. Karl Solger summarized this unified approach to human enquiry and creativity.

> Philosophy, art, and religion are the three necessary parts of a harmonious culture: Philosophy without art is means without purpose; art without philosophy is end without beginning; and both without religion are utterly debased, vile and godless: philosophy becomes insolence and violence, and art arrogant amusement.[92]

III SELF-REFLECTION, *BIOGRAPHIA LITERARIA* AND THE 'CONFESSIO FIDEI'

The winter of 1810 found Coleridge in utter despair. His marriage was wrecked and his health shattered by opium. He feared he would never break the habit and his shame knew no bounds. Earlier in the year publication of *The Friend* had ceased, and his will to work was finally broken when his beloved Sara Hutchinson left him for good. Dorothy Wordsworth wrote, 'We have no hope of him.'[93] It was in the depths of his despondency that Coleridge composed his 'Confessio Fidei', entered in his notebook on 3 November 1810,[94] and published twenty-six years later by his nephew H. N. Coleridge in the *Literary Remains* (1836–9). His current reading of English divines, particularly Robert South (1634–1716) and Jeremy Taylor (1613–67) is evident throughout the 'Confessio'.

Coleridge begins by asserting that man is a responsible and Free Agent, possessing a will, a Reason – that is a Law of Right and Wrong – and a sense of moral responsibility which constitutes the voice of Conscience. His conscience dictates it as a duty to believe in God, whose will is absolute, and properly with this absolute will of God man's free will lies in such a relation 'as a perfect Time-piece would have to the Sun'. Against this background Coleridge continues with the Creed of Natural Religion. The created world serves to remind man of the existence of God. The notion of God, however, is essential to the human mind, called forth by Conscience and evident to Reason. It is necessarily insusceptible of scientific demonstration, and just as all language presupposes in the intelligent listener those primary notions which it symbolizes, so the evidences of nature and the creation presuppose in the mind of man the notion of God.

Belief in God, inspired by conscience, has its origin in the moral sense. This is not the case in the realm of science. Conscience further dictates as the ultimate end of human actions, not the pains and pleasures of this life, but hopes for a future spiritual state of being. This ultimate perspective on life is guided not by intellectual arguments, in Coleridge's terms 'arguments acquired by my Understanding', but by reason of Conscience which is 'the sole fountain of certainty'.

From this, the 'Religion of all finite rational Beings', Coleridge proceeds to the Creed of Revealed Religion. A theme is here begun which was to find its full development in *Aids to Reflection*, that of man's fallen nature and his redemption 'in Christ Jesus'. 'Calvinism', Coleridge asserted, 'is *practically* a ... soothing and consoling system'.[95] Nevertheless, while yet in his despair he reached out to the divine omnipotence, his reading of Kant was not forgotten in his 'Confessio Fidei'. Kant it was who proposed for man an independent will, whose *Kritik der reinen Vernunft*, as Coleridge wrote on 3 November 1807 to John Ryland, 'has completely overthrown the edifice of Fatalism, or causative Precedence as applied to Action'.[96] Born a child of wrath, man is capable of moral evil, but not of himself of moral good. 'This fearful Mystery I pretend not to understand', Coleridge admits, that man remains free and morally responsible and yet in conscience is led to believe in a divinity whose will is absolute and by whose grace alone man is saved. The certainty of redemption is revealed to the conscience, yet not to the understanding, and Christ's life, crucifixion, death and resurrection are both the symbols and 'necessary parts of the aweful process' of this Redemption.

Coleridge makes a final point in the 'Confessio Fidei' before concluding with a lengthy analysis of the inadequacy of Unitarianism. The Trinity, he asserts, is a doctrine commended to us by our conscience. That is, belief in the mysteries of religion is declared to be 'real', as opposed to the acceptance of what is only conceptually clear. In a note made five months earlier in June 1810, Coleridge had affirmed the priority of the will or moral act over intellectual assent in religious matters. He concluded that note: 'Believe, says St Augustin, & most profoundly too – and thou wilt receive an intellectual conviction, (perception of its rationality) as the reward of thy Faith.'[97]

Such, in brief, was Coleridge's religious position in 1810. When he published *Aids to Reflection* fifteen years later, despite his original intention of compiling an anthology from Archbishop Leighton's works, he had ended up writing a book on the process of reaching a Christian belief, beginning with Need and concluding with Trial.[98] In his 'Author's Address to the Reader', he asks a series of questions of his 'fellow-Christian'.

> Has it led you to reflect? Has it supplied or suggested fresh subjects for reflection? Has it given you any new information? Has it removed any obstacle to a lively conviction of your responsibility as a moral agent? Has it solved any difficulties, which had impeded your faith as a Christian? Lastly, has it increased your power of thinking connectedly – especially on the scheme and purpose of the Redemption by Christ?[99]

Stephen Prickett has pointed out that what Coleridge was trying to establish about the mind in *Aids to Reflection* cannot be understood outside the context of his earlier poetic and critical work.[100] The title of the work is a deliberate *double entendre* between 'reflection' as a mode of thought and as the image cast by a mirror. In *Aids*, Coleridge defines 'thought' as:

the voluntary reproduction in our minds of those states of consciousness, or ... of those inward experiences, to which, as to his best and
most authentic documents, the teacher of moral or religious truth
refers us.[101]

Divine revelation may be given by reflection upon the reflected image of
God in man as an 'inward experience', to be perceived and shaped by the
creative imagination. Because of the divine qualities of infinity and
eternity, such reflection will expect an endless process of dislocation and
decreation as it challenges the formal limits imposed as devices of order
on the self, so that the self, reflecting infinitely upon the self, begins to
open and reflect truly the image of the Divine. Revelation is extended to
an interpretative act in which 'things' become signs or symbols.[102]

Northrop Frye in *The Anatomy of Criticism* (1957) argues for the
autonomy of criticism in culture, and its task of destroying the
intellectual idolatry of religion with its 'recurrent tendency ... to replace
the object of its worship with its present understanding and forms of
approach to that object'. Religions, claims Frye, despite their 'enlarged
perspective', cannot embrace the art and criticism which is limitless,
endlessly hypothetical, and he concludes that 'between religion's "this
is" and poetry's "but suppose *this is*", there must always be some kind of
tension, until the possible and the actual meet at infinity'.[103] Frye
criticizes Coleridge for making literary criticism a kind of natural
theology. That is, while he was right to think that the 'Logos', the
universal Word, was the goal of his critical work, he was wrong to
absorb this poetic Logos into the religious figure of Christ. For the
universal Word cannot be an object of faith or a personality, since it is
precisely the 'Fülle' or abundance of a process which is infinitely
becoming and expansive through the critical task of self-reflection. In
one sense Frye is right in his identification of Coleridge's goal. But he
seriously misrepresents Coleridge's approach to the figure of Christ,
which, if it were as simple as Frye suggests, would make the later
Christian writings both less problematic and less stimulating.[104]

At this stage it might seem that Coleridge is being identified as a kind
of early structuralist, concerned not with independently existing objects,
but with the relationships which are constructed and then perceived
between the observer and the observed, with the correlative that any
observer is bound to create something of what he observes: the divine
revealed in the inspired creative act. Dangerous though such comparisons always are, there is some truth in this. Yet the *Biographia Literaria*
takes us beyond the simple conclusion that Coleridge was a structuralist

before his time.

For Coleridge, to 'know' the truth was not simply a grasping of the facts, but involved the human subject. Experience must be subjected to a 'self-revising subjectivity',[105] to a critical knowledge which overcomes dogmatism and self-deception. Yet this 'secular' experience must be within a religious context: subjectivity going hand in hand with religion. It is this dual commitment which seems to lie at the root of the confusion felt by early critics of *Biographia*, 'that rambling, confused, and inconclusive work', as one reviewer of 1818 described it.[106] In the same journal, *Blackwood's*, John Wilson, better known as 'Christopher North' and Professor of Moral Philosophy at Edinburgh, had written the previous year at length on *Biographia*.

> We have felt it our duty to speak with severity of this book and its author – and we have given our readers ample opportunities to judge of the justice of our strictures. We have not been speaking in the cause of Literature only, but, we conceive, in the cause of Morality and Religion. For it is not fitting that he should be held up as an example to the rising generation ... who has alternately embraced, defended, and thrown aside all systems of Philosophy, and all creeds of Religion; who seems to have no power of retaining an opinion, no trust in the principles which he defend, but who fluctuates from theory to theory.[107]

Coleridge, it was felt, and quite rightly, could never rest in a religion with its identifiable, ecclesial traditions or in an intelligent subjectivity. Somehow he wanted it both ways, and critics like John Wilson could not see that the two might be co-inherent.

From his earliest writings, Coleridge had been concerned with 'Facts of mind'[108] and human experience in its 'inwardness', and asserted that 'the mind *acts & plays a part*, itself the actor & the spectator at once!'[109] It is habitually reflecting upon itself at work. In *The Friend* (1808–10), this sense of a reflective consciousness which precedes expression, yet is only perceived and articulated in expression, is applied principally to political and moral insight. In the *Lay Sermons* (1816–17) it is examined in the context of the public character of religion. It is the 'habitual unreflectingness' of public religion which as led to its 'spiritual slumber'.[110] The remedy is to be sought in the process of reading, whereby the individual is encouraged to reflect upon the limitations of his existing patterns of thought and assumptions, and, Coleridge concludes:

this enlargement and elevation of the soul above its mere self attest the presence, and accompany the intuition of ultimate PRINCIPLES alone. These alone can interest the undegraded human spirit deeply and enduringly, because these alone belong to its essence, and will remain with it permanently.[111]

Initially all that is required is an attitude of trust, a 'first act of faith . . . scarcely less than identical with its own being'.[112] Thus, the self is required to engage in an endless self-transcendence until faith is given not only to the initial attitude of trust, which is 'enunciated in the word, GOD', but to the identical and sole sufficient 'other', God himself, towards which the self-transcending mind is reaching. Religion is the 'interpreter' of this endless process of self-reflection, representing 'the concentration of All in Each – a Power that acts by a contraction of universal truths into individual duties' (Appendix C, p. 64). Religion is drawn towards Coleridge's theory of the imagination for its language and expression.

This reflective self-consciousness which was characteristic of Coleridge's philosophizing and theologizing was given early and detailed attention in America by James Marsh, Professor of Philosophy at the University of Vermont, whose 'Preliminary Essay' to *Aids to Reflection* introduced Coleridge's writings to Ralph Waldo Emerson (1803–82) and the transcendentalists of New England. Through Marsh, *Aids* became 'a seminal text in American intellectual history'.[113]

> The first principles [wrote Marsh], the ultimate grounds, of these, so far as they are possible objects of knowledge for us, must be sought and found in the laws of our being, or they are not found at all. The knowledge of these, terminates in the knowledge of ourselves, of our rational and personal being, of our proper and distinctive humanity, and of that Divine Being, in whose image we are created. 'We must retire inward,' says St Bernard, 'if we would ascend upward.' It is by self-inspection, by reflecting upon the mysterious grounds of our own being, that we can alone arrive at any rational knowledge of the central and absolute ground of all being.[114]

The same principle proved fertile in directions far removed from Emersonian transcendentalism. In England, the philosopher Shadforth H. Hodgson published his *Philosophy of Reflection* (1878), dedicated to Coleridge, 'my Father in Philosophy'. It is, says Hodgson, through 'self-consciousness' or the 'principle of reflection' that 'all conscious beings are agents who help to make the unseen world. . . . Their volitions are evidences of its otherwise unknown nature.'[115] Rather later in Germany, Charlotte Broicher's 'Anglikanische Kirche und deutsche Philosophie', [116] which devotes considerable attention to *Biographia Literaria*, not only identifies Coleridge as a precursor of William James on the 'innere Beglaubigung' (interior verification) of religious truth (p. 228), but also of Keble, J. H. Newman and Hurrell Froude on the imagination in religious belief, on the illative sense, and on the will as man's spiritual centre (pp. 458–93).[117]

In the 'Confessio Fidei', Coleridge writes that it is to the conscience, and not to the mere understanding, that the certainty of redemption is revealed. The religious quest, indeed, like the quest for philosophic unity, is not merely intellectual but also emotional and volitional. Man, possessing will, reason and a sense of moral responsibility (that is, conscience), reflects upon hs own nature until, led back repeatedly to a sense of his own limitations, ultimate self-expression is revealed, in hope, as 'a God, that is, a Being in whom Supreme Reason and a most holy Will are one with an infinite Power. . . . that all holy Will is coincident with the Will of God, and therefore secure in its ultimate Consequences by his Omnipotence'.[118] The process of self-reflection will ultimately reveal the Divine, the only sufficient Other.

While in *The Friend* Coleridge's subject is primarily political and moral, in the *Lay Sermons* religious, *Biographia Literaria* might be identified as an exercise in the processes of self-reflection through the act of reading. It is a book about reading which makes conscious in the reader the experience of the interaction of artist and spectator. He becomes thus a part of the created work of art. A primary element in Coleridge's endeavour to demonstrate the mind's self-consciousness is metaphor, which is addressed in the first instance to the imagination. A metaphor is a linguistic transference, describing one thing in terms of another, and the process whereby words construct a 'reality' from within themselves and impose this on the world in which we live.[119] By the 'shaping spirit' of the Imagination, a metaphor first links many diverse elements into a unity and gives language the expressive power 'to conquer a realm beyond the immediate world perceived by the eye'. As the metaphor sinks into and reflects the reader's experience, it requires of him a creative act 'so as to make him lose the consciousness of words – to make him *see* everything'.[120]

Here is an extended metaphor descriptive of the act of thinking.

Most of my readers will have observed a small water-insect on the surface of rivulets, which throws a cinque-spotted shadow fringed with prismatic colours on the sunny bottom of the brook; and will have noticed, how the little animal *wins* its way up against the stream, by alternate pulses of active and passive motion, now resisting the current, and now yielding to it in order to gather strength and a momentary *fulcrum* for a further propulsion. This is no unapt emblem of the mind's self-experience in the act of thinking.[121]

Just as irony may disintegrate old relationships and perceive new, so metaphor can illustrate and prompt a new perspective and understanding of the perceiving self. The human mind is here described in terms of the complex action by which the water-insect propels itself upstream. Precisely because the description is metaphorical and indirect – mediated through an illustration which experience can grasp – it demands the exercise of the very mental processes which it describes. The truth of the metaphor can only be grasped in the active appreciation of it: consciousness precedes expression, and expression alone makes consciousness available. Thus the self-conscious mind develops. Furthermore, it illustrates and exercises the form of mental energy which is required to read *Biographia*. Such metaphors, therefore, are 'fulcra' on which the mind is consciously turned in order to propel itself actively against the current of the book.[122]

Part of the difficulty of reading *Biographia* lies in its repeated pressure on the reader to think about what he is doing as he reads. More than that, the structure is deliberately incomplete. 'You have been obliged', Coleridge warns, 'to omit so many links, from the necessity of compression, that what remains, looks ... like the fragments of the winding steps of an old ruined tower.'[123] In the act of climbing we create the missing stairs. This constructive work is further described in Thesis VI of Chapter 12, in which Coleridge tries to define the I AM, otherwise identified as spirit, self and self-consciousness.

In this, and in this alone, object and subject, being and knowing are identical, each involving, and supposing the other. In other words, it is a subject which becomes a subject by the act of constructing itself objectively to itself.[124]

At this point, it can be said that Coleridge is not simply a primitive structuralist, for structuralists are interested primarily in relationships, while it seems that Coleridge's attention is focused firmly upon the reader, rather in the manner suggested by Stanley Fish in his paper 'Literature in the Reader: Affective Stylistics'.[125] Indeed, the principles underlying Fish's method should by now be familiar: the denial of a point of termination; the adhesion to a process; the appeal to and creation of experience. Fish's open-endedness, however, would not be ultimately embraced by that which, in Coleridge, frustrated and confused his early critics in *Blackwood's*, the religious horizon which laps the repeatedly experienced finitude of secularity in the context of an infinite divinity. Coleridge must return, in the end, to the ultimately constitutive nature of the 'ideas' of 'God', 'Freedom', 'Immortality' and 'Self'. And so, like Schelling and unlike Kant, he was looking for an intuitive knowledge in which a subjective idea ultimately authenticated its own objective validity.[126]

Finally, the discussion of self-consciousness should be linked with the concluding paragraph of the 'Confessio Fidei' on the Trinity, a doctrine commended to us by our conscience and 'real' beyond what is conceptually clear. 'The Idea of God involves that of a Tri-unity', wrote Coleridge in 1806.[127] In the principle of polar causality 'the cause remains present in the effect, and is, from one point of view, identical with it'.[128] They are distinguished, however, by their relative positions. In his examination of cognition and consciousness, Coleridge limits conceptual clarity, attainable by the understanding, to the principle of identity, the mere fact of being. But the principle of polarity, lying at the root of the 'multeity in unity', defines the content of self-consciousness as tri-une, three 'in' one and one 'in' three.[129] In tri-unity is realized the actual self, the will which is ultimately coincident with the Will of God. Coleridge sums it up in a note on Donne's Sermon XXXIV.

Being, Mind, Love in action = holy Spirit are ideas distinguishable tho' not divisible, but *Will* is incapable of distinction or division: it is equally implied in 1. vital Being, 2. in essential intelligence, and 3. in effluent Love or holy Action. Now Will is the true principle & meaning of *Identity*, of *Selfness*: even in our common language. The Will, therefore, being indistinguishably one, but the possessive Powers triply distinguishable, do perforce involve the notion expressed by three *Persons* and one *God*.[130]

The purpose of *Biographia Literaria* might be defined as self-construction. If its subject-matter is the imagination, its method is to encourage the reader to experience the imagination at work. Nevertheless, it should not be taken in isolation from the rest of Coleridge's work, lest indeed the *subjective* Pole of the Dynamic Philosophy outgrow itself.[131] For it was intended only as a prelude to his major project. 'It will', wrote Coleridge, 'be an important Pioneer to the great Work on the *Logos*,

Divine and Human, on which I have set my Heart and hope to ground my ultimate reputation'.[132] Jerome Christensen describes the method of *Biographia Literaria* as 'marginal', an investigation into 'the contingency of living in a borrowed home'. As an exercise in self-reflection it sheds light on the point that 'all philosophical certainties have inconsistencies and interruptions; all texts have margins'.[133] Through this openendedness Coleridge sought to focus on the theological matter of the relationship between the finite and contingent, and the infinity of the divine. How far Coleridge recast a true Christian theology in a romantic tradition which saw the need for a modern mythology and, as has been argued, rejected the structural plot and symbolic imagery of the Judaeo-Christian literary tradition,[134] will be a major theme of Chapter 7.

6 Three Later Poems

I 'LIMBO' AND 'NE PLUS ULTRA'

In his book *Coleridge as Religious Thinker* 1961), James D. Boulger dismisses Coleridge's later poetry as of little value on the ground that, after 1810, Coleridge was not emotionally at home in the abstract world of spiritual Christianity into which he had thought himself by philosophical reflection and self-reflection. The poet, it might be said, failed to conjoin the necessary elements of 'lofty and abstract truths' with 'impassioned feelings'.[1] Boulger's comments, faithful to the traditional criticism of Coleridge as a poetic failure after 'Dejection: An Ode' (1802), fail to appreciate his emotional commitment to Christian doctrine in his later years and the integral part played by his poetic inspiration in the resolution and sustenance of his belief. Nor do they give due credit to his continued development as both philosopher and religious thinker long after the publication of *Biographia Literaria*, and, not least, the refinement of his poetry from an art in which subjective, internal experiences are transformed, and reflected upon, as external, public object, to a creative activity in which the finite form of the poem functions as a window on infinity. In his 'Essays on the Principles of Method' in *The Friend* (1818), Coleridge wrote:

> The finite form can neither be laid hold of, nor is it anything of itself real, but merely an apprehension, a frame-work which the human imagination forms by its own limits, as the foot measures itself on the snow.[2]

Instead of focusing on the solid image, whether palace dome or albatross, Coleridge's later poetry, often deliberately fragmentary, intimates, with a delicate and translucent purity, a greater mystery and repeatedly invites the reconstruction of a wholeness of being of which it is the symbolic indication.

The origins of the poems 'Limbo' and 'Ne Plus Ultra' are obscured by a chaotic notebook entry dated by Professor Coburn as April–May 1811.[3] Ernest Hartley Coleridge dates their composition as 1817 and '?1826' respectively. However, internal evidence apart, the existence of a

gloss on 'Limbo' in a notebook entry for 1814,[4] its close parallels with
the concluding chapter of *Biographia Literaria*, together with a strong
repudiation of the religious ideas of both poems in a letter written to
J. H. Green in September 1818, suggest that the earlier date is more
accurate. Furthermore, the poetry reflects the spiritual evolution
undergone by Coleridge during the crisis years 1810–11, and through
which he had grown by the end of the decade. His spiritual growth was
part and parcel of his poetic development, each balancing the other. The
evolution of the poetry, which was characterized by 'progressive
realization' rather than simply an 'aggregation of words',[5] irrigated his
own theology of revealed religion which, in turn, to some extent repaired
the fragments of the later poems. The poet guided the believer who
restored the romantic's sense of ruin.

In the manuscript form of these two poems, it is clear that Coleridge
laboured hard in their creation, beginning with the themes of corruption, damnation and privation in a pastiche entitled 'On Donne's first
Poem', and running into what was later published as 'Limbo', which, in
turn, is a companion-piece to the poem 'Sole Positive of Night', entitled
'Ne Plus Ultra' by E. H. Coleridge. The version here given of 'Limbo'
follows Coleridge's final manuscript form.

> Tis a strange Place, this Limbo! not a Place,
> Yet name it so – where Time & weary Space
> Fetter'd from flight, with night-mair sense of Fleeing
> Strive for their last crepuscular Half-being –
> Lank Space, and <scytheless> Time with branny Hands
> Barren and soundless as the measuring Sands,
> Mark'd but by Flit of Shades – unmeaning they
> As Moonlight on the Dial of Day –
> But that is lovely – looks like Human Time,
> An old Man with a steady Look sublime
> That stops his earthly Task to watch the Skies –
> But he is blind – a statue hath such Eyes –
> Yet having moon-ward turn'd his face by chance –
> Gazes the orb with moon-like Countenance
> With scant white hairs, with fore-top bald & high
> He gazes still, his eyeless Face all Eye –
> As twere an Organ full of silent Sight
> His whole Face seemeth to rejoice in Light/
> Lip touching Lip, all moveless, Bust and Limb,
> He seems to gaze at that which seems to gaze on Him!
>
> (ll. 11–30)[6]

What is here almost certainly a poetic self-portrait in the old man, finds a remarkable parallel of theme in the early 'Ode to the Departing Year' (1796) which was probably influenced by Coleridge's reading of Boehme and the Cabala and wherein is a godhead whose 'stormy blackness' of Power contains within itself Love and Light.[7] The theme is further developed in 'Ne Plus Ultra'. More significant, however, is the close parallel between 'Limbo' and Coleridge's prose attempt to develop a metaphysical grounding for his thoughts on time in Chapter 24 of *Biographia Literaria*.

The sense of Before and After becomes both intelligible and intellectual when, and *only* when, we contemplate the succession in the relations of Cause and Effect, which, like the two poles of the magnet manifest the being and unity of the one power by relative opposites, and give, as it were, a substratum of permanence, of identity, and therefore of reality, to the shadowy flux of Time. It is Eternity revealing itself in the phenomena of Time: and the perception and acknowledgement of the proportionality and appropriateness of the Present to the Past, prove to the afflicted Soul, that it has not yet been deprived of the sight of God, that it can still recognize the effective presence of a Father, though through a darkened glass and a turbid atmosphere, though of a Father that is chastening it.[8]

Already in the *Biographia*, following Schelling, Coleridge had asserted that the 'free will' or 'absolute self' was supratemporal and experienced '*time per se*'. Such despatialized time is, according to Schelling, not extended but rather concentrated into one moment or compresent.[9] Now the similar moral intelligibility of eternity, blessed in its puzzling involvement with time, is contrasted with the 'state of the reprobate spirits' which is described by the 'mystic theologians' as 'a dreadful dream in which there is no sense of reality ... – an eternity without time, and as it were below it – God present without manifestation of his presence'.[10]

A more general note should be made on Coleridge's reading of Schelling and also Jacob Boehme as a background to 'Limbo', before considering more precisely the contribution of poetry and poetic form to the poem's effect. In *Vom dreifachen Leben des Menschen* (1620), ch. 4:32, Boehme describes how 'when God set the will in the *Fiat*, then the wheel of the eternal essences went forth into a substance and there the time had its beginning, which was *not* from eternity'.[11] Coleridge associated theories of 'internal time' with Boehme, commenting in *The Philosophical Lectures* on 'Böhmen's ideas of the Horology or innate

Time in all creatures'.[12] The 'Human Time' of 'Limbo' seems to derive directly from Boehme's *Psychologia vera, oder Viertzig Fragen Von der Seen* (1620, trans. J. Sparrow, 1647), in which Question 34 ('What is the miserable and horrible condition of the Damned Souls?') states that 'their number is not the number of any human time', and that 'they have a sport ... though indeed there is no time'.[13]

Underlying and integral to Coleridge's poetic processes in the second decade of the nineteenth century are his philosophical and theological investigations.

In its manuscript form the final line of 'Limbo' seems to have been written with fresh ink and a fresh quill ('A fear, a future fate. Tis *positive Negation!*'), making it appear as a title to the next notebook entry which continues in the same quill as the manuscript of 'Ne Plus Ultra'. In this way the two poems may almost be regarded as one. Once again, the version here given of 'Ne Plus Ultra' follows Coleridge's final manuscript form.

> Sole Positive of Night!
> Antipathist of Light!
> Fate's only Essence! Primal Scorpion Rod!
> The one permitted Opposite of God!
> Condensed Blackness, and Abysmal Storm
> Compacted to one Sceptre
> Arms the Grasp enorm,
> The Interceptor!
> The Substance, that still costs the Shadow, Death!
> The Dragon foul and fell!
> The unrevealable
> And hidden one, whose Breath
> Gives Wind and Fuel to the fires of Hell!
> Ah sole Despair
> Of both th'Eternities in Heaven!
> Sole Interdict of all-bedewing Prayer,
> The All-compassionate!
> Save to the Lampads seven
> Revealed to none of all th'Angelic State,
> Save to the Lampads seven
> That watch the Throne of Heaven![14]

As with 'Limbo', the sources of 'Ne Plus Ultra' are to be found in Behmenist cosmology, although no similar precise references can be found for the poem's expression of the paradoxical polarity of the Godhead. Yet this polarity is indeed central to Boehme's philosophy and laid down in his earliest work *Aurora oder Morgenröte im Aufgang* (1612, trans. J. Sparrow, 1656), in which the world is subjected to two opposing principles, good and evil, light and darkness, both of which are aspects of God. More precisely in *De electione gratiae, oder Von der Gnaden-Wahl* (1623, trans. J. Sparrow, 1655), Chapter 4, Boehme describes the movement from an undifferentiated and unmanifest eternity to the external Principles of Fire and Light, existing only mutually, to the third Principle, manifested through 'sevens'. However, there seems to be no immediate source for the terrifying reality of the non-existent hell of 'Ne Plus Ultra', an insubstantiality which is Interceptor, sole Despair, and sole Interdict of prayer. The poem needs to be read in the context of its companion-piece 'Limbo', to balance its positive negation, partly, indeed, relieved by the Lampads seven, with the poetic irony which affirms what looks like Human Time – an affirmation expressed in manifest and revealed deity.

The letter already mentioned, written to J. H. Green on 30 September 1818, repudiates this Behmenist notion of paradoxical polarity within the divine unity, and provides a sound argument for an earlier dating of the poem. It is a clear attack on pantheistic tendencies in Boehme, Schelling and Coleridge's own reflections on 'bi-polar knowledge' in *Biographia*. He now categorically rejects the two opposing principles as aspects of the one God.

> Our first point therefore is – steadily to deny and clearly to expose, the Polarity as existing or capable of existing in the unity of a perfect Will or in the Godhead as ens realissimum. *The divine Unity* is indeed the indispensable CONDITION of this Polarity; but both its *formal* and it's immediate, *specific* CAUSE is in the contradictory Will of the Apostasy. (Fichte was far nearer the truth than Schelling – . . .)[15]

Writing to C. A. Tulk on 24 November 1818, Coleridge condemns Schelling as a mere pantheist in the mould of Boehme. For their polarity is, in Coleridge's later language, a 'contrariness', finding itself in the divine unity not as an equipoise of opposites but as a disharmony within a universal similarity. 'Polar forces,' he was to observe, ' – that is, opposite, not contrary, powers – are necessarily *unius generis*, homogeneous.'[16] Though split they tend towards reunion because each opposite has been generated from the other, and thus the interest of progressiveness is upheld. But in the interest of permanence,[17] in Boehme nature is the manifestation of the polar conflict in the deity, God dwelling in nature as the soul dwells in the body. So, too, in Schelling, 'Natur-Philosophie' is in the end mere Pantheism, 'or "gemina Natura quae fit et facit, creat et creatur", of which the Deity itself is but an Out-birth'.[18]

The development of Coleridge's religious thought was, in this case, prompted by an increasingly profound sense of the nature of evil, which becomes for him far more real and independent of the Godhead than the sinister nothingness of 'Ne Plus Ultra'. However, if theology moved beyond this paradoxical polarity of the deity, the 'trichotomous logic' of Coleridge's later poetry and prose continued to explore the paradoxes of oppositions which were really not contradictions, and the reconciliation of apparent opposites. Quoting a marginal note made by Coleridge on Kant's *Allgemeine Naturgeschichte*, Professor J. H. Muirhead in his book *Coleridge as Philosopher* (1930) describes the workings of 'trichotomy':

'seek first for the Unity as the only source of Reality, and then for the two opposite yet correspondent forms by which it manifests itself. For it is an axiom of universal application that *manifestio non datur nisi per alterum*. Instead therefore of affirmation and contradiction, the tools of dichotamic logic, we have three terms Identity, Thesis and Antithesis'. It is only by this principle that he [Coleridge] conceived it possible to advance beyond the limitations of Logic or the science of Understanding to a Noetic, or science of the Reason, which should also be a science of Reality.[19]

So far this study has explored the background to 'Limbo' and 'Ne Plus Ultra' in Coleridge's philosophical and theological reading, suggesting that his understanding of Schelling and Boehme developed beyond the cosmology of the poems. Yet a further important point remains to be made, that the poetic processes at work were exercising a powerful counterforce as a mode of reflection about reality. The aesthetic activity of the poetry intensifies ordinary experience and perception, a point which lies at the root of the distinction between primary and secondary Imagination in *Biographia*. Thus, even while it continued to develop, Coleridge's religious thought was irrigated by the processes in the later poetry of self-reflection and reflection on experience. Such critical self-consciousness, as it has been explored in the critical prose and the verse, was an ever-present defence against the forms of custom, prejudice and mere understanding divorced from reason which are dangers always lurking in the degeneration of Christian doctrine as it slides into sterile dogma.

'Limbo' and 'Ne Plus Ultra' are fragments and create fragmentation. The public form of the doctrine that gives 'Limbo' its name is violated by the poetic, creative energy. Coleridge, in a letter to the younger James Gillman, of 24 October 1826, describes the mind as a kaleidoscope bringing symmetry out of a chaos of shapes from the past.[20] As themselves poetic fragments the poems exemplify important romantic formulations concerning poetry.[21] The fragment both creates an impulse to reconstruct the intimated whole, and also, together with paradox, resists this hypothetical completeness since the poems' achievement is precisely in a challenging inachievement. Behind this sense of the paradoxical nature of existence lies, of course, the German Romantic tradition of higher irony.

In the poems, fragmentation and polarity operate at a number of levels. There are the basic polarities of theme – time and eternity, darkness and light, the power of God and the weakness of man, heaven and hell. There are the polarities of language – 'positive Negation', 'positive of Night'. There is also – looking back to 'The Ancient Mariner' – a polarity in the artist as both controller and controlled, the critical spectator–artist. The poem is about the poem, through creative experience of which the divine is glimpsed and thereby more effectively perceived. The sight–blindness paradox of 'Limbo' and its companion-piece are employed as a means of escape both from 'Understanding's Phantom logic' and from Coleridge's earlier poetic process of externalizing subjective experiences in the description of natural objects. What is created, then, is a purely symbolic work, wherein the images interrelate meaningfully through 'passion or universal logic' and not through 'the logic of grammar'.[22]

In the published form of 'Limbo', Coleridge begins his poem with a series of pronouns which lack any antecedent meaning.

> The sole true Something – This! In Limbo's Den
> It frightens Ghosts, as here Ghosts frighten men.

By line 19, 'This' is rediscovered transformed:

> But that is lovely – looks like Human Time.

The immediate demonstrative pronoun has, in the poetic process, become distanced and set apart so that it may seem to have a form and aesthetic grace. But at least the poetry has endowed the terrifying blankness of the initial 'This' with recognizable features – just as Limbo, though no place, is named so by the poem – so that it becomes a 'that' with which some relationship is possible.

The blind old man, recognizably Coleridge himself, embodies both spiritual deprivation and potential spiritual fulfilment. Two letters, one of 1799 and the other of 1832, illustrate the development of this ambivalent sense of blindness as a metaphor.

i. I have, at times, experienced such an extinction of *Light* in my mind, I have been so forsaken by all the *forms* and *colourings* of Existence, as if the *organs* of Life had been dried up; as if only simple BEING remained, blind and stagnant!

ii. in Christ only did he build a hope – yea, he blessed the emptiness, that made him capable of his Lord's Fullness, gloried in the Blindness that was receptive of his Master's Light.[23]

There is no serene spiritual vision enjoyed by the old man of the poem. All the language of perception is highly qualified. If that which is lovely merely looks like Human Time, so 'He seems to gaze at that which seems to gaze on him'. Accepting man's inability to know spiritual truth with certainty and acknowledging the limitations of poetic language, nevertheless the poet indicates through the blindness of the old man a possible willed means of finding God. Poetic creativity, from the very light that comes from within man, provides intimations which reflect in themselves the divine splendour which, he surmises, shines down upon our blindness.

The contrast with Limbo is starkly projected:

> No such sweet sights doth Limbo den immure,
> Wall'd round, and made a spirit-jail secure,
> By the mere horror of blank Nought-at-all.
>
> (ll. 31–3)

The minifest deity which in 'Limbo' looks like man's true time, is linked in 'Ne Plus Ultra' with the Lampads Seven wherein the fullness of being is contrasted with hellish negation. Again, it is an intimation of the divine splendour. The Lampads are elsewhere referred to by Coleridge in 'Ode to the Departing Year' (ll. 76–7), and in the tenth of the *Philosophical Lectures*.

the Deity as manifested, as expanding <in at> least <seven> ways, they [the Cabalists] represented as the seven spirits or the seven

Sephiroth. The last, which was to be the Messiah or the Shekinah, was to be the same as the second person of the triad, and to be in the Shekinah a concentration of all the seven spirits of the manifestation, a doctrine which must have been very early indeed in the Church, because we find a clear reference to it in the beginning of the Apocalypse.[24]

This last quotation links the concern for Christian doctrine with the poetic contribution to Coleridge's religious development. As poetry, reflective and self-reflective, joins the interest of art and imagination to that of reality and perception, so the fragmentary nature of the poems prompts a fulfilment that is at once divine and on the edge of human experience. As Coleridge writes in the 'Essays on the Principles of Method', 'there is *method* in the fragments'.[25] The paradoxical sensations which underlie the poetic discipline of 'Limbo' and 'Ne Plus Ultra' are expressed in a note of September 1808.

For Love, passionate in its deepest tranquillity, Love unutterable fills my whole Spirit, so that every fibre of my Heart, nay, of my whole frame seems to tremble under its perpetual touch and sweet pressure, like the string of a Lute – with a sense of vibratory Pain distinct from all other sensations, a Pain that seems to shiver and tremble *on the threshhold of some Joy, that cannot be entered into while I am embodied* – a pain of yearning which all the Pleasure on earth could not induce me to relinquish, even were it in my power[26]

The poems, true to Coleridge's principles of method, actually create and develop their own subject (which is themselves), and finally point beyond their own fragmentariness. Such a poetic method implies a 'progressive transition' which is the antithesis of 'mere dead arrangement',[27] and continually undermines the static tendencies of religious doctrinal form. But this is not to deny that such form has its part to play in the paradoxical quality of a confessed faith, and Coleridge had, indeed, composed his 'Confessio Fidei' on 3 November 1810.[28] Referring again to the Lampads Seven in 'Ne Plus Ultra', and their association with early Christian doctrine in the *Philosophical Lectures*, the concerns of doctrine and the poetic perception of reality seem to be linked in a comment which could almost stand as a moral of the poem: 'Without faith in the only begotten Son of God no rational conviction of reality in any subject is possible'.[29]

Coleridge's best later poetry does not confirm the suggestion that he was not at home emotionally in the abstract religious world into which he had thought himself. Rather it sustains the highly articulate and self-conscious emotional and spiritual development of Coleridge's theological and philosophical reflections.

II 'CONSTANCY TO AN IDEAL OBJECT'

The later poetry explores the creative process of thinking rather than thought and the paradoxes of reflection about a reality which demands self-reflection. In 'Constancy to an Ideal Object' (which may have been written as early as 1805, or as late as 1828), the ideal object is not an entity, but an act – a consciousness which links subject and object in a joining of opposites which does not cancel them out. Such poetry enables us to 'see', to experience and think about the self and the world across the barriers of sense and finitude, for, as Coleridge defined it in *The Statesman's Manual*, Appendix E, an Idea 'is an educt of the Imagination actuated by the pure Reason, to which there neither is or can be an adequate correspondent in the world of the senses'.[30]

If the beloved Sara Hutchinson lies behind 'Constancy to an Ideal Object', it is not the lady herself who is the ideal object. Coleridge's concern is not with Sara's physical presence, but with the thought of her, with love itself and not love's embodiment. In a letter, probably dating from November 1819, he describes the creative process by which emotion and experience are focused and by which the poet comes to 'see'.

> For from my very childhood I have been accustomed to *abstract* and as it were unrealize whatever of more than common interest my eyes dwelt on; and then by a sort of transfusion and transmission of my consciousness to identify myself with the Object – ... it was a pride and a place of Healing to lie, as in an Apostle's Shadow, within the Eclipse and deep substance-seeming Gloom of 'these dread Ambassadors from Earth to Heaven, Great Hierarchs'![31]

Love becomes objectless as the creative poet, abandoning the stock rhetorical abstractions of the early verse, explores the experience of relationship (finite/infinite: subject/object) in a poetry which is symbolic, partaking of the reality which it renders intelligible.

'Constancy to an Ideal Object' contrasts two conditions as it addresses the 'loveliest friend'. Coleridge oscillated between them throughout his life.

> The peacefull'st cot, the moon shall shine upon,
> Lulled by the thrush and wakened by the lark,
> Without thee were but a becalmed bark,
> Whose Helmsman on an ocean waste and wide
> Sits mute and pale his mouldering helm beside.
>
> (ll. 20–4)

Rural domestic bliss is contrasted with the fate of the Ancient Mariner, and the Mariner, we recall, came to experience love and loveliness precisely in things most hateful, the slimy sea-creatures. Similarly here the tone of the poem changes after its protracted lament that that which is most dear is an illusion. Now, as the Mariner accepted the water-snakes, the poet accepts the illusion: 'And art thou nothing?'

The ambiguity is explored in the phenomenon of the Brocken Spectre. It had haunted Coleridge since his ascent of the Brocken in the Harz mountains in May 1799[32] and he refers to it as late as 1825 in *Aids to Reflection*. In the rising or setting of the sun, when its rays are almost horizontal, a man's shadow may be thrown onto a bank of mountain mist, his head haloed with a ring of light or a 'glory':

> . . . as when
> The woodman winding westward up the glen
> At wintry dawn, where o'er the sheep-track's maze
> The viewless snow-mist weaves a glist'ning haze,
> Sees full before him, gliding without tread,
> An image with a glory round its head;
> The enamoured rustic worships its fair hues,
> Nor knows he makes the shadow, he pursues!
>
> (ll. 25–32)

Boulger, who had dismissed the later poetry as emotionally distinct from the later abstract spirituality, dismisses also 'Constancy to an Ideal Object' as a recognition that the ideal object of the poet is but the 'self-generating illusion of the rustic'.[33] Yet the tone of the lines describing the Brocken Spectre contradicts Boulger's reading. It is one of triumph and energy. The image of the Spectre is there for all to see ('sees full before him'). 'Glory' is a word descriptive of religious and spiritual value, adding a richness to the image making for richness and worth. The rustic responds to the richness eagerly, and being 'enamoured', worships its beauty. The last word of the poem, 'pursues', emphasizes his energy and vitality.

Clearly something important is happening, not to be dismissed merely as a 'self-generating illusion'. Describing genius in *Aids to Reflection*, Coleridge remarks that 'the beholder either recognizes it as a projected form of his own Being, that moves before him with a Glory round its head, or recoils from it as from a Spectre'.[34] The ambiguity is all, while in the poem the ideal object, as an act of consciousness, is the uniting of the meditative mind and its object of meditation, opposites yet one in the poetic creation. Furthermore, to emphasize the polarity, the 'glory' on a Brocken spectre may be seen only by the person to whom it belongs, even though the shadow of the figure may be seen by all.[35] Thus, while the 'objectivity' is preserved, it remains uniquely personal.

Coleridge's poem is about the nature of poetic perception and creativity. The poem, enabling us to 'see', is not merely descriptive, but creative and illuminative (if we will allow it), enlightening our abstractions from what we perceive so that perception becomes a realization of the eternal through and in the temporal, the divine illumination no vision but a 'state of consciousness' or an 'inward experience'.[36] Paralleling the Ideal Object or 'Idea' of the poem with the description of 'symbol' in *The Statesman's Manual*, it may be characterized as 'the living *educt* of the Imagination', 'incorporating the Reason in Images of the Sense, and organizing (as it were) the flux of the Senses by the permanence and self-circling energies of the Reason'.[37]

The Ideal Object as it has been explored in this late poem, a process and not a thing, forged in the poet's creative genius, is the 'visible tip of the ontological iceberg'.[38] The shadowy ambiguities of the Brocken Spectre reflect back to Plato's cave-myth which finds a reference in 'The Destiny of Nations', begun by Coleridge as early as 1796. If there be no divinity or eternal, then the polarity and ambiguity ceases to be creative, the rustic pursues in vain and the glory becomes an illusion indeed. And yet the energy and the glory remain, obstinately. Indeed they presuppose and render intelligible the Reality not as it appears but as it is. Referring to the chariots of Ezekiel, Coleridge wrote in *The Statesman's Manual*: 'The truths and the symbols that represent them move in conjunction and form the living chariot that bears up (for *us*) the throne of the Divine Humanity.'[39]

This final reference raises a problem to which Coleridge gave some attention in his later writings. From what has been suggested, it might be said that the creative imagination of the poet is equally with the Bible a source of 'revelation'. Swiatecka, indeed, while acknowledging that Coleridge held the Bible in very high regard, believes that he never really tackled the problem of its parity with other works wherein inspiration may reveal 'symbols of Truth, actual tho' dim perceptions of it'.[40] Yet it must be recognized that Coleridge had described the Bible as 'the Best Guide to Political Skill and Foresight' in the subtitle to *The Statesman's Manual*, and confessed in the posthumously published *Confessions of an Inquiring Spirit* (1840) that 'in the Bible there is more that *finds* me than I have experienced in all other books together'.[41] In what way, therefore, is the Bible a more valuable, or even a more certain, source of divine revelation and illumination of the relationship between God and man, the infinite and finite, than any poetic process whose end is not so much a poem (an artifact), but a new awareness of Being and an intuition of the spiritual in man?

7 The Later Prose and Notebooks

Confessions of an Inquiring Spirit is Coleridge's principal attack upon Bibliolatry, that unthinking reverence for the Bible which offends the rights of reason and rejects interpretation by means of an external frame of reference. His devotion to Scripture arises from an appeal to the whole experience of man, the Bible received inasmuch as it *finds* him 'at greater depths' of his being, bringing with it 'an irresistible evidence of its having proceeded from the Holy Spirit'.[1] Revelation must be authenticated in man's human essence. 'Make a man feel the *want* of it; rouse him, if you can, to the self-knowledge of his *need* of it.'[2] The first part of this chapter will examine how, in the task of reflection and self-discovery, man necessarily employs his faculties of reason and will in responding to divine initiative. The authentication of revelation, therefore, is the assent in a new and objective form to that to which he is already subjectively related.[3]

Second, and to return to the question with which Chapter 5 concluded, did Coleridge, poet and writer of narrative, reject the structure of what M. H. Abrams calls the 'circuitous journey' from paradise through the Fall, redemption and back to paradise in the Judaeo-Christian tradition? Anne Mellor believes he did.[4] Abrams himself holds to the structure but in a purely secularized form.[5] However, the present argument, while maintaining Abram's anatomy of the Christian – or, more strictly, Biblical – pattern of history, would suggest that it flourished in Coleridge's imagination in the context of that 'polarity' which was his constant preoccupation, and that together they found their final expression in the Trinitarian profession of faith and the Polar Logic of his last years.

The final section of the chapter will give some consideration to Coleridge's great work, so long planned and unfulfilled. On 12 September 1814, he wrote to Daniel Stuart:

The Title is: Christianity the one true Philosophy – or 5 Treatises on the Logos, or communicative Intelligence, Natural, Human, and

Divine: – to which is prefixed a prefatory Essay on the Laws & Limits of Toleration & Liberality illustrated by fragments of *Auto*-biography –. The first Treatise – Logos propaideuticos – or the science of systematic Thinking in ordinary Life – the second, Logos architectonicus, or an attempt to apply the constructive, or mathematical, Process to Metaphysics & Natural Theology – the 3rd – (the divine Logos incarnate) a full Commentary on the Gospel of St. John, in development of St. Paul's doctrine of preaching Christ alone, & him Crucified – the 4th, on Spinoza with a Life of B. Spinoza – this entitled, Logos Agonistes. 5th and last, Logos alogos (i.e. logos illogicus) or on modern Unitarianism, it's causes & effects. ... The purpose of the whole is – a philosophical Defence of the Articles of the Church, as far as they respect Doctrine, or points of Faith.[6]

It is arguable that through the literary development of his theory of symbol and the imagination, Coleridge left no real place in his thinking for the historical elements of Christianity, or for the particularity of Jesus Christ.[7] Coleridge, certainly, was well aware of this danger, expressing a hope, in 1805, 'that my mind may be made up as to the character of Jesus, and of historical Christianity, as clearly as it is of Christ the Logos and intellectual or spiritual Christianity'.[8]

It will be suggested that, by his Polar Logic, Coleridge recognized both the 'ideal' and the historical element of Christianity, that revelation was neither wholly outward nor wholly inward,[9] and that, like the poles of a magnet, these two elements suppose and require each other in the Christian profession.

I   REVELATION AND RADICAL EVIL

Coleridge's comments on revealed religion in *Confessions of an Inquiring Spirit* as 'in its highest contemplation the unity, that is, the identity or co-inherence, of Subjective and Objective', have been briefly noted in Chapter 5.[10] He described it further as 'at once inward life and Truth, and outward Fact and Luminary'. The second section of this chapter will be more concerned with this 'outward Fact and Luminary' of revealed religion, that is, Coleridge's views on the Trinity or the incarnation and its place in the scheme of redemption. For the present, attention will be given to the 'inward life and Truth', and more particularly to Coleridge's later understanding of an early preoccupation, original sin in man: also to the means, in man, by which it may be overcome and grace received. Comparison will be made between Coleridge's writings and the work of Kant in *Die Religion innerhalb der Grenzen der blossen Vernunft* (1793) and, to a lesser extent, Fichte in *Versuch einer Kritik aller Offenbarung* (1792), which was first thought to have been the work of Kant.[11] In no sense is this intended to be an exhaustive examination of Coleridge's relationship with the Germans, but a specific and highly selective study of his thinking on revealed religion in one doctrinal area.

As a poet, Coleridge kept distinguished company with others who, in various ways, had defended the authority of revelation. To this end, John Dryden, a convinced Roman Catholic, had composed *The Hind and the Panther* (1687). Blake, religiously idiosyncratic, declared that 'there is no natural religion'[12] and that revelation was not something invented but given. This study has traced the continuous processes in Coleridge's poetry and prose which culminated in his later years in his clear affirmation of a Christian belief. His practice as a poet and literary critic may not be separated from his philosophical reading embracing Boehme, the Cambridge Platonists, David Hartley, and finally Kant and German idealism. It was on the foundations of a revised epistemology learned principally from Kant and Fichte, that Coleridge established his poetic defence of a revealed religion on a philosophical basis. However, what for him provided the confirmation of Christian belief, implied for these Germans the ultimate withering away of positive religion, for it was the requirements of rational morality which lay at the heart of their philosophy of religion. Epistemological considerations apart, however, there is clear evidence that Coleridge's experience of a life wrecked by opium, an ill-advised marriage and constitutional indecision, led him to a deep sympathy with Kant's assertion of radical evil in human nature, the innate tendency to depart from the maxims of morality, the 'Antitype of a the [*sic*] moral Law' as Coleridge described this 'Kantian idea'.[13] It was a view which Kant himself explicitly connected with the traditional Christian sources of the doctrine of original sin.[14] Thus when Coleridge, in the 'Confessio Fidei' asserts that 'I believe, and hold it as the fundamental article of Christianity, that I am a fallen creature', he is following Kant, and in a more veiled form Fichte, in their identification of moral evil as a necessary precondition of religion.[15]

Religion is essentially concerned with the problem of how man is to overcome the radical evil within him which diverts him from fulfilling the moral law. In *Biographia Literaria* Coleridge drew heavily on Schelling's *System des transcendentalen Idealismus* (1800) in the philosophical demonstration of the saving intuition which is reached, not by the processes characteristic of the 'understanding', but by a sudden revelation. Schelling had written:

> All misunderstanding of the transcendental philosophy is due, not to any unintelligibility in that philosophy, but to a lack of the organ by which it must be apprehended. ... Unless a man already brings the transcendental way of thinking with him, the transcendental philosophy must always be found unintelligible. It is therefore necessary that one insert oneself into this manner of thinking at the outset, through an act of freedom.[16]

The operation of rescue from man's fallen state, which is the primary task of religion, is achieved in a manner parallel to the acquisition of philosophical apprehension, by an initial 'act of freedom' through which the light of revelation shines. Coleridge is paraphrasing Schelling in *Biographia* when he writes:

> To an Esquimaux or New Zealander our most popular philosophy would be wholly unintelligible. The sense, the inward organ for it, is not yet born in him. So is there many a one among us, yes, and some who think themselves philosophers too, to whom the philosophic organ is entirely wanting. To such a man philosophy is a mere play of words and notions, like a theory of music to the deaf, or like the geometry of light to the blind.[17]

This act of freedom by which man learns to receive what revelation presents is dealt with at length in *Aids to Reflection* (1825), where it is described as faith. Drawing upon Kant, modified by Friedrich Jacobi,[18] Coleridge distinguished between 'understanding' and 'reason' to make the point that man's unassisted powers of understanding are inadequate, but that, drawn through this inadequacy, he may reach a faith in unseen realities. Repeatedly in *Aids*, Coleridge asserts that faith is not reason *per se*, but reason acting together with the will. In the same way in 'Kubla Khan' the poetic vision must be structured by the will, the conscious, recollective act of the poet. Coleridge had also stated this long before in an early marginal note on Kant's *Religion*: 'The total *Energy* of // Will, the one act of the whole Being, which alike can produce this state, is Gospel *Faith*. By Faith we are justified.'[19]

Faith, therefore, while dependent on divine initiative, employs man's total capability of reason and will. It is not indeed an inferior sort of knowledge, but rather a knowledge at first hand. A contemporary commentator on Jacobi described it succinctly.

> Of actual existence there are not two kinds of knowledge, an *a priori* and an *a posteriori*, but only one, the *a posteriori*, through sensation (*Empfindung*). And since all knowledge which does not arise *a priori* is faith, therefore all real knowledge depends upon faith, since things must first be *given* before one is in a position to apprehend relations between them.[20]

Coleridge adopts precisely this position in *The Friend* (1818), where he asserts that religion 'through her sacred oracles' confirms that 'all effective faith pre-supposes knowledge and individual conviction'.[21] Later in the same essays he refers to St Paul for whom perfection is the 'intuitive beholding of truth in its eternal and immutable source' (p. 105). Since this intuitive beholding is also the necessary exercise of man's will and reason, Coleridge is drawn towards the vision of the divine which both enhances and is conveyed by man's knowledge and control of himself.[22] As has already been noted, this image of reflection is elaborately explored in the poem 'Limbo', and implied in the double meaning of the title *Aids to Reflection*.

These remarks on St Paul, which first appeared in *The Friend*, no. 5, 14 September 1809, appear to have been drawn from a lengthy notebook entry entitled 'On Certainty', dating probably from August–September 1809.[23] Certainly, the condition of the true believer, which is the 'fixed and necessary Relation of Object to Subject', is established:

> not merely from the logical completeness of my Intuitions, Notions, Judgements and Elementary Positions in themselves and in their relation to my particular conviction, but far more from the degree of my confidence in their absolute truth, in their independence on choice and chance and individual temperament, that my conduct is determined.

Faith which is inspired by certainty, as Coleridge remarked in a letter to De Quincey, is 'intuitively distinguished from a mere delusive *feeling* of *Positiveness*'.[24] It is a gathering of the intelligence and faculties in a willed response to that which is given and ultimately determines the conduct of life. While intuition plays an essential role in the establishment of certainty, Coleridge clearly affirms that such faith is the response of 'a well-disciplined mind', and, as has already been suggested, such a *willing* suspension of disbelief is central to his literary theory.[25] In the experience of dramatic performance, as in the reception of revealed religion, there is no mere falling into idle delusion, but a conscious and intelligent respect for intuition, 'a voluntary Lending of the Will to this suspension of one of it's own operations'.[26] Some sixty years after Coleridge wrote *The Friend*, Cardinal Newman in the *Grammar of Assent* (1870) was expounding the role of the 'illative sense', that is the faculty of judging from given facts by processes outside the limits of strict logic, in reaching religious certitude. Newman was well acquainted with Coleridge's writing and aware of its importance.[27] Considering, therefore, Coleridge's aesthetic and literary concerns in his developing notions of faith and certainty, it may be worth noting that in the early drafts of the *Grammar of Assent*, what became the distinction between notional and real assent, had been between notional and imaginative assent.[28] In a manner in which Coleridge would undoubtedly have approved, Newman describes the act of real assent as 'imaginative' because it is a creative act by which the fullness of personal identity is achieved. Such a completed personality, by drawing many things into one, becomes 'a whole complete in itself' [29] and is given an absolute value.

Faith is the result of a combination of intelligence receptive to a given revelation. Returning to the essay in *The Friend* (1818) with its suggestion of St Paul as a mystic, Coleridge is careful to maintain a balance between intellect and intuitive response in religious matters.

> Not that knowledge can of itself do all! That light of religion is not that of the moon, light without heat; but neither is its warmth that of the stove, warmth without light.

The same point had been made in a notebook entry as early as the late summer of 1802.[30]

Having examined that faith whereby man may achieve the fullness of being of which he is deprived by inherent evil, the value to Coleridge of Kant and Fichte in the formulation of his theological response to sin and evil must now be demonstrated. The principal texts for this are *The Friend* in the 'rifacimento' of 1818 and the *Philosophical Lectures* delivered in 1818–19. In *The Friend* Coleridge regards the act of commitment to religion as a balance of faculties involving two poles. The Sun, indeed, 'makes all objects glorious on which it looks' (they *reflect* its glory), while faith 'presupposes knowledge and individual conviction'. Indeed as 'in every work of art there is a reconcilement of the external with the internal',[31] the historical assurance received from revelation must be fused with the individual as a moral and responsible person. Later in *The Friend*, in the 'Essays on the Principles of Method', faith as affirming and affirmed, is described as

> an eternal and infinite self-rejoicing, self-loving, with a joy unfathomable, with a love all comprehensive. It is absolute; and the absolute is neither singly that which affirms, nor that which is affirmed; but the identity and living copula of both.[32]

Thus the 'Law of Polarity' is established as an important philosophical foundation for both *The Friend* and the *Philosophical Lectures*. In the posthumously published *Confessions of an Inquiring Spirit* its centrality in the matter of religion is reaffirmed, inasmuch as Religion has 'its objective, or historic and ecclesiastical pole, and its subjective, or spiritual and individual pole', in a 'harmony of correspondent Opposites'.[33]

In *The Friend* and the *Philosophical Lectures*[34] Giordano Bruno is credited with the promotion and application of the law of polarity to 'Logic', 'Physics' and 'Metaphysics'. Coleridge expands the basic definition that 'all opposition is a tendency to re-union':

> The Principle may be thus expressed. The *Identity* of Thesis and Antithesis is the substance of all *Being*; their *Opposition* is the condition of all *Existence*, or Being manifested; and every *Thing* or Phaenomenon is the Exponent of a Synthesis as long as the opposite energies are retained in that Synthesis.[35]

'Polar logic' links the many facets of Coleridge's thinking and practice. The characterization of symbol in the Scriptures in *The Statesman's Manual* as the 'translucence of . . . the General in the Especial' closely resembles the description in *The Friend* of Shakespeare's genius for portraying utterly individual characters springing from a firm foundation in the universal.[36] It hints at what, in a letter of 1817, is promised for the third volume of *The Friend* – that is a discussion of 'the great *results* of this Philosophy [of the law of polarity] in it's relation to Ethics and Theology'.[37] In *The Friend* it is barely dealt with, and hardly alluded to in the *Philosophical Lectures*. The promise comes closest to fulfilment in the elusive, deeply religious and prayerful later notebooks, at present still only available in manuscript form in the British Library.

In the *Philosophical Lectures* Coleridge is reported to have affirmed that 'there is through all nature, and we must assume it as a ground of all reasoning, a perpetual tendency at once to individualize and yet to universalize'.[38] This stated was expanded into his 'trichotomous logic' in the context of Christian doctrine in 'On the Philosophic Import of the Words Object and Subject' (*Blackwood's Edinburgh Magazine*, LVI (1821) 246–52), and at more length in the still unpublished Notebook 26 which also dates from the early 1820s. The two poles of the act of commitment, the universal assurance from revelation and the moral and intelligent response of the individual, raise the question of the will and the relationship between the individual and the Absolute Will, and further how free the individual is to fall into sin or choose the way of salvation. The logical figure drawn in the notebook introduces the mesothesis of the Self as 'the point of indifference' between the positive pole of 'actual good' and the negative pole of 'potential evil'. Man finds himself in this neutral position as a result of the Fall. There was a time when 'the individual will in harmony with the Absolute Will was in positive potency'. Then, indeed, the individual discovered himself most fully, and realized his potential in the universal. For such a state man still yearns. 'Negative potency', however, lies in the individual will 'willing itself individual' and forsaking its sense of harmony with the Absolute and the universal. Thus it falls 'into apostasy and Original Sin'.[39]

Such is man's position. Why, epistemologically, was Kant so attractive as Coleridge moved towards a Christian response to the problem? Coleridge recognized in him a means of reconciling two hitherto opposing epistemological schools, the empiricist and the rationalist. For the former, truth was to be elicited only from experience; for the latter, only by deduction from *a priori* principles.[40] For Kant, experience was, indeed governed by, the *a priori* functions of the mind. Thus he preserved the polarity of the individual and the universal, and retained the possibility of harmony with the Absolute, with the corresponding escape from wilful individualism. Kant and Coleridge rejected the assumption that the mind of man was passive, a *tabula rasa*. For Kant, the mind generates things which in thinking, *a priori*, are logically presupposed by experience though not necessarily temporally antecedent.[41] Coleridge's annotations of the relevant passages in the *Kritik der Urtheilskraft* (1790) eventually appeared in the 'Essays on the Principles of Method'.

Nay, it must not be overlooked, that the assumption of the nexus effectivus itself originates in the mind, as one of the laws under which

alone it can reduce the manifold of the impression from without into
unity, and thus contemplate it as one thing.[42]

Both Kant and Coleridge, therefore, derive their position from Leibniz's
completion of the empiricist maxim, 'there is nothing in the mind that
does not come through the senses' – 'excipe, nisi intellectus ipse' (except
the mind itself).[43]

In his analysis of the knowing process in the *Kritik der reinen Vernunft*
(rev. ed. 1787), Kant provided a ladder for Coleridge to rebuild a
theology after the destructive processes of David Hume and the
empiricists. It was possible now to gather together the treasures of Ralph
Cudworth (1617–88) and the Cambridge Platonists who, like Coleridge
and Kant, had also believed in the activity of the mind. Coleridge was
also familiar with James Beattie (1735–1803) and the Scottish school of
philosophers who were opposing Hume. Beattie, in his once-celebrated
Essays on the Nature and Immutability of Truth (1776) had written:

> The argument a priori might be comprehended in the following
> works. If there be any creatures in human shape, who deny the
> distinction between truth and falsehood, or who are unconscious of
> that distinction, they are far beyond the reach, and below the notice
> of, philosophy, and therefore have no concern in this inquiry.
> Whoever is sensible of that distinction, and is willing to acknowledge
> it, must confess that truth is something fixed and determinate,
> depending not upon man, but upon the Author of nature. The
> fundamental principles of truth must therefore rest upon their own
> evidence, perceived intuitively by the understanding.[44]

Beattie, like Coleridge later, was arguing from a position of Christian
profession, but this fundamentally moral concern to establish an
absolute distinction between right and wrong lay at the root of the
pervasive influence of Fichte's more tangentially Christian *Versuch einer
Kritik aller Offenbarung* on *The Friend*. Coleridge commended Fichte in
Biographia for 'commencing with an *act*, instead of a *thing* or *substance*'
and thus supplying 'the *idea* of a system truly metaphysical, and of a
metaphysique truly systematic: (i.e. having its spring and principle within
itself)'.[45] This provided a foundation stone for the 'Essays on the
Principles of Method'. According to Fichte, 'The essential element of
revelation in general is the proclamation of God as moral lawgiver
through a supernatural effect in the world of sense.'[46] By setting up
moral examples, revelation can 'clothe its morality in narratives, and it

only meets the needs of man all the better when it does so'.[47] Coleridge
and Fichte believed that the matter of religion and Christian doctrine,
'such, for instance, as the tenets of original sin and of redemption, those
fundamental articles of every known religion professing to have been
revealed',[48] had a practical and moral application in the nature of things
and in the necessities of human nature. Coleridge required practical
assistance to enable him to face the tragedy of his life. Belief was a
necessity of life, not of speculation, and Fichte's strong moral emphasis
in his examination of revelation was suitably practical. Unfortunately he
sees religion, in the end, simply as that which brings clarity to morality, a
kind of supplementary moral incentive which may not even be
universally required.[49] For Coleridge, on the other hand, the 'mysteries
of faith' are fundamental to man's moral salvation.[50]

Kant, like Fichte, was limited for Coleridge's purposes, for while he
may have recognized the claims of psychology, his work is not open to
psychological interpretation. Coleridge, however, was a continuous and
acute psychological observer, and from his observations and reflections
emerge his need for religious assurance. It is true that throughout *The
Friend*, in *Biographia Literaria* and in *Omniana* (1812), Coleridge
specifically praises the Kantian *a priori*.[51] But his reading of Kant, as has
already been remarked, was modified by Jacobi who had gone so far as
to call reason faith, a definition with which Coleridge would have
concurred had Jacobi added to reason the element of the will, making it,
in short, reason in active operation. The Kantian *a priori*, with the
notion of 'ideas',[52] were for Coleridge matters of deep religious concern
in the life of man. It is clear that by 1820 he was developing what he had
learnt from Kant beyond the position of the master. What is begun in the
MS *Logic* (?1822–3) as a discussion of 'the reason ... as the source of
principles',[53] is continued in the three volumes of papers dating from
Coleridge's last years, housed in the library of Victoria College,
Toronto, and now described as the *Opus Maximum*. There, in an
extensive philosophical demonstration of the truths of Christianity,
Coleridge refers to the un-Christian elements in Kant. While for Kant
'moral law' is primary, for Coleridge it is 'good will'. The passage, with
its rejection of Kant's rigorism, is anticipated in a letter to J. H. Green of
13 December 1817.

I reject Kant's *stoic* principle, as false, unnatural, and even immoral,
where in his Critik der Practischen Vernun [f]t he treats the affections
as indifferent ('αδιάφορα).in ethics, and would persuade us that a man
who disliking, and without any feeling of Love for, Virtue yet *acted*

virtuously, because and only because it was his *Duty*, is more worthy of our esteem, than the man whose *affections* were aidant to, and congruous with, his Conscience. For it would imply little less than that things not the Objects of the moral Will or under it's controul were yet indispensable to it's due practical direction. In other words, it would subvert his own System. – Likewise, his remarks on PRAYER in his RELIGION innerhalb d.r.V.[54] are crass, nay vulgar; and as superficial even in psychology as they are low in taste. – But with these exceptions I reverence Immanuel Kant with my whole heart and soul.[55]

What, then, may be said of the relationship of Coleridge's notion of original sin to Kant's and Fichte's of radical evil? The linkage in Coleridge between his 'trichotomous logic' and the doctrine of the Fall with its evil consequences has already been noted. Furthermore in *The Friend*, the *Philosophical Lectures* and the *Logic* he locates the origin of this logic in Heraclitus, Giordano Bruno and the English divine Richard Baxter (1615–91). Whether or not his location is correct,[56] Coleridge is at pains to dissociate the trichotomy which is so central to his own thought from Kant and apply it to the Christian Baxter.[57] The pivot of the Coleridgean doctrine is the degree of freedom in the individual to fall into sin or to choose the way of salvation. It was noted in Chapter 5 that in the *Biographia*, and following Schelling, Coleridge writes of despatialized time or 'time *per se*', which is not 'extended' but concentrated into one moment or compresent. The true 'self' experiences everything simultaneously. He concludes that

> it would require only a different and appropriate organization – the *body celestial* instead of the *body terrestrial* – to bring before every human soul the collective experience of its whole past existence. . . . Yea, in the very nature of a living spirit, it may be more possible that heaven and earth should pass away, than that a single act, a single thought, should be loosened or lost from that living chain of causes, with all the links of which, conscious or unconscious, the free will, our only absolute Self, is co-extensive and co-present.[58]

For Coleridge, therefore, the 'free will' or 'absolute Self' was supratemporal. Kant's *Religion* was an attempt to give a philosophical justification for moral freedom. Rather like Coleridge, Kant denied that true freedom could exist in the spatio-temporal world since there subjection to the laws of causality would make every action dependent on its antecedent. Freedom presupposes something in the individual which is absolutely uncaused,[59] and must be attributed to a 'noumenal Ego'. (Coleridge in his marginalia on Kant distinguishes at length between the 'Homo Νουμενον' and the 'Homo φαινομενον'.[60]) Yet this freedom manifests itself in man's temporal behaviour as a whole, without interfering with the activity of antecedent causes in the determination of that behaviour.

Although in his discussion of radical evil Kant more than once refers to the biblical account of the Fall,[61] the connection between 'radical evil' and 'original sin' must not be regarded as identification. Emil L. Fackenheim neatly summarizes Kant's position:

Original sin is a state in which I am obligated to a law which I am nevertheless unable to obey. It is a paradoxical condition. Man can recognize but not overcome this condition; to overcome it requires an act of divine grace. To Kant the state of original sin is a moral and metaphysical impossibility. For he categorically denies the possibility of a situation in which there is a moral obligation without a corresponding moral freedom.[62]

Above all Kant is concerned to preserve man's moral freedom. A religious doctrine which assumed a sinfulness inherited from Adam and a restoration effected ultimately only by the unmerited grace of God, was to him intolerable. Moral action lies at the core of the religious life, and anything other than good conduct done to please God is mere 'pseudo-service'.[63] For Fichte, the task of revelation is to bring morality to the soul,[64] and in the end religion merely provides a supplementary incentive to moral obedience, while for Kant it serves also the purpose of clarifying the final aims of morality. What is clear is that for both men, redemption is seen primarily in moral terms and is an act of self-redemption, although Kant does hint at a doctrine of divine grace.[65] However, the original perversion toward evil and the act of self-conversion in its rejection are both undeniably unintelligible, actions *ex nihilo*, yet, Kant maintains, 'A man (can) reverse ... by a single unchangeable decision, that highest ground of his maxims whereby he was an evil man (and thus put on the new man).'[66]

This chilling conclusion, wherein man is burdened with a lonely responsibility to choose between good and evil, could hardly be expected to satisfy Coleridge, deeply sensible as he was of himself as a miserable sinner. Indeed, in his treatment of depravity and the sinner who actively wills evil he is in basic disagreement with the sentimentalism of the eighteenth-century moralists – Shaftesbury, Hartley, Price, Priestley,

Paley and Godwin – for whom innate evil is little more than weakness. It is true that Kant himself in the *Kritik der praktischen Vernunft* (1788) had proposed an account of moral freedom in which man's propensity to evil was due not so much to an act of will as to a lack of will, a weakness rather than a villainy.[67] This view he later rejects in the *Religion* since it does not account for a genuine freedom and responsibility to choose between good and evil. Coleridge, taking his cue from the distinction between reason and understanding, adopted Kant's placement of radical evil in the noumenal Ego, problematically related to the sequence of natural events. But here, where Kant's purpose was to give an adequate philosophical justification of moral freedom, Coleridge parts company with him inasmuch as for him the traditional religious notion of original sin is upheld. His purpose was certainly not the philosophical demonstration of individual freedom, for at variance with this freedom were his acceptance of the Augustinian doctrine of creation (and therefore of the Fall) and his sense of the divine omnipresence.[68] His real concerns are hinted at in the marginal note on Kant's *Grundlegung zur Metaphysik der Sitten* (1785).

> If I say, I doubt this independence of Love on the Will, and doubt even Love's being in it's essence merely eine Sache der Empfindung, a mere matter of *feeling*, i.e. a somewhat *found* in us which is not of and from us (*Emp* (= in sich) – Findung, I mean only that my Thoughts are not distinct much less adequate on the subject – and I am not able to [con]vey any ground of my Belief of the contrary. But the contrary I *do* believe. What Kant // affirms of Man in the state of Adam, an ineffable act of the will choosing evil & which is underneath or within the *consciousness* tho' incarnate in the *conscience*, inasmuch as it must be conceived as taking place in the Homo Νουμενον, not the Homo φαινομενον – something like this I conceive of Love – in that highest sense of the Word.[69]

Coleridge is at pains to deny that he is pursuing a philosophical argument. 'Love' is found in us yet not of or from us and should best be equated with divine grace acting independently on the will in contradiction to the ineffable operations of original sin. Thus Coleridge deduces from the presence of radical evil in man the necessity for a supernatural and vicarious means of redemption which is communicated by divine revelation. His Christian conclusion is summed up in the 'Confessio Fidei'.

I receive with full and grateful Faith the assurance of Revelation, that the Word which is from all eternity with God and is God, assumed our human nature in order to redeem me and all mankind from this our connate Corruption. My reason convinces me, that no other mode of redemption is conceivable, and, as did Socrates, would have yearned after the Redeemer, tho' it would not dare expect so wonderful an Act of Divine Love, except only as an effort of my mind to conceive the utmost of the infinite greatness of that Love![70]

Elinor Shaffer has suggested that in *Aids to Reform* Coleridge was arguing specifically against Kant in *Die Religion innerhalb der Grenzen der blossen Vernunft*.[71] Basing himself on Kantian epistemology, Coleridge's task was to develop and justify a mode of thought which was religious, aesthetic, and moral without sacrificing rationality. The present argument assumes, as does Shaffer, the legitimacy of Coleridge's tendency to read Kant as a cold rationalist, while aware that such a reading is, to say the least, questionable.[72] The argument in *Aids* focuses upon the problem of radical evil in man and the means of dealing with it. For Coleridge, the belief in freedom through self-determination is merely an assertion of the finite will. True freedom is only to be found as the individual will draws nearer and becomes one with the Absolute Will. Thus the paradoxes that 'service is perfect freedom' and 'in His will is our peace' were endlessly fascinating to Coleridge.

Coleridge certainly does not want to exclude speculative reason from theology,[73] nor would he see any contrariety between Revelation and Understanding.[74] But this is not to deny the intuitive and unfinished nature of religious experience and that 'Christianity is not a Theory, or a Speculation; but a *Life*; not a *Philosophy* of Life, but a Life and a living Process'.[75] The willing and thinking individual is a pilgrim on a road which, ultimately, must exclude Kant's pride of reason, and wherein grace, which for Kant may not have been impossible but was certainly unprovable, was divinely offered to be received with humility[76] and not as man makes himself morally able to receive it. Shaffer links Coleridge's position with Erasmus's delicate humanism which Luther denied. This allowed room for the exercise of the free will in the context of unmerited divine grace, leaving, indeed, an important task for human endeavour and merit while avoiding 'the self-defeating presumption of Kant's religion of reason'.[77]

Let Coleridge himself have the final word in an entry in his last notebook, dated March 1834, some four months before his death.

O grace of God! if only a believing mind were thoroughly purged from the refracting film of nominalism; if it could indeed be possessed by and possess, the full Idea of the Reality of the Absolute State, the Good. [The] yet higher shall I see [or] deeper [this] *reality*, the [State(?)] as the gound essentially causative of all *real* Being, and therefore essentially of it's own Being – the [state] super-personal, and transcending all relations, and by an eternal act affirming [its] own Being, eternally self-personal, the *I AM* and by the adjunct of personeity & the absolute Good with the Holy I AM – as the *Good* absolutely begotten [his] adequate Image in the True, the supreme *Reason.*[78]

II 'O MYSTERY OF LOVING-KINDNESS!': POLAR LOGIC IN THE LATE NOTEBOOKS

According to M. H. Abrams the biblical pattern of history has five distinctive attributes.[79] First it is finite, representing events happening once for all and uniquely, as opposed to the doctrine that history simply repeats itself. In Coleridge's own narrative poetry it is the arbitrariness and uniqueness of events which is stressed; the shooting of the albatross, or Christabel's discovery of Geraldine. Second, the design of biblical history is a well-formed plot carried through by a clear sequence of dramatic events. The sequence of fall, restoration and reintegration shapes both 'The Ancient Mariner' and the 'Confessio Fidei'. Third, behind the biblical history is a hidden author, its director and the guarantor of the future. Again, such is implied in the counterpointing of narrative levels in 'The Ancient Mariner' or the blurring in 'Kubla Khan' of the poet's conscious creative act with the infinite mystery of his vision. Fourth, the key events of the biblical narrative are abrupt and precipitous. Suddenly, out of nothing the world is created by divine fiat. Abruptly, the reader is thrown into the middle of the great narrative poems: 'It is an ancient Mariner': ''Tis the middle of night by the castle clock' ('Christabel'). Finally, the biblical scheme is symmetrical, concluding where it began in 'a new Earth and new Heaven'. And if the beginning is retrospective, the end is infinitely prospective, stretching out to embrace a universal vision, ever fulfilled and ever waiting to be fulfilled anew.

As will be seen, in his last writings – copious notes on the Pentateuch, the Pauline epistles, the Acts of the Apostles and the Fourth Gospel – Coleridge returned to his life-long study of the Scriptures which, above all other writings, illuminate human experience and the highest demands of our moral nature. It was the design of biblical history in the Old and New Testaments which nourished his most creative poetry, and it was from his experience as a poet that, as critic, philosopher and theologian, Coleridge began to articulate his Polar Logic. This, in turn, provides the foundation for the Trinitarian faith of the late notebooks, which is expounded with such passion and prayerfulness.

The origins and pattern of Polar Logic have been well rehearsed, and it lies outside the purposes of the present study to repeat them at length. Owen Barfield, in a book whose purpose might be described as the demonstration that polarity is at the root of what Coleridge thought, argues from that, that the content of self-consciousness is always tri-une.[80] In Polar Logic, the 'higher third' or the Identity is the point of reconciliation of the two poles, and in the notebooks Christ is repeatedly described as the Identity of the divine tri-unity. Coleridge's progress towards Trinitarian orthodoxy by the metaphysical path of Polar Logic is first fully exemplified as early as October 1806, in a letter to Thomas Clarkson.

> God is the sole self-comprehending Being, i.e. he has an Idea of himself, and that Idea is consumately adequate, & superlatively real. ... This Idea therefore from all eternity co-existing with, & yet filiated, by the absolute Being ... is the same, as the Father in all things, but the impossible one, of self-origination. He is the substantial Image of God, in whom the Father beholds well-pleased his whole Being – and being substantial (ὁμοούσιος) he of divine and permanent Will, and a necessity which is the absolute opposition of compulsion, as delight-edly & with as intense LOVE contemplates the Father in the Father, and the Father in himself, and himself in the Father. But all the actions ... proceed co-eternally both from the Father and the Son – & neither of these Three *can* be conceived *apart*, nor *confusedly* – so that the Idea of God involves that of a Tri-unity.[81]

Both Owen Barfield and David Newsome have examined in some detail the origins of Coleridge's Polar Logic, whether Giordano Bruno (as Coleridge claims in *Biographia Literaria*[82]), Richard Baxter, Schelling or the Pythagorean *tetractys*.[83] Whatever the truth, Newsome warns of the difficulty of following Coleridge through the various figures which he employs in the description of polarity, for he 'frequently employed more figures than three, sometimes setting out his position as a pentad, occasionally as a heptad, and based them all on the mystical Pythagorean symbol of the *tetractys*, a triangular figure of ten points, rising from a base of four, the whole representing the Supreme Being'.[84]

The commonest of these figures is the Noetic Pentad, already described in Chapter 5.[85] Newsome and Boulger, as well as J. Robert Barth in *Coleridge and Christian Doctrine* (1969), have variously described the importance of the Noetic Pentad, or dialectical triad in the final development of Coleridge's interpretation of Christian doctrine. Only David Pym, in *The Religious Thought of Samuel Taylor Coleridge* (1978) would dissociate the Trinity of the Coleridge of faith from that of the philosopher, from 'the over-ambitious side of Coleridge's mind, the weakness in indulging in idle speculation'.[86]

In fact, Coleridge's late notebooks are a remarkable example of a wholeness of being, and the creation of unity out of diversity which characterizes all his work. Philosophy, theology, imagination and faith are drawn together with intellectual and scholarly humility. A valuable introduction to them might be the description of the Pentad of Operative Christianity with which he prefaces *Confessions of an Inquiring Spirit*.

> The Scriptures, the Spirit, and the Church, are co-ordinate; the indispensable conditions and the working causes of the perpetuity, and continued renascence and spiritual life of Christ still militant. The Eternal Word, Christ from everlasting, is the *Prothesis*, or identity; – the Scriptures and the Church are the two poles, or *Thesis* and *Antithesis*; and the Preacher in direct line under the Spirit, but likewise the point of junction of the Written Word and the Church, is the *Synthesis*.
> This is God's Hand in the World.[87]

Page after page of Coleridge's last notebook consist of an extended meditation on this figure, in a tone of rapt devotion. They focus upon the mystery of Jesus Christ, the Prothesis or Identity, which gives coherence to all polarity; the self (Ipseity) and the other (Alterity), the subjective and objective, the individual and ecclesiastical, the historical and the 'ideal'.

> Unity and Disunity in the *Alterity* of the Infinite in essence α Finite in *form* – α thus absolute – and in the Identity in the Ipseity begets itself as Ipseity in the Alterity, yet still as Alterity – and hence the [adoration definitely] in unity of the absolute $<>$ and the Universal, of the Center and the *Sphere* – o how with inspired wisdom and eloquence set forth in the first chapter of St. John's Gospel[88]

The biblical commentaries which form such a large part of these later notebooks are no dry, academic exercises. Coleridge distinguishes between the 'historico-critical *intellective* study' of Scripture, and 'the praying of the same', the latter being 'in the spirit of appreciation to our own wants and troubles'.[89]

The same Notebook 41 is given over almost entirely to a consideration of the Pauline epistles and to 'the establishing of sound principles of interpretation'.[90] In Notebook 42, Coleridge embarks on the Pentateuch, first endeavouring to define the 'Christian philosopher'. He is:

> a Man of Science, a Physiologist, Naturalist, well studied in Geology and Oryctognosy – Lastly, he is a sound Biblical critic, who prizes and reverences the Bible tho' not a bibliolater.[91]

Throughout these commentaries, Coleridge applies a 'philosophic imagination',[92] a combination of poetic insight and academic rigour in an over-arching context of prayer, thanksgiving and a sense that sin is a universal condition requiring the action of divine grace.[93] Notebook 46 contains a commentary on Numbers 36, Psalms 107 and 91. Coleridge's reflections on the psalms give rise to a comment on the 'two laws of the imagination':

> first, that we recollect co-incidents, rather than incidents without any co-incident – α second, that a part being given, the excited imagination tends to produce a whole.[94]

Scripture, like many other works of literature, is a product of the imagination, both as insight and creative power, authoritative inasmuch as it provides the basic design for subsequent narrative and because, even in the fallible record of the Bible, 'whatever *finds* me, bears witness for itself that it has proceeded from a Holy Spirit'.[95] This reference to the imagination leads into Coleridge's final note on the psalms, which is a return to the figure of the *tetractys*, combining man's imaginative creativity and religious aspirations.

In each form of the *tetractys* we find a distinct object of aspiration:

1 – The Absolute Subject	– the Good
2 – The I AM	– Duty
3 – The Word	– Light
4 – The Spirit	– Life.[96]

Through Coleridge's Polar Logic and its derivatives, the Pentad and the *tetractys*, man aspires to gaze upon eternity which is given focus in the Identity, transcending both thesis and antithesis, and that One in which polar forces are discovered to be necessarily *unius generis*. It is in the Fourth Gospel that Coleridge perceives most clearly that Christ, the Word is this Identity or Prothesis, and it is this which confirms this Gospel as his final principal subject of attention.

One momentous point of superiority in John is his clear insight into the identity of the *Word* and the Universal Light, or the substantiality and personeity of Reason.

The 3 first Gospels seem rather to contain the prefatory truths, the moral principles necessary in order for Christianity, and the Epistles have all the appearance of occasional writings, presupposing a previous communication of the scheme, and the constituent articles of faith, that formed it's exposition.[97]

In a sense, all these notebooks of 1827–34 are the prayer of a man who is tragically aware of his own inadequacies, and whose desperately won faith in the Divine mystery was the culmination of a life-long intellectual struggle.

Before God I prostrate myself in the dust, thankfully confessing that my sufferings have been in no proportion to my demerits, and that the Graces & Comforts, that have been vouchsafed me, have been beyond all utterance His free and sovereign Goodness – without a pretence of claim on my part – coals of fire heaped on my unworthy will to melt it down by gracious force into – what? O marvel! O mystery of loving-kindness![98]

III   CHRISTIANITY THE ONE TRUE PHILOSOPHY

I therefore go, and join head, heart and hand,
Active and firm, to fight the bloodless fight
Of Science, Freedom, and the Truth in Christ.[99]

The purpose so boldly expressed in 1796 was to remain with Coleridge throughout his life, until its unfulfilment was finally recognized in the last, sad comment of the *Table Talk*, dated 10 July 1834, only two weeks before his death:

so I own I wish life and strength had been spared to me to complete my Philosophy. For, as God hears me, the originating, continuing, and sustaining wish and design in my heart were to exalt the glory of his name; and, which is the same thing in other words, to promote the improvement of mankind. But *visum aliter Deo*, and his will be done.[100]

The three manuscript volumes in the Library of Victoria University in Toronto are the fragmentary remains of Coleridge's 'Great Work', called by him variously the 'Logosophia', 'Eidoloclastes', 'Assertion of Religion', *magnum opus* and *Opus Maximum*.[101] These, with other fragments, are now being edited by Thomas McFarland for the *Collected Works*. But, as has already been noted, *Biographia Literaria* seems to have been originally envisaged as a prelude to the main work.[102] Arguably, the same is true of *Aids to Reflection*, *Logic* and *Theory of Life*.[103] All, indeed, of Coleridge's major work is subsidiary to the great, uncompleted fragment. Coleridge's task may, indeed, have been, in the end, impossible; or perhaps the *Opus Maximum* should be placed beside 'Kubla Khan' and 'Christabel', as a fragment which is a Romantic form and a part of a whole which can only be intimated in the fragment. The critical history of the work seems to suggest that it is extremely difficult to resist the impulse to reconstruct the whole, and to supply the missing stairs in the winding steps of the old ruined tower.[104] Sam Barnes, who suggests that the *Theory of Life* is, perhaps unintentionally, Coleridge's nearest approach to accomplishing his projected work, admits that he finally falters when he approaches the projected conclusion, the 'truth in Christ' that man, as the highest form of individuation in Nature, was to return to God.

> *Thus*, then, Life itself is not a *thing* – a self-subsistent *hypostasis* – but an *act* and *process*; which, pitiable as the prejudice will appear to the *forts esprits*, is a great deal more than either my reason would authorize or my conscience allow me to assert – concerning the Soul as the principle both of Reason and Conscience.[105]

In the end, therefore, the *Opus Maximum* must, almost by definition, remain a fragment, enunciating the whole of which it is the representative.

Coleridge's letter of September 1814 to Daniel Stuart, which outlines in detail his plans for the great work has already been noted. There are, scattered through the letters and notebooks, numerous similar sketches, dividing the project variously into four, five or six sections.[106] In a note, dated by Professor Coburn as 1815–16, Coleridge remarks on his '6 Discourses on the Logos', establishing a rough system for collecting and organizing material for the work.[107] What is noteworthy is the devotional tone of the comments, which are directed against institutional Christianity and its abuses. His purpose is:

> In the 'Logos' to reperuse Taylor's Works, especially his sermons, in order to expose the errors and the sources of the errors, of Judaizing Christianity – or the return to the beggarly Elements. – Till the Light of Immortality was brought by Christ.

In some ways the task was done many years later in *Aids to Reflection* which is, essentially, the fresh perusal of another seventeenth-century divine, Archbishop Leighton. In fact, *Aids* is linked to the *Opus Maximum* on a number of occasions by Coleridge. On 12 April 1824, he wrote to Wordsworth that he was working hard on his 'Leighton' and his 'Logic' as a preparation for the greater work which was to follow.[108] A year later he wrote to his nephew, John Taylor Coleridge, that his principal concerns in both *Aids* and the projected work is the Trinity, but that *Aids* is merely a preparatory stage.

> In the 'Aids to Reflection' I have touched on the Mystery of the Trinity only in a *negative* way. That is, I have shewn the hollowness of the arguments by which it has been assailed ... But the positive establishment of the Doctrine as involved in the Idea, God – together with the *Origin* of EVIL, as distinguished from Original Sin ... and the Creation of the visible World – THESE as absolutely requiring the habit of abstraction, and *severe Thinking*, I have reserved for my larger Work.[109]

As early as 1806, Coleridge had described his purpose of articulating a 'vital head-and-heart FAITH' which was Trinitarian and *practical* inasmuch as it effected redemption by the 'necessary assumption of humanity by the Word'.[110] In the same letter to George Fricker, he had vowed that his work would contradict the mode of defending Christianity adopted by the Dutch theologian Hugo Grotius (1583–1645) and by Paley, which encouraged men to look out of themselves and of their nature instead of looking into their own souls. The demand for 'evidences' – rejected so impatiently in *Aids* – was to be a major point of attack in the *Opus Maximum* and in 1827, Coleridge continued to refer to his purpose of undermining the 'Grotian and Paleyan defences' of 'the philosophy and history of Christianity'.[111]

For at least thirty years, then, Coleridge displays a remarkable consistency in his plans for the great work. Towards the end of his life the devotional note which is heard in the notebook entry of 1815–16 becomes clearer. In 1827 he wrote to J. Blanco White in despair of ever bringing the chaos of his thoughts into order. Yet the fervour which the growing sense of his own inadequacies engenders may be for the best.

> I have but a few hours back announced myself to my friend, as the author of a SYSTEM of Philosophy on Nature, History, Reason, Revelation; on the Eternal, and on the Generations of the Heaven and the Earth, and I am unable to solve the problem of my own Dreams! ... Well for me if these vexations of the Night increase the dread of being suffered to fall back upon the wild activities and restless chaos of my own corrupt Nature! Well, if they increase the fervency with which I pray, *Thy* kingdom come! in the world within me![112]

Four months later, a letter to George Skinner, a fellow of Jesus College, Cambridge, locates Coleridge's final labours on the *Opus Maximum* firmly within the devotional, almost enraptured, mood of the later notebooks.

> I have been for some time past swallowed up in the one anxiety of arranging and increasing my huge pile of Manuscripts, so that the *substance* at least of the results of my logical, physiological, philoso-phical, theological, biblical, and I hope I am entitled to add *religious* and *Christian* studies and meditations for the last 20 years of my life might be found in a state capable of being published by my dear Friend Mr Green ... I thank God that this is so far effected that should He call me tomorrow, I shall leave the world in the humble trust that my daily morning and evening supplications offered in the very words of the Psalmist (Psalm 71st.) had been heard ... and that the power & life of Christ our Redeemer will so *precipitate* the remaining evil of my corrupt nature as that cleansed by his spiritual blood my spirit may rise a pure capacity of *him*, blind to be irradiated with *his* light, empty to be filled from his fullness, and naked to be clothed with *his* Righteousness – in him & thro' him to be united with the Eternal *One* the Author of my Being and its ultimate *End*.[113]

The religious fervour, however, did not mean the abandonment of intellectual rigour. In a very business-like letter to J. H. Green of 1829, which quotes Eichhorn and refers to a careful study of the Greek of the New Testament, Coleridge outlines in detail the biblical studies which form the substance of his last notebooks, studies well versed in contemporary biblical criticism, and deeply devotional.[114]

The point of stressing the devotional and prayerful qualities which are increasingly apparent in the last years of Coleridge's writings and his growing sense of the religious purpose of the *Opus Maximum*, is not merely to suggest that as an old man he became a more devout Christian. Rather, the energies involved reflect his life as a poet and critic of the imagination. It has been suggested that his preoccupation with the *Opus Maximum* tended to draw off his poetic energies, resulting in a drying up of the poetry,[115] and it is true that at one stage, at least, Coleridge's anxiety to proceed with his 'great philosophical work' led him to feel that 'poetry is out of the question'.[116]

However, Coleridge continued to write poetry which in both form and image continued to reflect and explore his philosophical and theological preoccupations, and to warm them with a shaping spirit of imagination. It was as a poet, uniting head and heart, that Coleridge continued to feel the need for Christianity, the one true philosophy. An example of the cross-currents between the later poems and the later religious verse is the image of himself as 'blind to be irradiated with *his* light' in the letter to George Skinner in 1828. It is found again and explored more fully in the 'old Man with a steady Look sublime' in 'Limbo'.[117] Blind, the old man gazes and irradiates the light of some divine inward experience, and so, by reflection he appears to contemplate the Divine – 'He seems to gaze at that which seems to gaze on Him!' (l. 30). Or again, the rustic who experiences the Brocken Spectre in 'Constancy to an Ideal Object' might be Coleridge himself in his last years, 'enamoured' of the great truths which he 'pursues' in the illumination of his consciousness and reflections.

Perhaps most significant, however, is a long and complex discussion of the *Opus Maximum* in a letter to J. H. Green written on 12 August 1829. In essence it follows the pattern and themes of the many other plans for the work. It is religious in its concern with God and the Spirit. It also develops the discussion at length in terms of polarity and the *tetractys*. But it is all shifted into the sphere of aesthetics, the beautiful and 'a complete Theory of the Fine Arts'. Coleridge's concern is the Idea of the Beautiful.

> The only thought indeed that I can recollect which possibly *might* have led me to the true Idea ... was an anticipation and half perception that in the distinctities of the Godhead the Beautiful or Essential Beauty belonged to the SPIRIT, or the Indifference (Mesoth-

esis) of Will and Mind in the form of celestial Life, and in accordance with this and no less a consequence or corollary of your view, 1. the Good (= the Holy one, the abysmal Will) is the *Absolute* Subject – 2. the Father, = I am, the Subjective: 3. the word or Reason (ὁ ἀληθής) the Objective: 4. the Spirit, or Life = Love, the Subjective Objective.

the Beautiful is an *Idea* – the *spirit* of this or that object – but not the object in toto – as Beauty adequately realized. As you truly observed, it is the subjective in the form of the objective – a fortiori, not the objective in contradistinction from the Subjective. We behold our own light reflected from the object as light bestowed *by* it. The Beauty of the object consists in its fitness to reflect it.[118]

Once again Coleridge meditates upon the theme of the blind old man in 'Limbo', the reflection of light between observer and observed, subject and object. An Idea, whether of the Beautiful, or of God, Self or Freedom,[119] is that 'which is given by the knowledge of *its ultimate aim*', may be true without ever having been realized as a historical 'fact', and may only be realized at infinity.[120] The Beautiful as an Idea involves in some way a resolution between the terms subjective and objective. Here, therefore, in the realm of art and aesthetics, linked with an underlying discussion of the Divine as Trinity, Coleridge is discussing what is the essential purpose of the *Opus Maximum*, which is a 'hope of achieving a systematic reconciliation of the 'I am' and the 'it is'.[121] And if this purpose of the great work is finally theological, its crown to be 'a detailed commentary on the Gospel of St. John',[122] Coleridge's language in his preparatory discussions, as in the letter to J. H. Green, is closely related also to his most important discussion on the nature of the primary and secondary Imagination in *Biographia Literaria* ('the Father = I am, the Subjective': 'a repetition in the finite mind of the eternal act of creation in the infinite I AM.').

Another, slightly later, letter to Green develops the discussion of subjective/objective into the realm of the doctrine of revelation.

My principle has ever been that Reason is *subjective* Revelation, Revelation *objective* Reason – and that *our* business is not to *derive* Authority from the *mythoi* of the Jews & the first Jew-Christians (i.e. the O. and N. Testament) but to *give* it to them – never to assume their stories as facts, any more than you would Quack Doctors' affidavits on oath before the Lord Mayor – and very in point of the old Bailey

Evidence this is a flattering representation of the Paleyan Evidence –
but by *science* to confirm the Facit, kindly afforded to beginners in
Arithmetic. If I lose my faith in *Reason*, as the perpetual revelation, I
lose my faith altogether. I must deduce the objective from the
subjective Revelation, or it is no longer a revelation for me, but a
beastly fear and superstition.[123]

Where the eighteenth century demanded external evidence and proof
rather than reason which is its own evidence,[124] Coleridge's appeal was
to experience and the developing self-consciousness of the human
subject. While for his predecessors an image might be merely the work of
the fancy, recreated from what is simply remembered, its use perhaps
only decorative, for Coleridge the image or symbol could be the product
of the creative imagination, pointing beyond itself to a scarcely
perceived whole or absolute. Finally, where religion had been shrivelled
by a dry eighteenth-century rationalism with its basis in Locke's
epistemology, and which 'failed to state the rightful place of the
imagination in human experience',[125] Coleridge refounded the authority of the Bible in the reflective experience of man and human
subjectivity. Belief was thus reasonable, aesthetic and ethical. In the
Opus Maximum, above all, would this coherence be demonstrated, for
there, in Stephen Happel's words,

> he would be able to show a doctrine of God and all things in relation to
> the Divine as the infinite coherence of subjectivity and self-objectifica-
> tion – an infinite "I AM" – the Absolutely Adequate, Self-revising
> Subject, upon which, through which, and in which all take their
> meaning.[126]

Thus the reader of a book which is largely about poetry, the *Biography
Literaria*, is prepared by Coleridge's deliberate enhancement of the
consciousness of the reading process for a deeper understanding of the
doctrine of revelation and of the Divine.

Laurence Lockridge, in his book *Coleridge the Moralist* (1977),
criticizes the *Opus Maximum* manuscripts and suggests that in his moral
writings Coleridge tend to be personal and to avoid abstractions. His
concern, in other words, is the practical one of enabling people to
overcome the problems facing them in their human nature and, by
realizing their capacity to intuit and create, to excite them to a 'sense of
their individuality'.[127] In a letter of 1819, two of the 'Postulates'
Coleridge establishes for his great work are that it should be '*grounded*'

and that it should not be grounded in an *abstraction*.[128] At the root of this practical purpose behind his most important work is his old sense of failure and personal inadequacy, and his need for a Redeemer. He had written to his brother George in 1802 that he clung to his faith: 'not because I *understand* it; but because I *feel*, that it is not only suitable to, but needful for, my nature and because I find it clearly revealed'.[129] In March 1830, Notebook 43 opens with a long 'prayer to the Redeemer'.[130]

Although in the 1825 letter to his nephew, which is quoted above, Coleridge suggests a distinction between the origin of evil and original sin, his extended discussion of the subject in *Aids to Reflection* fails to make this distinction clear. What is clear from *Aids* is that neither evil nor moral guilt are begotten of God, for if they were, they would be co-eternal with him.[131] The Fall is defined as willing actuality in the self, rather than God, and sin is the enslavement of the will by the rejection of its own law (for it is ultimately coincident with the will of God) in favour of mere natural inclination. The task of the Redeemer is to enable the resumption of this law, and the nature of the Redeemer is the final point of focus of Polar Logic and the *Opus Maximum*.

And I believe in the descension and condescension of the Divine Spirit, Word, Father, and Incomprehensible Ground of all – and that he is a God who *seeketh* that which was lost, and that the whole world of Phaenomena is a revelation of the Redemptive Process, of the Deus *Patiens*, or Deitas *Objectiva* beginning in the separation of Life from Hades, which under the control of the Law = Logos = Unity – becomes *Nature*, i.e., that which never *is* but *natura* est, is to be, from the brute Multeity, and Indistinction, and is to end with the union with God in the Pleroma.[132]

The means of achieving this ultimate aim of union with God in the Pleroma is clarified by a marginal note which Coleridge made in Derwent Coleridge's copy of the 1818 *Friend*. Christ is described as 'the Logos, Deitas *Objectiva*, *centered* Humanity (always pre-existing in the Pleroma)'.[133] He alone is capable of bringing about man's union, in the Pleroma, with God. The Incarnation is the manifestation in time of an eternal, or timeless act, and here it is necessary to recall that Coleridge's 'free will' or 'absolute *self*' is supratemporal, that is 'co-extensive and co-present';[134] that 'time *per se*' is compresent in one moment which is also eternal. By his *Life*, manifested in time, Christ becomes 'the *Light* = Reason, of mankind'. Coleridge concludes his marginal note that Christ '[was made flesh: John 1:14] – & dwelt among men, an individual Man, in order that he might dwell *in* all his Elect, as the Root of the divine Humanity in time.'[135]

Coleridge is well aware of the necessary paradox of the Incarnation that it is in history and particular, yet also an ideal and of eternity. It is simply not true that, as David Pym argues,

> so eager was he to view revelation in terms of the 'existential now', expressed in the language of a Platonist metaphysic, that he stated the Incarnation as a union of the Logos with 'ideal man' and lost the essential New Testament, and especially Pauline, teaching of the 'once-for-allness' of the Christ event, as an occurrence in space and time'.[136]

This argument fails to perceive that Coleridge changed his views on St Paul and developed a much more sophisticated approach to his Epistles than Pym supposes. In Notebook 39 (1829), Coleridge admits that, as opposed to the Fourth Gospel, Paul did indeed contemplate 'the Protogenes only as a Person, *subjectively*'.[137] As his commentary on Romans developed, however, he admitted that this was an inadequate appraisal. Later in 1829 he wrote:

> I think now I understand this 5th Chapter. The Apostle's purpose was to prepare the minds of the converts for that more spiritual character of Our Lord by which he *dwells* in the Faithful that he who *dwelt* among men for a short time *dwelleth* in the elect always.[138]

After his early 'rage for metaphysics', Coleridge, with increasing insistence, emphasizes the need to establish the historical basis of Christianity, with its focus in the character of Jesus, and the necessary assumption of human nature by the Logos. If, indeed, the *Opus Maximum* was to achieve the reconciliation of the 'I am' and the 'it is', these poles were to be represented by the Fourth Gospel and the pantheistic Spinoza, and,[139] reflecting upon his early philosophical years, Coleridge admitted that 'my head was with Spinoza' while 'my whole heart remained with Paul and John'.[140]

Paul and John, then, were drawn together in Christ the 'Λόγος θεάνθρωπος'. The historical, human Jesus requires the ideal Christ; Polar Logic ensures their homogeneity, and that they are *unius generis*. In the Pentad of Operative Christianity, Christ, the Word is the prothesis, the identity of thesis and antithesis and the one of which the many are parts. Furthermore, like the symbol as it is defined in *The Statesman's Manual*, Christ's individuality in history is the necessary particular through which the universal is perceived, his temporality a reflection on eternity. In Christ 'that union and interpenetration of the universal and the particular' point to an infinity, and the figure in history acts as a mirror to God's enlightenment.[141] The drawing together of all human energies in a faith which culminates in the meeting of God and man, is finally described in the 'Essay on Faith' which was first published in *The Literary Remains* (1838–9), possibly as a part of the uncompleted 'Supplementary volume' which Coleridge refers to in *Aids to Reflection*.

Faith must be a Light originating in the Logos, or the substantial Reason, which is co-eternal and one with the Holy Will, and which Light is at the same time the Life of men. Now, as *Life* is here the sum or collective of all moral and spiritual acts, in suffering, doing, and being, so is Faith the source and the sum, the energy and the principle of the fidelity of Man to God, by the subordination of his human Will, in all provinces of his nature, to his Reason, as the sum of spiritual Truth, representing and manifesting the Will Divine.[142]

Christ, the Logos, is the sum of spiritual Truth – Christianity the one true philosophy.

8 Conclusion: Inspiration and Revelation

> If religion is concerned with the relation between man and nature, or between man and God, if it must explore the difference between time and eternity, between goodness and badness, between the helplessness and the power of human beings, between their deep solitude and their superficial sociability, then knowledge of such things must come from the significance we find in our sensory experience, in what we actually see and hear.[1]

Thus wrote Mary Warnock in an article published in *Theology* in November 1980, entitled 'Imagination – Aesthetic and Religious'. This study has sought to trace in Coleridge's writings his endeavours to perceive the nature of divine revelation in his experience of poetic inspiration and creativity. His habits of self-reflection prompted his insights into the psychology of belief, and his concern for language as a poet led him to a concern for the nature of 'God-language' in theology and religious discourse. This final chapter is not so much a conclusion in a formal sense, as it does not attempt to draw together and sum up the arguments of those which precede it. Rather, it seeks to illustrate the continuing importance of those matters which concerned Coleridge, as a Christian thinker who worked primarily through the categories of literature and poetry. Its approach is not historical, nor does it attempt to describe writers and theologians who have, in some way, been directly influenced by Coleridge,[2] not least because, invariably, Coleridge is greater than any example given, slipping through its confines with an elusive abundance of creativity.[3]

Austin Farrer's work in our century may be regarded as the practical working out, in a deeply literary theologian, of Coleridge's notion of Polar Logic. There is little direct evidence of Coleridge's influence on Farrer, and he is chosen, in part, to illustrate the universality of Coleridge's concerns. Farrer was fascinated by the analogy between divine self-disclosure and human self-disclosure,[4] and by the processes

144

of reflection upon the self as made in God's image. He recognized the similarity in the processes of poetry and divine inspiration and the importance of perceiving that while they are ultimately necessarily different, they also require and suppose each other. Farrer was a theologian who read the Bible as a work of literature and whose faith and theology was profoundly affected as a result. Coleridge, in his own day, was a poet who discovered in the literature and poetry of the Bible an enlightening mystery which uniquely illuminated the religious matter of the relationship between man and God, the finite and the infinite.

I METAPHYSICAL PHILOSOPHY, SCRIPTURAL REVELATION AND POETRY: AUSTIN FARRER'S *THE GLASS OF VISION* (1948)

> The lectures which follow are no more than a modest attempt to state what I do, in fact, think about the relation borne to one another by three things – the sense of metaphysical philosophy, the sense of scriptural revelation, and the sense of poetry.... These three things rubbing against one another in my mind, seem to kindle one another, and so I am moved to ask how this happens.[5]

These opening words of Austin Farrer's Bampton Lectures for 1948, *The Glass of Vision*, immediately link it with the themes of the present study of Coleridge. There were two major critical attacks on *The Glass of Vision* in the 1950s, one theological by H. D. Lewis in his book *Our Experience of God* (1959), one literary by Dame Helen Gardner in her Riddell Memorial Lectures, *The Limits of Literary Criticism* (1956). Farrer defended himself against both his critics in his paper 'Inspiration: Poetical and Divine' (1963). But the debate has not ended there, for it has been renewed in the recent exchanges between Professor Frank Kermode, whose book *The Genesis of Secrecy* (1979) rests heavily on Farrer's work on St Mark's Gospel, and again Helen Gardner, in her latest book *In Defence of the Imagination* (1982). This argument involves now a conservative defending herself against a structuralist criticism – and it is the structuralist who looks back to Farrer.

But first the earlier debate should be considered in outline. Professor Lewis first turns his attention to Farrer's statements about the authority of certain images whose terms 'are taken from our finite experience but which have a reference beyond that experience'.[6] Farrer's point in *The Glass of Vision* had been quite clear: 'The choice, use and combination of images made by Christ and the Spirit must be simply a supernatural work.... The images are supernaturally formed, and supernaturally made intelligible to faith.'[7] Lewis respects Farrer's development of his position, that a religious image may be capable of accretions of meaning in new contexts and almost a life of its own. But his questionings begin with what he regards as Farrer's inability to distinguish between these regulative religious images and other images.[8] Lewis's criticism can readily be illustrated from *The Glass of Vision*. Does it help to make the required distinction, for example, when Farrer asserts that 'within the field of revealed truth, the principal images provide a canon to the lesser images'? (p. 111). Or again, that natural theology may provide a rule of 'a highly general kind', affording analogies for supernaturally formed images and 'a rule by which to regulate our intuition of what they mean'? (p. 110).

Lewis does, however, admit the role which natural theology must play. Presumably he would not quibble with Farrer's suggestion that:

The apostles were not, indeed, philosophers: but the philosophy of natural knowledge presupposes the knowledge it analyses and refines, and that natural knowledge, in abundant measure, the apostles had. What God bestowed on them through Christ was revelation of God's particular action. They had not known before that God would send his Son for us men and our salvation, but they had known that God was God; and what they now learnt was not that some superhuman Father had sent his Son, but that God had done so. Natural theology, then, provides a canon of interpretation which stands outside the particular matter of revealed truth.   (pp. 110–11)

This reflects almost exactly Coleridge's position in the 'Confessio Fidei'. Lewis follows Farrer thus far, but as soon as he moves into the realm of particularity he begins to ask questions. Lewis points out that if the course of God's particular action can simply be educed out of the idea or knowledge of his *being*, then revelation is barely necessary. The question must be asked again, what principle of selection is to be applied to distinguish between the 'principal' and the 'lesser' images?

Lewis criticizes the ambiguity of Farrer's account of religion as the 'supernaturalizing of events in the existing world',[9] since Farrer appears to want it both ways – that an event be supernaturalized and also retain the fullness of its independent natural character. It is at this point that he begins to write in terms of 'a double personal agency in our one activity' (p. 33), that is of seeing happenings in the world as acts both of God and of man. This concept of double agency rests upon something very like Coleridge's Polar Logic, 'opposite, not contrary powers', and seeing the universal in the particular and the particular necessarily requiring the universal. Farrer, in his way, was a poet – and Professor Lewis does not seem to respond readily to what is poetic.

Farrer lays the primacy firmly upon the images, and revelation presents 'the extreme example of irreducible imagery'.[10] Lewis seems to assume that, if this is the case, such images must necessarily be self-authenticating. But for Farrer, as for Coleridge of biblical revelation,[11] this need not be so. For Farrer certainly does not subscribe to what naturally follows from this, that we take the substance of the Bible and biblical imagery, *ab initio*, as ultimate and beyond question. Images, rather, are to be tested by experience and must answer to the deepest demands of man's spirit. Lewis himself believes that God works primarily in the world through 'the very substance of living' rather than 'given images'.[12] Images, therefore, are generated in the context of human activity. Farrer – content again to live with paradox – suggests that particular 'given images', when tested in universal experience, will be discovered to characterize man as he properly is, made in God's image. Revelation must be found in both image and experience, and not simply experience untreated by a necessary and 'irreducible imagery'.

Lewis's final criticism of *The Glass of Vision* is in the context of his discussion of art and religion. He refers particularly to Farrer's distinction between poetry and prophecy, and, once again, he has a one-sided view. For Lewis, poetry and prophecy are ultimately one and the same, so that poetry and religion will, in the end, merge into one another.[13] But he fails to perceive the delicacy of Farrer's distinction. The prophet, certainly, is not necessarily the poet, and of the prophet Farrer writes that

> What he has got to say is determinate and particular, it is what the Lord God declares and requires on the day which he speaks. It is designed to evoke not an exquisite and contemplative realization of human existence, but particular practical responses to God.[14]

Nevertheless, Farrer continues, 'the poetical character of the prophetic utterance' is not immaterial, since 'poetry, for the prophet, is a technique of divination, in the poetic process he gets his message' (p. 128). Thus, what the prophet and poet share is the technique of inspiration. Both, writes Farrer, 'move an incantation of images under a control' (p. 129). But all poetry is not therefore prophetic or religious. Literature and its insights may indeed irrigate the religious imagination, at the heart of which remains the irreducible mystery. Farrer might even go so far as to suggest that as the controlling images are tested in experience, so divine illumination is not so much a vision, but, as Coleridge expressed it, a 'state of consciousness' or an 'inward experience'.[15] Yet it has a particularity perceived in the common experience – again the Polar Logic: poetry and religion, necessarily different while supposing and requiring each other.

In *The Limits of Literary Criticism*, subtitled *Reflections on the Interpretation of Poetry and Scripture*, Helen Gardner criticized *The Glass of Vision* in her role as literary critic. She concentrated upon one point only, Farrer's discussion of the ending of St Mark's Gospel, and writes:

> He approaches the literary criticism of the New Testament with a mind steeped in secular literature both ancient and modern, and he shows himself fully aware of the parallels between what he is doing and what is being done by modern critics of poetry. How whole-heartedly he had adopted the methods of modern literary criticism can be seen from his handling in *The Glass of Vision* ... of a classic problem in the New Testament.[16]

Farrer treats the abrupt ending of St Mark, the words '*ἐφοβοῦντο γάρ*', as a literary question, examining parallels and structures, or what he calls the 'formal recurrences of St Mark's poetical magic'.[17] The Gospel then demands that we see it as an overall pattern, 'all cohering in a structure of meaning'.[18] Farrer parallels the Marcan narrative with the Old Testament story of Joseph, the last words of the Gospel echoing the Septuagint version of the reaction of Joseph's brothers when his true identity in Egypt is revealed – '*ἐφοβοῦντο γάρ*' – 'for they were afraid'.

Helen Gardner's criticism is primarily historical. In all these literary parallels and structures, what we see, she says, is not the 'mind and imagination of St. Mark, but the "lively and fertile mind and ... profoundly poetic and Christian imagination" of Dr. Farrer'.[19] True, she admits that Farrer does say that 'the principal importance of St. Mark's Gospel lies in its historical content', yet nevertheless his 'method is often oblivious of, and impatient with, the historical' (p. 36). Coleridge, similarly has been criticized inasmuch as 'he failed to conceive of [Jesus Christ] as being *a particular* man with his own peculiar characteristics'.[20] Helen Gardner, however, concludes with some curious remarks.

It is surely an odd phrase to speak of St. Mark's imagination being 'controlled' by facts. If we believe that what he is recording *are* facts – and that is the crux of the matter between Christian and non-Christian – then it is surely filled by the wonder of those facts, and not merely respectful to them. It is curious that the study of images, which began from a high theory of the imagination's power to apprehend the truth and value of experience, and to express its apprehension of the world, has led only too often in practice to an ignoring of the primary imagination, which degrades the secondary, or creative, imagination into an instrument for perceiving analogies and making connexions.   (p. 37)

It is strange that her criticism of Farrer should conclude by calling up Coleridge on the primary and secondary Imagination, since Farrer in many ways might have been schooled by Coleridge. For Helen Gardner, history is composed of irrefutable facts, and Christianity must stick to them. But she does not seem to be aware of the problem and paradox of the incarnation as the ahistorical and atemporal breaking into history. The particularity of Christianity is always a problem for the poet, and Helen Gardner, like Professor Lewis, fails to see that image and imagination play upon the historical, seeing the eternal through the temporal and the universal through the particular.

Farrer replied to Lewis and Gardner in his paper 'Inspiration : Poetical and Divine'.[21] He was unrepentent and vigorous in his defence of *The Glass of Vision*. Once again, he draws close parallels between the *processes* of 'religious seers and secular poets'. But, he continues:

it is most necessary to emphasize the limitations attaching to the parallel. Religious seers and secular poets may be led to seek inspiration in these similar ways; but the fact casts no light whatsoever on the fundamental mystery of divine inspiration. Shelley uses certain methods to set his imagination acting; and this gives his imagination scope to act. St. John uses similar methods; and this gives the Holy Ghost scope to move his imagination... Belief in inspiration is a metaphysical belief; it is the belief that the Creator everywhere underlies the creature, with the added faith that at certain points he acts in, as, and through the creature's mind. We have argued that if this really happens a part will be played by the imagination. Imagination, in such an employment, will be suppled and made responsive or creative; there will surely be an analogy here to the workings of the poetic mind. But that which obtains expression in the two sorts of case will be widely different; and so will be the significance of the product.[22]

This is both disturbing and yet, somehow, right and adequate. No doubt Lewis and Gardner will continue to say that he wants to have it both ways, and, in the end, how can we tell the difference between the religious seer and the secular poet? Certainly a common criticism levelled against Coleridge, despite his many writings on the Bible, is that Scripture, Nature and almost all literary and artistic products of the imagination are equally sources of 'revelation'.[23] Is 'The Rime of the Ancient Mariner' a religious poem, or not? Coleridge's answer is no less unsatisfactory and no less true than Farrer's; try it, and see! In literature, the Bible, he claimed, 'finds me at a greater depth of my being . . . [than] all other books put together'.[24] The difference, however, is one of degree. Where the principal images work with the Spirit within the poetic imagination they will work in a unique and unmistakable way upon man's spiritual constitution and needs.

But all this needs disinfecting with a strong dose of hard-headed criticism. It is supplied in the renewed debate in which Helen Gardner is engaged, on almost exactly the same ground, with Professor Frank Kermode. In 1969, Kermode published a paper in the journal *Modern Language Notes* entitled 'The Structure of Fiction'.[25] He begins thus.

The question is whether there is a chance that some mode of structural analysis can satisfy the requirements of criticism, if we take those to be: first, that there should be available for any work we take to be worthy of preservation and of public interest some fairly systematic account which is itself acceptable to an informed public; and secondly that this account should try to tell the truth and know how much of the truth it can tell.

Kermode takes his criticisms into the world of structuralism[26] and uses as one of his examples of the determination of structure and meaning Farrer on St Mark's Gospel in *The Glass of Vision* and *A Study of St. Mark* (1951). His concern is with typological structure and pattern, precisely those things which were regarded with such suspicion by Helen Gardner. Certainly he is very well aware of her fears that the study of the Gospel by structural analysis (and Kermode groups Farrer with Lévi-Strauss and Roland Barthes as a 'structuralist') disastrously reduces the historical actuality and immediacy which most Christians seek in it. However, Kermode's contention is that the Gospel writer is dealing with a story in which nothing is merely *historisch*, all is *geschichtlich*.[27] The universal importance of the literal truth of the story is evoked by a deliberate and sometimes, indeed, artificial patterning and structuring which establishes necessarily (and not randomly, as in purely fictional narrative) the authority of the 'principal images', those peculiar to divine revelation. Thus the Gospel rest upon, and yet moves beyond, the plain facts, for, says Kermode:

> If Farrer is to be believed, a narrative which we should regard as of the highest historical importance merely as a plain account of what happened, is yet at the same time very elaborately structured. (p. 905)

It is precisely in this deep structure that the irreducible mystery which always eludes description is said to lie (p. 915).

Here Helen Gardner returns to the lists, and her complaints against Kermode in her latest book, *In Defence of the Imagination* (1982), are an almost exact repetition of her complaints against *The Glass of Vision* in 1956: that the author of St Mark's Gospel is reduced to 'a mere exemplar of timeless laws governing the development of narrative of all and every kind'.[28] Kermode had elaborated his defence of Farrer in an earlier series of the Charles Eliot Norton Lectures, published in 1979 as *The Genesis of Secrecy*. The issues remain the same. 'As to Farrer', Kermode sadly remarks,

> his work was rejected by the establishment, and eventually by himself, largely because it was so literary. The institution knew intuitively that such literary elaboration, such emphasis on elements that must be called fictive, was unacceptable because damaging to what remained of the idea that the gospel narratives were still, in some measure, transparent upon history ... [Farrer] assumes that there is an enigmatic narrative concealed in the manifest one.[29]

According to Helen Gardner, Farrer and Kermode offer a Jesus who is simply a mirror image of our contemporary selves, and the Gospel is merely a set of puzzles or diagrams, there to be decoded.

Indeed, for Kermode it would be true to say that the narrative possesses significance, not meaning, and that criticism must attend only to how what is said is written and not to what it is written about. It is in the intense thematic opposition of one puzzle after another that we are drawn back, inevitably, to those irreducible, primary images which so troubled Professor Lewis. For this opposition – Polar Logic again – keeps its meaning 'secret' by producing what is, precisely, irreducible – a secrecy which is to be perpetually reinterpreted.

Helen Gardner, on the other hand, demands of criticism the elucidation of meaning rather than significance, and wishes to safeguard as normative the 'main' or 'literal' sense. A narrative, for her, is not a source of inexhaustible meanings, although she admits that great books may be almost inexhaustibly fertile. The debate can almost be defined in terms of the biblical fundamentalist who holds to the primacy of the literal sense of scripture against the structuralist, bred upon the structured typology of Farrer's analysis of St Mark. John Coulson, in his review of Helen Gardner's book concludes that

> The underlying question is how we gain meaning when the form in which it is contained is the highly ambiguous one of metaphor, symbol or story. If the symbol [or image] gives rise to thought, who verifies that thought, and by what authority?[30]

Here is a return to the old question. Kermode, now the secular critic, side-steps the issue and refers, elusively, to 'control by an institution', whatever that means. Farrer and Gardner, therefore, are left facing each other once again. For Farrer the problem must be: by what authority are these particular images confirmed if the literal sense of scripture is continually disturbed by a shifting pattern of parallels and types? At base, the problem is one of faith, or rather, the nature of the connection between what we hold in the language of faith and what we explain in the derived and second-order language of belief. The simple structuralist denies the connection; the biblical fundamentalist denies the distinction. Farrer lies somewhere between these extremes, the mystery threatened by reductionism on either side, to pattern or single meaning. 'Pattern and meaning', writes Coulson, 'are dependent upon each other and are separable only for purposes of comprehension'. Once again it is Polar Logic, 'both ... and', not 'either ... or'.

Literature certainly can never be merely a pattern, but yet a pattern demanding perpetual reinterpretation is necessary to preserve narrative from the trap of a simple literalism or the fetters of normative meaning. Imagination given play over certain images which are rooted in a 'given' set of historical circumstances, obtains a release from a simple adhesion to fact, which is rediscovered afresh in an eternity of new circumstances. The mystery is recognized anew, not in propositional faith or an assent to metaphysical assertions elicited from the primary, literal meaning of scripture, but in the perpetual demand of the structure for re-examination in the light of experience. Terence Hawkes sums up structuralist thinking in this way:

> At its simplest, it claims that the nature of every element in any given situation has no significance by itself, and in fact is determined by its relationship to all the other elements involved in that situation. In short, the full significance of any entity or experience cannot be perceived unless and until it is integrated into the *structure* of which it forms a part.[31]

Again, it is significance, not meaning, which is sought for; the significance of what is going on between God and man in revelation through the processes of inspiration and poetry. Farrer concludes *The Glass of Vision* on precisely this point.

> Poetry and divine inspiration have this in common, that both are projected in images which cannot be decoded, but must be allowed to signify what they signify of the reality beyond them.... Inspiration does not merely stand at a midway point between poetry and metaphysics; it actively communicates with both. The subjective process of inspiration is essentially poetical, the content it communicates is metaphysical.... But what inspiration reveals, it reveals about God, so that the thought of the sheer deity of God is embedded in the revelation. To think this thought out is to enter on a metaphysical enquiry. Even if we do not think it out, the thought of sheer deity is still the raw material of metaphysics, that is to say, it belongs to the natural knowledge of God. Without it no supernatural revelation can be either received or understood.[32]

Coleridge, as he sang and snuffled of 'om-m-mject' and 'sum-m-mject' would have approved of this.[33] For God, and man made in God's image as a living and creative soul, as opposites, the one generated from the other, have a tendency to reunion, as 'all polar forces, *i.e. opposite*, not *contrary*, powers, are necessarily *unius generis*, homogeneous'.[34]

II   A FINAL COMMENT

The influence of Coleridge on the nineteenth and twentieth centuries is extremely difficult to estimate. In 1842, F. D. Maurice wrote 'I rejoice to think that those who have most profited by what he has taught them, do not and cannot form a school'.[35] In England, a wide diversity of people acknowledged their debt to him; philosophers like J. S. Mill, theologians like Julius Hare and F. J. A. Hort, or literary men like George MacDonald. In the Church, Broadchurchmen and Tractarians felt his attraction. The young E. B. Pusey drew extensively, if critically, upon his reading of Coleridge for his *Lectures on Types and Prophecies of the Old Testament* (1836), which were much admired by Keble, Newman and Isaac Williams, among others. In America, Emerson's respect alone would have ensured Coleridge's prestige. Yet, by 1884, H. D. Traill was casting doubt on the reality of the Coleridge legend. He wrote:

> A few mystics of the type of Maurice, a few eager seekers after truth like Sterling, may have gathered, or fancied they gathered, distinct dogmatic instruction from the Highgate oracles; and no doubt, to the extent of his influence over the former of these disciples, we may justly credit Coleridge's discourses with having exercised a real if only transitory effect upon nineteenth-century thought.[36]

The legend, nevertheless, persisted and continues to persist, irrigating theological and literary discussion. Thus, George Watson in his book *The Literary Critics* (1962) has described 'a mind passionately in love with free enquiry, concentrated and disciplined in its determination to decipher the secret of poetic discourse'.[37]

In the twentieth century, investigation is led to seek not merely his identifiable influence but the wide diversity of thinkers whose work bears an affinity with what Coleridge thought. In the fields of phenomenology and philosophy, Thomas McFarland has traced valuable similarities in Edmund Husserl's *Ideas: General Introduction to Pure Phenomenology* (English trans. 1958), in Jaspers and in Heidegger. [38] In theology, Paul Tillich among others, has spoken of religious language with awareness of similar processes in poetry and other arts.[39] Nor is Coleridge irrelevant in the more recent theological discussion focusing upon the work of Don Cupitt, concerning the notion of revelation and in the description of Jesus as ironist.[40] Finally, poets and literary critics have continued to find in Coleridge hints and prophecies which seem to be patient of almost limitless expansion and suggestiveness.

But it is Coleridge, the wrecked man seeking the assurance of salvation to which the letters and notebooks increasingly point. The vast intellectual effort and the tireless project of self-reflection are religious tasks lasting a lifetime. To some he remains an enigmatic failure, a scavenger in the minds of greater men, and a bad husband and father. 'Old Sam was only a poet, you know, never did anything practical that was any good to anybody, actually not thought of much in the family, a bit of a disgrace in fact, taking drugs and not looking after his wife and children. Of course STC must have been a *wonderful man* – in a way.'[41] Somehow, Lord Coleridge has characterized the man perfectly. Yet, three weeks before his death, Coleridge wrote to his godson Adam Steinmetz Kennard, summing up, perhaps, a lifetime of toil under the sense of sin and failure and how these are to be overcome by the paradoxes of Christian believing.

And I thus, on the brink of the grave, solemnly bear witness to you, that the Almighty Redeemer, most gracious in his promises to them that truly seek Him, is faithful to perform what He has promised, & has preserved under all my pains and infirmities, the inward peace that passeth all understanding, with the supporting assurance of a reconciled God, who will not withdraw his spirit from me in the conflict, & in his own time will *deliver* me from the Evil One. O my dear Godchild! eminently blessed are they who begin *early* to seek, fear, & love their God, trusting wholly in the righteousness & mediation of their Lord, Redeemer, Saviour, & everlasting High Priest, Jesus Christ. O! preserve this as a legacy & bequest from your unseen Godfather & friend,

S. T. Coleridge[42]

Notes

NOTES TO CHAPTER 1: INTRODUCTION

1. Thomas De Quincey, *Confessions of an English Opium Eater*, ed. Alethea Hayter (1821; Harmondsworth, 1971) pp. 105–6.
2. *CL*, III, p. 541.
3. Walpole, *Anecdotes of Painting in England*, vol. 4 (Strawberry Hill, 1762–71); quoted in Mario Praz, Introductory Essay to Peter Fairclough (ed.), *Three Gothic Novels* (Harmondsworth, 1968) pp. 16–17.
4. See: William Vaughan, *Romantic Art* (London, 1978) pp. 32–6; Jørgen Andersen, 'Giant Dreams, Piranesi's Influence in England', *English Miscellany*, 3 (Rome, 1952), quoted in Mario Praz, op. cit., p. 16; Philip Hofer, Introduction to Giovanni Battista Piranesi, *The Prisons* [*Le Carceri*] (New York, 1973) p. viii.
5. Hofer, op. cit., p. xii.
6. Thomas De Quincey, 'Samuel Taylor Coleridge', *Tait's Edinburgh Magazine*, Sep 1834–Jan 1835; repr. in *Reminiscences of the English Lake Poets*, ed. John E. Jordan (London and New York, 1961) p. 10.
7. Quoted in Alec R. Vidler, *F. D. Maurice and Company: Nineteenth-Century Studies* (London, 1966) p. 222.
8. *Fortnightly Review*, n.s. XXXVII (1885) 11–25, 223–33.
9. A. C. Swinburne, *Essays and Studies* (London, 1875) p. 274.
10. Charles Lamb to William Wordsworth, 26 Apr 1816; see Edwin W. Marrs, Jr (ed.), *The Letters of Charles and Mary Anne Lamb*, 3 vols to date (Ithaca, N.Y., 1975–8) vol. III, p. 215.
11. Leslie Stephen, *Hours in a Library*, vol. III, 3rd edn (1879; London, 1909) p. 343.
12. E. P. Thompson, review of David V. Erdman (ed.), *Essays on His Times* (Princeton, 1978), in *The Wordsworth Circle*, 10 (1979) 261–5.
13. Stephen Happel, 'Words Made Beautiful by Grace: On Coleridge the Theologian', *Religious Studies Review*, 6 (1980) 201–10.
14. Mary Midgley, *Heart and Mind: The Varieties of Moral Experience* (Brighton, 1981) p. 44.
15. See Milton C. Nahm, 'The Theological Background of the Theory of the Artist as Creator', *Journal of the History of Ideas*, VIII (1947) 365.
16. *BL* vol. 1, p. 202.
17. Nahm, op. cit., p. 372.
18. *Lay Sermons (CC)*, p. 49.
19. Ibid., p. 50.
20. Owen Barfield, *What Coleridge Thought* (Middletown, Conn., 1971) pp. 144–57.

21. Pamela Vermes, *Buber on God and the Perfect Man* (Providence, RI, 1980) pp. 81–5.
22. Northrop Frye, *The Great Code* (London, 1982) pp. 14, 17, 29.

NOTES TO CHAPTER 2: THE ROMANTIC CONTEXT

1. J. S. Mill, 'Coleridge', *London and Westminster Review*, Mar 1840; repr. in J. B. Schneewind (ed.), *Mill's Essays on Literature and Society* (New York, 1965) p. 291.
2. William Wordsworth, *Poetical Works*, ed. Thomas Hutchinson, rev. Ernest de Selincourt (Oxford, 1969) p. 744.
3. Novalis, *Fragmente aus den letzten Jahren 1798–1800, in Gesammelte Werke*, ed., Carl Seelig, 4 vols (Zürich, 1946) vol. 4, no. 3056, p. 302.
4. Pierre-Simon Ballanche, *Orphée*, in *Oeuvres complètes*, Slatkine reprints (Geneva, 1967) vol. 6, pp. 82, 96.
5. W. H. Wackenroder, *Herzensergiessungen eines kunstliebenden Klosterbruders* (1797), ed. A. Gillies (1797; Oxford, 1948) p. 55.
6. P. B. Shelley, *A Defence of Poetry* (1821); repr. in *English Critical Essays (Nineteenth Century)*, ed. Edmund D. Jones (Oxford, 1968) pp. 132, 134–5, 123.
7. Novalis, *Blütenstaub* (1798), in *Gesammelte Werke*, (Zurich, 1945) vol. 2 no. 71, p. 25.
8. *CL*, I, p. 352.
9. Ballanche, op. cit., p. 96.
10. 'Monody on the Death of Chatterton' (*c.* 1790–6), *PW*, pp. 13–15.
11. Alfred De Vigny, 'Dernière nuit de travail du 29 au 30 juin 1834', in *Chatterton*, ed. A. H. Diverres (London, 1967) p. 59.
12. *Stello*, Ch. 17, in *Oeuvres complètes*, ed. F. Baldensperger (Paris, 1950) vol. 1, p. 627.
13. F. Schlegel, 'Athenäum Fragment', no. 44, *Kritische – Ausgabe*, vol. II: *Charakteristiken und Kritiken (1796–1801)*, ed. Hans Eichner (Munich, 1967) p. 260.
14. Wordsworth, Preface to *Lyrical Ballads*, *Poetical Works*, p. 738.
15. Shelley, op. cit., pp. 105–6.
16. Letter to John Thelwall, Apr 1796, *CL*, I, p. 205.
17. *BL*, vol. 1, p. 202.
18. Blake, letter to Dr Tusler, 23 Aug 1799, *Complete Writings*, ed. Geoffrey Keynes (Oxford, 1966) p. 793.
19. Blake, *A Vision of the Last Judgement* (1810), *Complete Writings*, p. 617.
20. *Letters of John Keats*, ed. Frederick Page (Oxford, 1954) p. 49.
21. Victor Hugo, *Oeuvres poétiques*, ed. Pierre Albouy and Gaetan Picon (Paris, 1964) vol. 1, p. 265.
22. A. W. Schlegel, *Vorlesungen über schöne Kunst und Literatur* (1801), in *Kritische Schriften und Briefe*, ed. Edgar Lohner (Stuttgart, 1963) vol. 2, p. 90.
23. *Vorlesungen über dramatische Kunst und Literatur* (A Course of Lectures on Dramatic Art and Literature) (1809), in *Kritische Schriften* (Stuttgart, 1967) vol. 6, p. 109; trans. John Black, rev. A. J. W. Morrison (London, 1846) p. 340.

24. See *Sh. Crit.*, vol. 1, p. 198.
25. Victor Hugo, op. cit., vol. 1, pp. 281–2.
26. *BL*, vol. 2, pp. 238–9.
27. Novalis, *Fragmente des Jahres* (1798) in *Gesammelte Werke*, vol. 3, no. 807, p. 23.
28. *Lay Sermons(CC)*, p. 30.
29. *BL*, vol. 2, p. 230.
30. F. Schlegel, 'Athenäum Fragment', no. 116, *Kritische Ausgabe*, vol. 2, p. 183.
31. Ludwig Tieck, *Nachgelassene Schriften*, ed. R. Köpke (Leipzig, 1855) vol. 2, p. 238.
32. *Marginalia*, p. 200.
33. *Lay Sermons (CC)*, p. 30.

NOTES TO CHAPTER 3: THE EARLY WRITINGS

1. *CL*, I, p. 349.
2. *CN*, I 273.
3. George Whalley, 'The Bristol Library Borrowings of Southey and Coleridge, 1793–8', *The Library*, IV (1949) 124.
4. Quoted in W. Schrickx, 'Coleridge and the Cambridge Platonists', *Review of English Literature*, 7 (1966) 81, using the edition *Faksimile – Neudruck der Ausgabe von London 1678* (Stuttgart, 1964).
5. *BL*, vol. 1, pp. 80, 87.
6. See Lucyle Werkmeister, 'The Early Coleridge: His "Rage for Metaphysics"', *Harvard Theological Review*, 54 (1961) 122.
7. Letter to Ludwig Tieck, 4 July 1817, *CL*, IV, p. 751. For further discussion of *Aurora*, see below, Ch. 6.
8. *CL*, I, p. 302.
9. Ibid.
10. Austin Farrer, *The Glass of Vision*, Bampton Lectures for 1948 (Westminster, 1948) p. 148.
11. *CL*, I, p. 310.
12. Letter of 9 October 1797, *CL*, I, p. 347.
13. Letter of 16 October 1797, *CL*, I, p. 354.
14. 'Frost at Midnight', *PW*, p. 242 (l. 52).
15. Charles Lamb, 'Christ's Hospital, Five and Thirty Years Ago', in *Essays of Elia* (1823; London, 1903) pp. 40–1.
16. *BL*, vol. 1, p. 9.
17. Werkmeister, op. cit., p. 106.
18. Plotinus, *Ennead*, II, 3.8, Loeb Classical Library (London, 1966) p. 72.
19. 'Easter Holidays' (1787), *PW*, p. 2 (ll. 25–30).
20. 'Anthem for the Children of Christ's Hospital' (1789), *PW*, p. 6 (l. 11).
21. 'To a Friend [Charles Lamb]' (1794), *PW*, p. 79 (ll. 26–8).
22. See S. F. Gingerich, 'From Necessity to Transcendentalism in Coleridge', *Publications of the Modern Language Association of America*, n.s. XXVIII (1920) 10–11.
23. Letter to John Thelwall, 19 Nov 1796, *CL*, I, p. 260.

24. Marginal note in the 1797 edition of *Poems*, *PW*, p. 79.
25. *Friend(CC)*, I, p. 457.
26. Stephen Prickett, *Coleridge and Wordsworth: The Poetry of Growth* (Cambridge, 1970) pp. 183–4.
27. *AR (II)*, p. xvii.
28. Coleridge, *Poetical Works*, ed. E. H. Coleridge (Oxford, 1912) vol. II, pp. 516–17.
29. Kelvin Everest, *Coleridge's Secret Ministry: The Context of the Conversation Poems 1795–8* (Sussex, 1979) p. 19.
30. 'The Eolian Harp' (1795), *PW*, p. 102 (l. 64).
31. Mario Praz would see it in these terms:

> Coleridge, who at first had preached fervently in favour of liberty and against violence and the sceptred and bloody tyrants, fell back later upon a defence, Christian ideal, with 'Fears in Solitude' (1798). The beginning and the ending of this poem, inspired by a love of his own land in the gentler and humbler aspects of its landscape, have a pastoral tone, a tone of elegiac quietism that might well be termed Biedermeier. (*The Hero in Eclipse in Victorian Fiction*, trans. Angus Davidson (Oxford, 1969) p. 39).

32. See below, Ch. 7.
33. 13 November 1795, *CL*, I, p. 168.
34. *Lectures(CC)*, p. 83.
35. Ibid., p. 177.
36. Ibid., p. 115.
37. Ibid., p. 91.
38. *CN*, I 6.
39. 21 October 1794, *CL*, I, p. 113.
40. *Lectures(CC)*, pp. 204–5.
41. Ibid., p. 160.
42. See H. A. Pistorius's notes and additions to David Hartley, *Observations on Man: His Fame, His Duty, and His Expectations*, 3 vols (1791) III, 598–629. Also see Hartley, ibid., II, 146–8.
43. *Lectures(CC)*, p. 109. See also letter to John Thelwall, 17 Dec 1796: 'Christianity regards morality as a process. . . . There is no resting-place for Morality' (*CL*, I, pp. 282–3).
44. 'The whole administration of divine providence in this world is evidently a *process*; and those things which are most perfect in their kind are the slowest in coming to maturity' – John Prior Estlin, *Evidences of Revealed Religion, and Particularly Christianity, Stated, with Reference to a Pamphlet Called the Age of Reason* (Bristol, 1796) p. 15.
45. *Watchman(CC)*, pp. 130–40.
46. 'Lecture on the Slave Trade', *Lectures(CC)*, pp. 235–6.
47. *BL*, vol. 1, pp. 164–6, 202. See also I. A. Richards, *Coleridge on Imagination* (London, 1934) Ch. 1.
48. *Watchman(CC)*, p. 132.
49. Ibid., p. 210.
50. Ibid., p. 272. Adapted from *Outlines of an Historical View of the Progress of*

the Human Mind (1795), Introduction. Coleridge's early ambivalence towards the doctrine of 'perfectibility' is illustrated by his marginalia on Malthus's first *Essay on Population* (1798), which was written mainly as an argument against the theories of Godwin and Condorcet. He first mentions reading Malthus in a letter of 1799, and his copy of the *Essay* was an 1803 edition. See George Reuben Potter, 'Unpublished Marginalia in Coleridge's Copy of Malthus's *Essay on Population*', *Publications of the Modern Language Association of America*, 51 (1936) 1061–8.

51. *Watchman(CC)*, p. 242.
52. *CN*, I 22; 'Religious Musings', *PW*, p. 111 (ll. 62–3); letter to Thomas Poole, *CL*, I, p. 203.
53. Letter to Mrs S. T. Coleridge, 10 March 1799, *CL*, I, p. 472.
54. See C. A. van Peursen, *Leibniz*, trans. Hubert Hoskins (London, 1969) pp. 17–18, 24.
55. *BL*, vol. 1, p. 89.
56. Whalley, op. cit., p. 119.
57. See *Lectures(CC)*, pp. 66, 235–6.
58. 'Lewesdon Hill' (1788) p. 9; quoted in C. G. Martin, 'Coleridge and William Crowe's "Lewesdon Hill" ', *Modern Language Review*, 62 (1967) 401.
59. *The Pleasures of Imagination*, I, l. 221.
60. *Lectures (CC)*, p. 338.
61. See *Watchman(CC)*, p. 12, on 'detached metaphysical systematizers'.
62. Letter to Robert Southey, 11 Dec 1794, *CL*, I, p. 137.
63. See Jerome Christensen, *Coleridge's Blessed Machine of Language* (Ithaca, N.Y., 1981) Ch. 2: 'Hartley's Influence on Coleridge', pp. 58–95. Christensen notes that Coleridge's response to Hartley is complicated by his reading *Observations on Man* in two editions by Priestley and Pistorius (p. 29). He further remarks on Hartley's writing on the divine inspiration of Scripture (pp. 46–7), and its effect on Coleridge, whose mature statement on the subject was not made until the end of his life in *Confessions of an Inquiring Spirit* (1840).
64. *CL*, II, p. 821.
65. *Watchman(CC)*, pp. 139, 332.
66. Ibid., pp. 168–9.
67. Ibid., p. 269.
68. See also J. B. Beer, *Coleridge the Visionary* (London, 1959) pp. 80–3.
69. Preface to *Poems on Various Subjects* (London, 1796); repr. in *Poetical Works*, vol. II (Oxford, 1912) p. 1136.
70. Letter to John Thelwall, 17 Dec 1796, *CL*, I, p. 285.
71. Introduction to 'A Sheet of Sonnets', *Poetical Works*, vol. 2, p. 1139.
72. See also W. K. Wimsatt, 'The Structure of Romantic Nature Imagery', *The Verbal Icon* (1954), repr. in M. H. Abrams (ed.), *English Romantic Poets: Modern Essays in Criticism* (New York, 1960) p. 28.
73. Preface to the Second Edition of *Poems* (London, 1797); repr. in *Poetical Works*, vol. 2, p. 1145.
74. Ibid., pp. 1145–6.
75. *Monthly Mirror*, II (1796) 97, quoted in J. R. de J. Jackson (ed.), *Coleridge: The Critical Heritage* (London, 1970) p. 38.

76. *Monthly Review*, XX (1796) 194–5, quoted in Jackson (ed.), op. cit., p. 37.
77. *Critical Review*, XVII (1796) 209–12; *Analytical Review*, XIII (1796) 610–12; *Critical Review*, XXIII (1798) 266–8; quoted in Jackson, op. cit., pp. 35, 33, 42.
78. *Monthly Mirror*, II (1796) 97; quoted in Jackson, op. cit., p. 38.
79. See below, pp. 52–3.
80. *PW*, p. 101.
81. Humphrey House, *Coleridge*, the Clark Lectures, 1951–2 (London, 1953) pp. 75–6.
82. See above, p. 21.
83. *CL*, IV, pp. 750–1.
84. Duane B. Schneider, 'Coleridge's Light–Sound Theory', *Notes and Queries*, CCVIII (1963) 182–3; J. B. Beer, 'Coleridge and Boehme's *Aurora*', ibid., 183–7.
85. See John Beer, *Coleridge's Poetic Intelligence* (London, 1977) pp. 24–32.
86. To C. A. Tulk, *CL*, IV, p. 807.
87. See Richard Haven, 'Coleridge and Jacob Boehme: a Further Comment', *Notes and Queries*, CCXI (1966) 176–8; Henri Nidecker, 'Notes Marginales de S. T. Coleridge, IV. En marge de Steffens', *Revue de Littérature,* XII (1932) 856–71.
88. *Marginalia*, pp. 564–5.
89. Ibid., pp. 598, 646.
90. Ibid., p. 639.
91. See below, pp. 105–7; also *Marginalia*, p. 672.
92. Ibid., pp. 667, 668–9.
93. Letter to Daniel Stuart, 7 Oct 1815, *CL*, IV, p. 592.
94. Transcribed by Alice D. Snyder, 'Coleridge on Böhme', *Publications of the Modern Language Association of America*, 45 (1930) 618.
95. *CL*, IV, p. 592. See also Thomas McFarland, *Coleridge and the Pantheist Tradition* (Oxford, 1969) Excursus XIX: 'Coleridge and Boehme', pp. 325–32.
96. Dedication of 'Ode to the Departing Year' (1796), to the Revd George Coleridge; quoted in M. H. Abrams, 'Coleridge's "A Light in Sound": Science, Metascience, and Poetic Imagination', *Proceedings of American Philosophical Society*, CXVI (1972) 458.
97. McFarland, op. cit., p. 191. See also below, Ch. 7.
98. *BL*, vol. 1, pp. 173–88.
99. See also M. H. Abrams, 'Coleridge's "A Light in Sound" ', p. 466.
100. *CN*, II 927.
101. *CN*, II 2264; *Friend(CC)*, II, p. 82; see also Alice D. Snyder, 'Coleridge on Giordano Bruno', *Modern Language Notes*, XLII (1927) 427–37.
102. *BL*, vol. 2, p. 219.
103. Ibid., vol. 1, p. 170. See also W. M. Ploplis, 'The Great Name of God: A Study of the Element of the Kabbala in Samuel Taylor Coleridge's Theogony and its Influence on the Theodicy and Cosmogony of his Major Poetry' (Loyola University of Chicago unpublished PhD dissertation, 1981): Ch. 4: 'Coleridge's Appreciation of the Kabbalist Tradition', pp. 266–73.
104. *AR (II)*, p. 261. Within the Christian tradition, Donald MacKinnon has

defended the validity of the mystic's private inspiration: 'mystical experience is properly spoken of as one in which the opposition of subject and object is overcome. . . . It is through the work of communication that the mystic's inclusive vision is defined, not once for all, but in the stumbling imperfection that demands continual correction.' ('Some Epistemological Reflections on Mystical Experience', in Stephen T. Katz (ed.), *Mysticism and Philosophical Essays* (London, 1978) pp. 136–9.

105. See Frances A. Yates, *The Art of Memory* (Harmondsworth, 1969) p. 224.
106. For further discussion of Coleridge's use of Asiatic 'mysteries', in a lecture probably dating from 1818, see William K. Pfeiler, 'Coleridge and Schelling's Treatise on the Samothracian Deities', *Modern Language Notes*, 52 (1937) 162–5.

NOTES TO CHAPTER 4: 'KUBLA KHAN', 'THE ANCIENT MARINER' AND 'DEJECTION'

1. See Wordsworth and Coleridge, *Lyrical Ballads* (1798), ed. W. J. B. Owen, 2nd edn (Oxford, 1969) p. 119.
2. *CL*, I, p. 387.
3. Herbert Read, *The Forms of Things Unknown: Essays Towards an Aesthetic Philosophy* (New York, 1960) pp. 124–40.
4. *Sh*, p. 76.
5. See A. D. Snyder in a letter to *The Times Literary Supplement*, 2 Aug 1934, p. 541; Irene H. Chayes, ' "Kubla Khan" and the Creative Process', *Studies in Romanticism*, VI (1966) 1. MS now in the British Library.
6. Quoted by E. L. Griggs, *CL*, I, p. 349.
7. *CL*, I, pp. 349–50.
8. Preface to 'Kubla Khan', *PW*, p. 296, ll. 22–3.
9. D. F. Rauber, 'The Fragment as Romantic Form', *Modern Language Quarterly*, 30 (1969) 221. On the Romantic fragment in Coleridge's later poetry, see below, Ch. 6
10. *BL*, vol. 1, p. 20.
11. 30 May 1815, *CL*, IV, p. 575.
12. See below, Ch. 5.
13. First pointed out by Elisabeth Schneider, *Coleridge, Opium and 'Kubla Khan'* (Chicago, 1953) pp. 245–6.
14. *Ion*, in Eric H. Warmington and Philip G. Rouse (eds), *Great Dialogues of Plato*, trans. W. H. D. Rouse (New York, 1956) p. 19.
15. Kathleen Raine, 'Traditional Symbolism in "Kubla Khan" ', *Sewanee Review*, 72 (1964) 640–2.
16. Humphrey House, *Coleridge*, the Clark Lectures, 1951–2 (London, 1953) p. 115.
17. *BL*, vol. 2, p. 12.
18. Ibid., vol. 1, p. 77.
19. 'Limbo', ll. 20–30, *PW*, p. 430. See also below, Ch. 6
20. See further K. M. Wheeler, *The Creative Mind in Coleridge's Poetry* (London, 1981) pp. 39–41.

21. Coleridge takes the phrase from Theocritus, I. 145: "ἐς ὕστερ ν ἄδιον ἀσῶ." (*PW*, p. 297).
22. *BL*, vol. 2, p. 258.
23. Mary Rahme, 'Coleridge's Concept of Symbolism', *Studies in English Literature*, IX (1969) 627.
24. Coleridge, 'On the Prometheus of Aeschylus', *Literary Remains*, ed. H. N. Coleridge (London, 1836–9) vol. 4, p. 362.
25. *TT*, p. 211.
26. See below, Ch. 5.
27. David Jones, 'An Introduction to "The Ancient Mariner"' (1963–4), in *'The Dying Gaul' and Other Writings*, ed. Harman Grisewood (London, 1978) p. 208. Also see Thomas McFarland, *Coleridge and the Pantheist Tradition* (Oxford, 1969), Excursus XIII: 'Coleridge's Theory of the Imagination', p. 308.
28. For example: Dorothy Waples argues for the persuasive influence of David Hartley's associationist psychology, admiringly summarized by Coleridge in the early poem 'Religious Musings' (1795), which speaks of unity, necessity, Hartley and the associationist stages of character building (*Journal of English and Germanic Philology*, 35 (1936) 337–51). J. A. Stuart argues for the theological influence of Augustine's doctrines of original sin and grace (*Harvard Theological Review*, 60 (1967) 177–211). David Jones grounds his discussion on the Passion, the Eucharist and the doctrine of redemption. Robert Penn Warren suggests that the two major functions of the poem are the creation of a sacramental universe by means of creative imagination and the operation within this universe of the Christian pattern of Fall and Redemption (*A Poem of Pure Imagination: An Experiment in Reading* (New York, 1946)).
29. *Sh*, p. 222.
30. See W. B. Gallie, *Philosophy and the Historical Understanding* (London, 1964) Ch. 2: 'What is a Story?'.
31. See above, n. 25.
32. See E. S. Shaffer, *'Kubla Khan' and the Fall of Jerusalem* (Cambridge, 1975) p. 291, and Stephen Prickett, *Romanticism and Religion* (Cambridge, 1976) Ch. 1: '"The Living Educts of the Imagination": Coleridge on Religious Language'.
33. *CL*, I, p. 396.
34. *The Letters of Charles and Mary Anne Lamb*, ed. Edwin W. Marrs, Jr, 3 vols to date (Ithaca, New York, 1975–8) vol. 1, p. 97.
35. *CN*, III 4005. See below, Ch. 5.
36. *Sh*, p. 241.
37. Maud Bodkin, *Archetypal Patterns in Poetry* (1934, Oxford, 1963) p. 307.
38. *BL*, vol. 1, p. 4.
39. Ibid., vol. 2, p. 6.
40. David Jones, op. cit., p. 224.
41. *Critical Review*, XXIV (1798) 197–204; quoted in J. R. de J. Jackson (ed.), *Coleridge: The Critical Heritage* (London, 1970) p. 53.
42. Attrib. Charles Burney, *Monthly Review*, XXIX (1799) 202–10; quoted in Jackson, op. cit., p. 56.

43. *British Critic*, XIV (1799) 364–5; quoted in Jackson, op. cit., pp. 57–8.
44. See letter to Southey, 8 Nov 1798, *The Letters of Charles and Mary Lamb*, vol. 1, pp. 142–3; and one of the series 'Essays on the Lake School', *Blackwood's Edinburgh Magazine*, VI (1819) 3–12; quoted in Jackson, op. cit., pp. 436–51.
45. 'Confessio Fidei', *CN*, III 4005.
46. Frank Kermode, *The Sense of an Ending: Studies in the Theory of Fiction* (1966; Oxford, 1979) pp. 58ff., 63.
47. Prickett, op. cit., p. 6.
48. John Coulson, *Newman and the Common Tradition* (Oxford, 1970) p. 4.
49. Line 17, of the version revised for *Sibylline Leaves* (London, 1817).
50. See D. W. Harding, 'The Theme of "The Ancient Mariner"', *Scrutiny*, IX (1941) 334–42.
51. *CN*, III 4005.
52. See letter to William Lisle Bowles, 16 Mar 1797, *CL*, I, p. 318.
53. *The Monk: A Romance* (London, 1796) vol. 2, pp. 60–1:66. Coleridge's review appeared in the *Critical Review*, XIX (1797) 194–200.
54. *BL*, vol. 2, p. 184.
55. Quoted in H. D. Traill, *Coleridge*, English Men of Letters, Series 1884 (London, 1909) p. 186.
56. For example: Graham Hough, *The English Mind* (Cambridge, 1964) p. 181. For comment on the 'great Coleridgean position' see Prickett, op. cit., pp. 11–12.
57. *PW*, p. 391, ll. 49–52.
58. Ibid., p. 365, ll. 47–8.
59. See Allan Grant, *A Preface to Coleridge* (London, 1972) p. 119.
60. *Lay Sermons (CC)*, p. 30.
61. *BL*, vol. 1, p. 202.
62. Nicholas Lash, *Theology on Dover Beach* (London, 1979) p. 160.
63. To Joseph Cottle, *CL*, III, p. 480.
64. *Confessions*, pp. 91–2.
65. Revd Alexander Dyce, from an account by Wordsworth, published in a note on 'The Ancient Mariner' in the 1852 edition of Coleridge's *Poems*; quoted in J. L. Lowes, *The Road to Xanadu*, rev. edn (London, 1978) pp. 203–4.
66. *CN*, I 174.
67. To Thomas Poole, 13 Dec 1796, *CL*, I, p. 273.
68. Gloss to ll. 131–4.
69. Allan Grant, op. cit., p. 124. More generally on Cudworth and Burnet see W. Schrickx, 'Coleridge and the Cambridge Platonists', *Review of English Studies*, 7 (1966) 71–91, and J. H. Muirhead, 'The Cambridge Platonists' I and II, *Mind*, n.s. 36 (1927) 158–78, 326–41.
70. See below, Ch. 5, p. 81.
71. *The Castle of Indolence*, Bk. I, stanza XXXIX, ll. 343–4, 350–1. See also George Dekker, *Coleridge and the Literature of Sensibility* (London, 1978) p. 103; A. H. Thompson, 'Thomson and Natural Description in Poetry', in Sir A. W. Ward and A. R. Waller (eds), *The Age of Johnson*, The Cambridge History of English Literature Series, vol. X (Cambridge, 1932) pp. 101–2.

72. Thomas McFarland, *Romanticism and the Forms of Ruin: Wordsworth, Coleridge and Modalities of Fragmentation*, Second Landing Place: 'The Place Beyond the Heavens: True Being, Transcendence, and the Symbolic Indication of Wholeness', pp. 382–418.

73. Plato, *Theatetus*, 173E.

74. Karl Jaspers, *Plato and Augustine* (New York, 1962) p. 30; McFarland, op. cit., pp. 395–6.

75. Don Cupitt, *The World to Come* (London, 1982) p. 110.

76. *Sh*, p. 234.

77. Ibid., p. 209.

78. Transcription of the marginalia in R. Florence Brinkley, 'Coleridge on John Petvin and John Locke', *Huntingdon Library Quarterly*, 8 (1945) 277–92, esp. 289.

79. George Dekker, *Coleridge and the Literature of Sensibility* (London, 1978) pp. 22–54.

80. See also *Poems*, pp. 257–8.

81. *PW*, p. 364, l. 27. The text quoted from is based on that published in *Sibylline Leaves* (1817).

82. Wordsworth, *Poetical Works*, pp. 737–8 (my italics).

83. Dekker, op. cit., p. 149.

84. See also, Stephen Prickett, 'The Religious Context', in Stephen Prickett (ed.), *The Romantics* (London, 1981) pp. 115–63.

85. Charles Wesley, *Short Hymns on Select Passages of the Holy Scriptures* (London, 1796), vol. II, p. 82.

86. Mark Akenside, *The Pleasures of Imagination*, I, ll. 64–73, in Robert Anderson (ed.), *The Works of the British Poets*, 14 vols (London, 1793–1807) vol. IX, p. 736.

87. *BL*, vol. 2, p. 258.

88. 'I still recollect his "object" and "subject", terms of continual recurrence in the Kantean province; and how he sang and snuffled them into "om-m-mject", and "sum-m-mject", with a kind of solemn shake or quaver, as he rolled along' (Thomas Carlyle, *Selected Writings*, ed. Alan Shelston (Harmondsworth, 1971) p. 317). See, for example, *BL*, vol. 1, pp. 175–80; 'On the Philosophic Import of the Words Object and Subject', *Blackwood's Edinburgh Magazine*, LVI (1821) 246–52. For comment, see Dorothy M. Emmet, 'Coleridge on the Growth of the Mind', in Kathleen Coburn (ed.) *Coleridge: A Collection of Critical Essays* (Englewood Cliffs, NJ, 1967) pp. 171–3.

89. Johnson's *Pocket Dictionary of the English Language* (Halifax, 1861) p. 126.

90. Wordsworth, *Tintern Abbey*, ll. 112–14, *Poetical Works*, p. 165.

91. *Phil. Lect.*, p. 179.

92. *PW*, p. 56.

93. *CN*, I 330.

94. Edward Kessler, *Coleridge's Metaphors of Being* (Princeton, NJ, 1979) p. 19.

95. *CN*, I 495.

96. *Church and State*, p. 16.

97. *Sh*, p. 206.

98. *Friend(CC)*, I, p. 343.
99. *BL*, vol. 1, pp. 85–6.
100. See below, pp. 99–100.
101. *BL*, vol. 1, p. 202. See also *Friend(CC)*, I, p. 457: 'The term, Method, cannot therefore, otherwise than by abuse, be applied to a mere dead arrangement, containing in itself no principle of progression.'
102. Kessler, op. cit., p. 31.
103. John Beer, *Coleridge's Poetic Intelligence* (London, 1977) pp. 84–94; and also his 'A Stream by Glimpes: Coleridge's Later Imagination', in Beer (ed.), *Coleridge's Variety: Bicentenary Studies* (London, 1974) pp. 227–9.
104. *Phil. Lect.*, p. 424.
105 *Church and State*, p. 26.
106. M. H. Abrams, *Natural Supernaturalism: Tradition and Revolution in Romantic Literature* (New York, 1971) p. 65. On the 'sacramental aspect of Romantic symbol', see J. Robert Barth, S.J., *The Symbolic Imagination: Coleridge and the Romantic Tradition* (Princeton, N.J., 1977) pp. 114–16.
107. 4 April 1804, *CL*, II, pp. 1115–16.
108. *CN*, II 2070.
109. *PW*, pp. 455–6. See below, Ch. 6.
110. *CN*, I 1827.

NOTES TO CHAPTER 5: THE CRITICAL PROSE

1. See Thomas McFarland, 'The Origin and Significance of Coleridge's Theory of Secondary Imagination', in Geoffrey H. Hartman (ed.), *New Perspectives on Coleridge and Wordsworth* (New York, 1972) pp. 195–246, esp. p. 204.
2. Ibid., p. 226, quoting *Kant's gesammelte Schriften*, ed. the Prussian Academy of Sciences (Berlin, 1902–) vol. III, p. 518.
3. Tetens, *Philosophische Versuche über die menschliche Natur und ihre Entwickelung* (Leipzig, 1777) vol. I, p. 117. The text used is from Coleridge's annotated copy in the British Library.
4. For example, 'I am much pleased ... with everything that overthrows & or illustrates the overthrow of that all-annihilating system of explaining everything wholly by association' *CN*, II 2093, May 1804).
5. Tetens, op. cit., vol. I, p. ix.
6. See also above, Ch. 3.
7. *BL*, vol. 1, p. 202.
8. D. M. MacKinnon, 'Coleridge and Kant', in John Beer (ed.), *Coleridge's Variety: Bicentenary Studies* (London, 1974) pp. 183–203, esp. p. 189.
9. M. H. Abrams, *The Mirror and the Lamp: Romantic Theory and Critical Tradition* (New York, 1953).
10. Kant, *The Critique of Pure Reason*, trans. Norman Kemp Smith (London, 1950) pp. 132–3.
11. Kwang-Sae Lee, 'Some Reflections on Apprehension, Reproduction and Production, and Recognition in *The Critique of Pure Reason*', *Akten des 5: Internationalen Kant-Kongresses Mainz 4–8 April 1981*, I.1. (Bonn, 1981) p. 240.

12. Kant, *The Critique of Judgement*, trans. James Creed Meredith (Oxford, 1928) p. 77.
13. Ibid., p. 86.
14. Austin Farrer, *Faith and Speculation: An Essay in Philosophical Theology* (London, 1967) p. 74.
15. *BL*, vol. 1, p. 99.
16. Hobbes, *Leviathan* (1651), ed. C. B. Macpherson (Harmondsworth, 1968) pp. 88–9.
17. Geoffrey H. Hartman, *Wordsworth's Poetry, 1787–1814* (New Haven, Conn., 1964) p. 39.
18. *TT*, p. 215.
19. See Roy Park, 'Coleridge and Kant: Poetic Imagination and Practical Reason', *British Journal of Aesthetics*, 8 (1968) pp. 336–7.
20. *Friend(CC)*, I, p. 112.
21. Benedetto Groce, *Aesthetic: As Science of Expression and General Linguistic*, trans. Douglas Ainslie (New York, 1955) p. 275.
22. *Lay Sermons(CC)*, p. 114.
23. Ibid., p. 62. See also *Phil. Lect.*, pp. 256–9.
24. James D. Boulger, 'Coleridge on Imagination Revisited', *The Wordsworth Circle*, IV (1973) 16.
25. Wordsworth, 'Essay, Supplementary to the Preface' (1815), *Poetical Works* (Oxford, 1969) p. 744.
26. See above, Ch. 3, and below, Ch. 7.
27. Kant, *The Inaugural Dissertation* (1770), in *Selected Pre-Critical Writings and Correspondence with Beck*, trans. G. B. Kerferd and D. E. Walford (Manchester, 1968) pp. 66, 70.
28. *BL*, vol. 1, p. 202.
29. Kant, *The Inaugural Dissertation*, p. 78.
30. Ibid., p. 91.
31. *BL*, vol. 1, pp. 79–80, esp. p. 87.
32. Kant, *The Inaugural Dissertation*, p. 89.
33. Ibid., p. 60.
34. BL.MS.ADD. 47540, Notebook 45, 27 May 1830, p. 21. See also *BL*, vol. 1, p. 187.
35. BL.MS.ADD. 47531, Notebook 36, 27 Nov 1827, p. 3.
36. *Theory of Life*, pp. 57–8.
37. *Logic*, p. 151. The quotation is untraced, but used also in 'On the Principles of Genial Criticism', *BL*, vol. 2, p. 230. J. R. de J. Jackson suggests *Of the Laws of Ecclesiastical Politie*, Bk II, §7: *Works* (1682) p. 119.
38. Kant, *Vermischte Schriften* (Halle und Königsberg, 1799–1807) vol. III, p. 80. Jackson also notes a similar definition in Fichte, *Das System der Sittenlehre* (1798).
39. *Logic*, p. 220.
40. Ibid., p. 220.
41. Ibid., p. 221.
42. *Lay Sermons(CC)*, p. 114. See also above, n. 22.
43. See J. Shawcross's note in *BL*, vol. 1, p. 272, quoting Schelling: 'Intelligence is productive in twofold wise, either blindly and unconsciously,

or with freedom and consciousness; unconsciously productive in the perception of the universe, consciously in the creation of an ideal world.'

44. Letter to John Murray, 27 Feb 1817, *CL*, IV, p. 706.
45. James Beattie, 'An Essay on Poetry and Music as They Affect the Mind' (1762), in *Essays* (Edinburgh, 1776) p. 52.
46. See above, Ch. 3.
47. See Anne K. Mellor, *English Romantic Irony* (Cambridge, Mass., 1980) p. 26.
48. *Friend(CC)*, I, p. 457.
49. See above, Ch. 2.
50. J. S. Mill, 'Coleridge', in *Mill's Essays on Literature and Society*, ed. J. B. Schneewind (New York, 1965) p. 318.
51. *The Literary Remains of Samuel Taylor Coleridge* (London, 1836) vol. 1, pp. 150–66.
52. *CN*, III 4498.
53. Schiller, *Kleinere prosaische Schriften* (Leipzig, 1800) vol. 2, p. 66.
54. See *Sh. Crit*, vol. 2, p. v; *Misc. Crit.*, pp. 3–228; *CN*, III passim.
55. See also *CN*, III 4192.
56. *Confessions*, p. 13. see also below, Ch. 7.
57. For further discussion of Herder, Eichhorn and Coleridge on this point, see E. S. Shaffer, *'Kubla Khan' and the Fall of Jerusalem* (Cambridge, 1975) p. 32.
58. *Confessions*, p. 91.
59. Wayne C. Booth, *A Rhetoric of Irony* (Chicago, 1974) p. 92
60. Northrop Frye, *The Great Code: The Bible and Literature* (London, 1982) p. xv.
61. *BL*, vol. 1, p. 102.
62. Ibid., p. 103.
63. *Sh. Crit.*, vol. 1, pp. 194–8.
64. *CN*, I 1255, and note; *BL*, vol. 2, p. 270.
65. G. N. G. Orsini, 'Coleridge and Schlegel Reconsidered', *Comparative Literature*, XVI (1964) 103.
66. Kant, *The Critique of Judgement*, pp. 168–9.
67. See Gabriel Marcel, *Coleridge et Schelling* (Paris, 1971) pp. 84–7.
68. *Sh. Crit.*, vol. 1, p. 197.
69. *Friend(CC)*, I, pp. 449–57.
70. A. W. Schlegel, *Lectures on Dramatic Art*, pp. 340, 342.
71. Ibid., p. 343.
72. A. W. Schlegel, *Kritische Schriften*, vol. 6, pp. 157–8.
73. *Sh. Crit.*, vol. 1, pp. 60–1. See above, Ch. 4, p. 63.
74. A. W. Schlegel, *Lectures on Dramatic Art*, p. 470.
75. *CN*, III 4388, and note.
76. F. Schlegel, *Literary Notebooks, 1797–1801*, ed. Hans Eichner (Toronto, 1957) p. 62.
77. *Church and State*, p. 100.
78. F. Schlegel, *Gespräch über die Poesie* (1800), in *Kritische Ausgabe*, vol. II, p. 313.
79. F. Schlegel, *Lyceums-Fragmente*, nos 42, 47 and 54, *Prosaische Jugends-chriften*, ed. J. Minor (Vienna, 1882) vol. II pp. 189–91. See also K. M.

Wheeler, *Sources, Processes and Methods in Coleridge's 'Biographia Literaria'* (Cambridge, 1980) p. 66.

80. This sense of 'genius' is precisely the opposite of that proposed by Kierkegaard in his *Edifying Discourse* (1849), 'On the Difference between a Genius and an Apostle', in which 'genius' becomes Schlegel's 'Bedingt', and 'apostle' his 'Unbedingt'.

81. F. Schlegel, *Literary Notebooks*, p. 93.

82. *Theory of Life*, p. 50.

83. Ibid., p. 42. The *Shorter Oxford Dictionary* does not attribute this meaning to 'individuation' until 1867, or a little later with the work of St George Jackson Mivart.

84. *Theory of Life*, 'Preface' pp. 11, 14.

85. *TT*, p. 238.

86. *AR (II)*, p. 118. See also, H. N. Coleridge (ed.), *Specimens of the Table Talk of S. T. Coleridge* (London, 1851) p. 172, 24 Apr 1832; *Confessions*, p. x.

87. *AR (II)* p. 225. See also letter to C. A. Tulk, Sep 1817, *CL*, IV, pp. 767–76.

88. 'An Essay on Faith', printed in *AR (II)*, p. 344.

89. Ibid., p. 118.

90. See, Booth, op. cit., p. 224, and Northrop Frye, *The Secular Scripture: A Study of the Structure of Romance* (Cambridge, Mass., 1976) p. 88.

91. Victoria University Library, Toronto. See, Laurence S. Lockridge, *Coleridge the Moralist* (Ithaca, NY, 1977) pp. 193–8: 'Irony and the Coleridgean Personality'.

92. K. Solger, *Nachgelassene Schriften und Briefwechsel*, ed. L. Tieck and F. von Raumer (Leipzig, 1826) vol. 1, p. 117. And see Wheeler, op. cit., p. 73.

93. Letter to Mrs Clarkson, 12 Apr 1810, *Letters of William and Dorothy Wordsworth: The Middle Years*, ed. Ernest de·Selincourt, rev. Mary Moorman (Oxford, 1969) vol. 1, p. 399.

94. *CN*, III 4005.

95. *17 Cent.*, p. 329.

96. *CL*, III, p. 35.

97. *CN*, III 3888. Augustine, *In Johannis Evangelium Tractatus*, XXIX, 6: 'Ergo noli quaerere intelligere, ut credas, sed crede ut intelligas', in J. P. Migne (ed.), *Patrologiae cursus completus ... Series Latina* (Paris, 1844–64) vol. XXXV, p. 1630.

98. See Basil Willey, *Samuel Taylor Coleridge* (London, 1972) p. 212.

99. *AR (I)*, p. xi.

100. Stephen Prickett, *Coleridge and Wordsworth: The Poetry of Growth* (Cambridge, 1970) p. 181.

101. *AR (II)*, p. 3.

102. See further Jonathan Culler, *Structuralist Poetics* (London, 1975) p. 130.

103. Northrop Frye, *The Anatomy of Criticism: Four Essays* (New York, 1969) pp. 127–8.

104. See below, Ch. 7.

105. Stephen Happel, 'Words Made Beautiful by Grace: on Coleridge the Theologian', *Religious Studies Review*, 6 (1980) 201. See also Thomas McFarland, *Coleridge and the Pantheist Tradition* (Oxford, 1969) pp. 379–80.

106. Anon, 'David Hume charged by Mr. Coleridge with Plagiarism from St. Thomas Aquinas', *Blackwood's Edinburgh Magazine*, III (1818) 653.
107. John Wilson (attrib.), 'Some Observations on the *Biographia Literaria* of S. T. Coleridge, Esq.—1817', ibid., II (1817) 18.
108. Letter to John Thelwall, 19 Nov 1796, *CL*, I, p. 260.
109. Letter to Thomas Poole, 6 May 1799, ibid., p. 493.
110. *Lay Sermons(CC)*, pp. 6–7.
111. Ibid., p. 23.
112. Ibid., p. 18.
113. John J. Duffy, 'Problems in Publishing Coleridge: James Marsh's First American Edition of *Aids to Reflection*', *New England Quarterly*, 43 (1970) 195.
114. James Marsh, 'Preliminary Essay' (1829), *AR (II)*, p. xxv.
115. S. H. Hodgson, *The Philosophy of Reflection* (London, 1878) vol. 1, p. 177; vol. 2, p. 235.
116. Charlotte Broicher, 'Anglicanische Kirche und deutsche Philosophie', *Preussische Jahrbücher*, 142 (1910) 205–33, 457–98.
117. For further discussion of the influence of Coleridge's reflective self-consciousness on nineteenth-century theology, see Philip C. Rule, *SJ*, 'Coleridge's Reputation as a Religious Thinker: 1816–1972', *Harvard Theological Review*, 67 (1974) 289–306.
118. *CN*, III 4005.
119. See Terence Hawkes, *Metaphor. The Critical Idiom*, 25 (London, 1972) p. 47.
120. *Sh.*, p. 66.
121. *BL*, vol. 1, pp. 85–6.
122. See further Wheeler, op. cit., pp. 83–4.
123. *BL*, vol. 1, p. 200.
124. Ibid., p. 183.
125. Stanley Fish, 'Literature in the Reader: Affective Stylistics', *New Literary History*, 2 (1970) 123–62.
126. See further Dorothy Emmet, 'Coleridge and Philosophy', in R. L. Brett (ed.), *Writers and their Background: S. T. Coleridge* (London, 1971) p. 205.
127. Letter to Thomas Clarkson, 13 Oct 1806, *CL*, II, p. 1196.
128. Owen Barfield, *What Coleridge Thought* (Middletown, Conn., 1971) p. 248.
129. See ibid., p. 145.
130. *17 Cent.*, p. 202.
131. See M. G. Cooke, '*Quisque Sui Faber:* Coleridge in the *Biographia Literaria*', *Philological Quarterly*, L (1971) 212.
132. Letter to John M. Gutch, 17 Sep 1815, *CL*, IV, p. 585.
133. Jerome Christensen, *Coleridge's Blessed Machine of Language* (Ithaca, NY, 1981) pp. 109, 117.
134. See, Shaffer, op. cit., p. 32, and Mellor, op. cit., p. 30.

NOTES TO CHAPTER 6: THREE LATER POEMS

1. Letter to John Thelwall, 17 Dec 1796, *CL*, I, p. 164.
2. *Friend(CC)*, I, p. 520.

3. *CN*, III 4073–4.
4. Ibid., 4213.
5. *Phil. Lect.*, p. 290.
6. *CN*, III 4073.
7. See further George M. Ridenour, 'Source and Allusion in Some Poems of Coleridge', *Studies in Philology*, 60 (1963) 87.
8. *BL*, vol. 2, pp. 207–8.
9. Ibid., vol. 1, p. 87, and see below, Ch. 7, p. 126.
10. Ibid., vol. 2, p. 208.
11. Jacob Boehme, *The High and Deep Searching Out of the Threefold Life of Man* (1620), trans. J. Sparrow, 1650 (London, 1909) pp. 100–1.
12. *Phil. Lect.*, p. 453.
13. See Ridenour, op. cit., p. 89, quoting from the second volume of the so-called 'Law edition' – *The Works of Jacob Behmen, the Teutonic Theosopher*, trans. J. Sparrow (London, 1761–81). It was the edition which Coleridge used.
14. *CN*, III 4074.
15. *CL*, IV, pp. 874–5.
16. *Church and State* (1830), p. 26.
17. See ibid., p. 16n.
18. *CL*, IV, p. 883.
19. J. H. Muirhead, *Coleridge as Philosopher* (London, 1930) p. 86.
20. *CL*, VI, p. 635.
21. See above, Ch. 2. Also, D. F. Rauber, 'The Fragment as Romantic Form', *Modern Language Quarterly*, 30 (1969) 212–21; Thomas McFarland, *Romanticism and the Forms of Ruin: Wordsworth, Coleridge and Modalities of Fragmentation* (Princeton, NJ, 1981).
22. *Misc. Crit.*, pp. 163–4. See also Edward Kessler *Coleridge's Metaphors of Being* (Princeton, NJ, 1979) pp. 90–120.
23. To Mrs S. T. Coleridge, 21 Mar 1799, *CL*, I, p. 470; to J. P. Kennard, 13 Aug 1832, ibid., VI, p. 922.
24. *Phil. Lect.*, p. 299.
25. *Friend(CC)*, I, p. 449.
26. *CN*, III 3370 (my italics).
27. *Friend(CC)*, I, p. 457.
28. *CN*, III 4005.
29. *Phil. Lect.*, p. 437.
30. *Lay Sermons(CC)*, pp. 113–14.
31. Letter to Unknown Correspondent, Nov 1819, *CL*, IV pp. 974–5.
32. See *CN*, I 430.
33. James D. Boulger, *Coleridge as Religious Thinker* (New Haven, Conn., 1961) p. 206. See also Stephen Prickett, *Coleridge and Wordsworth: The Poetry of Growth* (Cambridge, 1970) p. 23, taking Boulger to task.
34. *AR (II)*, p. 151.
35. A point made by Prickett, op. cit., p. 26.
36. *AR (II)*, p. 3.
37. *Lay Sermons(CC)*, p. 29.
38. M. Jadwiga Swiatecka, *The Idea of the Symbol: Some nineteenth century comparisons with Coleridge* (Cambridge, 1980) p. 59.
39. *Lay Sermons(CC)*, p. 29.

40. *CN*, II 2541; Swiatecka, op. cit., p. 65.
41. *Confessions*, p. 13.

NOTES TO CHAPTER 7: THE LATER PROSE AND NOTEBOOKS

1. *Confessions*, p. 13.
2. *AR (II)*, p. 272.
3. See Huw Parry Owen, 'The Theology of Coleridge', *Critical Quarterly*, 4 (1962) 59–67.
4. See above, Ch. 5, p. 102.
5. M. H. Abrams, *Natural Supernaturalism* (New York, 1971) pp. 65–71.
6. *CL*, III, pp. 533–4. E. K. Chambers suggests that *Biographia Literaria* presumably grew out of the 'fragments of *Auto*-biography' (*Samuel Taylor Coleridge: A Biographical Study* (Oxford, 1938) p. 270).
7. See David Pym, *The Religious Thought of Samuel Taylor Coleridge* (Gerrards Cross, 1978) p. 70; Geoffrey Rowell, *Hell and the Victorians* (Oxford, 1974) pp. 69–70.
8. *CN*, II 2448.
9. F. J. A. Hort, 'Coleridge', *Cambridge Essays* (London, 1856) p. 328.
10. *Confessions*, p. 91. See above, p. 84.
11. The texts used for these works by Kant and Fichte will be the translations by T. M. Greene and H. H. Hudson, *Religion within the Limits of Reason Alone* (New York, 1960), and by Garrett Green (of the second edition of 1793), *Attempt at a Critique of All Revelation* (Cambridge, 1978), respectively; cited henceforth as *Religion* and *Attempt*.
12. See Helen Gardner, *Religion and Literature* (London, 1971) p. 134.
13. *CN*, III 3510.
14. *Religion*, p. 25.
15. *CN*, III 4005. See also Aurel Kolnai, 'The Thematic Primacy of Moral Evil', *Philosophical Quarterly*, VI (1956) 27–42.
16. Schelling, *System des transcendentalen Idealismus*, trans. and quoted by A. O. Lovejoy, *The Reason, the Understanding and Time* (Baltimore, Md, 1961) p. 35.
17. *BL*, vol. 1, p. 173.
18. See *Friend(CC)*, I, pp. 154–61: The essay on 'Reason and Understanding', 'the leading thought of which', wrote Coleridge, 'I remember to have read in the works of a continental Philosopher' (p. 154). He refers to Jacobi, *David Hume ... oder Idealismus und Realismus: Werke*, vol. 2 (Leipzig, 1815) pp. 8–17; *Von den Göttlichen Dingen* Beilage A: *Werke*, vol. 3 (1816) pp. 429–35. See also F. J. A. Hort, op. cit., pp. 321–4.
19. Henri Nidecker, 'Notes Marginales de S. T. Coleridge', *Revue de Littérature Comparée*, 7 (1927) 142. The copy of the 1794 edition, annotated by Coleridge, is in the British Library.
20. T. A. Rixner, *Handbuch der Geschichten der Philosophie* (1823), trans. and quoted by Lovejoy, op. cit., p. 55.
21. *Friend(CC)*, I, p. 104; also, II, p. 71.
22. For a modern parallel, see K. E. Kirk, *The Vision of God: The Christian*

Doctrine of the Summum Bonum (New York, 1966) pp. 103–4, discussing II Corinthians 3:18, 'κατοπτρι ζόμενοι'. See also Ch. 4 for a discussion of Coleridge and mysticism.

23. *CN*, III 3592.
24. C. 25 Jan 1808, *CL*, III, p. 48.
25. *BL*, vol. 2, p. 6. See also 'On Poesy or Art', *BL*, vol. 2, p. 258, *Sh. Crit.*, vol. 1, p. 202.
26. Letter to Daniel Stuart, 13 May 1816, *CL*, IV, p. 642.
27. See Newman, *Apologia Pro Vita Sua* (1864; London, 1959) p. 169.
28. See John Coulson, *Religion and Imagination*: '*in aid of a grammar of assent*' (Oxford, 1981) p. 60.
29. Newman, *Historical Sketches* (London, 1872) vol. 3, pp. 41–2.
30. *Friend(CC)*, I, p. 105; *CN*, I 1233: 'Socinianism moonlight – Methodism a Stove! O for some Sun to unite heat & warm Light!'
31. 'On Poesy or Art', *BL*, vol. 2, p. 258.
32. *Friend(CC)*, I, p. 521.
33. *Confessions*, p. 92.
34. *Phil. Lect.*, p. 323.
35. *Friend(CC)*, I, p. 94.
36. Ibid., p. 457.
37. To C. A. Tulk, Sep 1817, *CL*, IV, p. 767.
38. *Phil. Lect.*, p. 357.
39. Notebook 26 (*c.* 1817–18) ff. 14–17. See further James D. Boulger, *Coleridge as Religious Thinker* (New Haven, Conn., 1961) pp. 154–7.
40. See G. N. G. Orsini, *Coleridge and German Idealism* (Carbondale, 1969) pp. 57–8.
41. Kant, *The Critique of Judgement*, trans. James Creed Meredith, (Oxford, 1980) Part II: 'Critique of Theological Judgement', §61, pp. 3–5.
42. *Friend(CC)*, I, p. 499.
43. See Orsini, op. cit., p. 63.
44. James Beattie, *Essays on the Nature and Immutability of Truth* – in *Opposition to Sophism and Scepticism* (Edinburgh, 1776) p. 89. On Beattie, see also above, Ch. 5, p. 81.
45. *BL*, vol. 1, p. 101.
46. *Attempt*, p. 127.
47. Ibid., p. 139.
48. *Friend(CC)*, I, p. 430.
49. *Attempt*, p. 144.
50. *Friend(CC)*, I, p. 433.
51. *BL*, vol. 1 p. 193; *Omniana*, no. 174: 'The Soul and its organs of Sense', pp. 181–5.
52. *Church and State*, pp. 3–6.
53. *Logic*, pp. 66ff.
54. Kant, *Die Religion innerhalb der Grenzen der blossen Vernunft*.
55. *CL*, IV, pp. 791–2. On Kant, see further H. J. Paton, *In Defence of Reason* (London, 1951) pp. 157–77; P. F. Strawson, *Freedom and Resentment* (London, 1974) pp. 178–88.
56. See David Newsome, *Two Classes of Men: Platonism and English Romantic Thought* (London, 1974) p. 101; Owen Barfield, *What Coleridge Thought*

(Middletown, Conn., 1971) Appendix: 'Polar Logic', pp. 179–93. Also, see above, Ch. 3.

57. *Logic*, pp. 241–2; *17 Cent.*, p. 89. See also J. H. Muirhead, *Coleridge as Philosopher* (London, 1930) pp. 84–5.

58. *BL*, vol. 1, pp. 87, 79–80.

59. *Religion*, p. 17.

60. Marginalia on *Grundlegung zur Metaphysik der Sitten* (1785); see Nidecker, op. cit., 337.

61. *Religion*, pp. 25, 36ff.

62. Emil L. Fackenheim, 'Kant and Radical Evil', *University of Toronto Quarterly*, 23 (1954) pp. 350–1.

63. *Religion*, pp. 142, 158.

64. *Attempt*, p. 116.

65. See letter to J. C. Lavater, 28 Apr 1775: 'God must have hidden some supplement to our deficiencies somewhere in the depth of His decrees' (Arnulf Zweig (ed. and trans.), *Kant's Philosophical Correspondence, 1759–99* (Chicago, 1967) p. 80). See also *Religion*, pp. 179–90; D. M. MacKinnon, 'Kant's Philosophy of Religion', *Philosophy*, 50(1975) 135–6.

66. *Religion*, p. 43.

67. See Kant, *Critique of Practical Reason*, trans. T. K. Abbott, 6th edn (London, 1909) p. 151.

68. See A. O. Lovejoy, 'Coleridge and Kant's Two Worlds', *Essays in the History of Ideas* (Baltimore, Md., 1948) p. 272.

69. Nidecker, op. cit., 337.

70. *CN*, III 4005.

71. Elinor Shaffer, 'Metaphysics of Culture: Kant and Coleridge's *Aids to Reflection*', *Journal of the History of Ideas*, 31 (1970) 199–218.

72. See Mary Midgley, 'The Objection to Systematic Humbug', *Philosophy*, 53 (1978) 147–69, esp. 151 Midgley criticizes the assumption often attributed to Kant, that our feelings do not concern morality. See also, Mary Midgley, *Beast and Man: The Roots of Human Nature* (London, 1980) pp. 258–61.

73. *AR (II)*, p. 122.

74. Ibid., p. 135.

75. Ibid., p. 134.

76. Ibid., p. 126.

77. Shaffer, op. cit., 212. See also Luther, *The Bondage of the Will* (1525), trans. J. I. Packer and O. R. Johnston (London, 1957) p. 270: 'And I do not accept or tolerate that middle way [mediocritatem] which Erasmus ... recommends to me, namely to allow a very little to free will, so that the contradictions of Scripture ... may be more easily removed.'

78. *BL*, MS.ADD 47550, Notebook 55, p. 25.

79. Abrams, op. cit., pp. 35–7.

80. Barfield, op. cit., p. 145.

81. 13 Oct 1806, *CL*, II, pp. 1195–6.

82. *BL*, vol. 1, p. 103.

83. Barfield, op. cit., Appendix: 'Polar Logic', pp. 179–93; Newsome, op. cit., Appendix C: 'Coleridge's "Trichotomous Logic"', pp. 100–10.

84. Ibid., p. 103.
85. See above, pp. 92–3.
86. Pym, op. cit., p. 27.
87. *Confessions*, p. x.
88. BL.MS.ADD. 47550, Notebook 55, p. 38.
89. Ibid., 47536, Notebook 41, June 1829, p. 87.
90. Ibid., p. 13.
91. Ibid., 47537, Notebook 42, 4 Sep 1829, p. 29.
92. Ibid., 47536, Notebook 41, p. 19.
93. Ibid., 47541, Notebook 46, 24 Aug 1830, p. 30.
94. Ibid., p. 20.
95. *Confessions*, p. 10.
96. BL.MS.ADD. 47541, Notebook 46, p. 30.
97. Ibid., 47534, Notebook 39, 1829, pp. 24, 71–2.
98. Ibid., 47535, Notebook 40, 21 June 1828, p. 53.
99. 'Reflections on having left a Place of Retirement' (1796) ll. 60–2, *PW*, p. 108.
100. *TT*, p. 261.
101. See: Alice D. Snyder, *Coleridge on Logic and Learning* (New Haven, Conn., 1929); Boulger, op. cit., pp. 121–4; T. McFarland, *Romanticism and the Forms of Ruin* (Princeton, NJ, 1981) pp. 342–81.
102. See above, p. 125.
103. See: letter to John Taylor Coleridge, 8 May 1825, *CL*, v, p. 444; McFarland, op. cit., p. 354; Sam G. Barnes, 'Was *Theory of Life* Coleridge's "Opus Maximum"?', *Studies in Philology*, 55 (1958) 494–514.
104. *BL*, vol. 1, p. 200. See above, Ch. 5.
105. *Theory of Life*, p. 94; Barnes, op. cit., p. 513.
106. There are at least three outlines almost contemporary with the letter to Stuart. See *CL*, IV, pp. 589–90.
107. *CN*, III 4003.
108. *CL*, VI, p. 1053.
109. 8 May 1825, *CL*, v, p. 444.
110. Letter to George Fricker, 4 Oct 1806, *CL*, II, p. 1189.
111. Letter to Unknown Correspondent, 9 June 1827, *CL*, VI, p. 691.
112. 28 Nov 1827, *CL*, VI, p. 715.
113. 16 Feb 1828, ibid., p. 724.
114. 7 Feb 1829, ibid., p. 784.
115. McFarland, op. cit., p. 343.
116. Letter to William Collins, 6 Dec 1818, *CL*, IV, p. 893.
117. See above, Ch. 6.
118. *CL*, VI, pp. 811–13.
119. Stephen Prickett, *Coleridge and Wordsworth: The Poetry of Growth* (Cambridge, 1970) p. 181.
120. *Church and State*, p. 4. See also Basil Willey, *Nineteenth-Century Studies: Coleridge to Matthew Arnold* (Harmondsworth, 1969) p. 53.
121. Thomas McFarland, *Coleridge and the Pantheist Tradition* (Oxford, 1969) p. 191.
122. Letter to Francis Wrangham, 5 June 1817, *CL*, IV, p. 736.
123. 29 Mar 1832, *CL*, VI, p. 895.

124. *BL*, vol. 2, p. 215.
125. D. G. James, *The Life of Reason: Hobbes, Locke, Bolingbroke* (London, 1949) p. 270.
126. Stephen Happel, 'Words Made Beautiful by Grace: on Coleridge the Theologian', *Religious Studies Review*, 6 (1980) 206.
127. Laurence S. Lockridge, *Coleridge the Moralist* (Ithaca, NY, 1977) pp. 25, 258–9. The concluding phrase Lockridge quotes from the *Opus Maximum* MS in the Victorian University Library, Toronto. OM, B₃, ff. 166–71.
128. Letter to Robert Southey, 31 Jan 1819, *CL*, IV, p. 917.
129. 1 July 1802, *CL*, II, p. 807.
130. BL.MS.ADD. 47538, pp. 4–5.
131. *AR (II)*, p. 170.
132. Letter to William Rowan Hamilton, 6 Apr 1832, *CL*, VI, p. 897.
133. *Friend(CC)*, I, p. 316.
134. *BL*, vol. 1, p. 80.
135. *Friend(CC)*, I, p. 316. Henry Nelson Coleridge dates the note as 1825. *Friend* (1837) vol. 2, pp. 171–2n.
136. Pym, op. cit., p. 71.
137. BL.MS.ADD. 47534, p. 24.
138. Ibid., 47536, p. 8.
139. See letter to Hugh J. Rose, 25 Sep 1816, *CL*, IV, p. 687.
140. See, McFarland, *Coleridge and the Pantheist Tradition*, p. 193.
141. *Lay Sermons(CC)*, p. 30; *Friend(CC)*, I, p. 457.
142. *AR (II)*, p. 349.

NOTES TO CHAPTER 8: CONCLUSION

1. Mary Warnock, 'Imagination – Aesthetic and Religious', *Theology*, LXXXIII (1980) 404.
2. For example, A. M. Allchin, 'The Theological Vision of the Oxford Movement', in Allchin and John Coulson (eds), *The Rediscovery of Newman: An Oxford Symposium* (London, 1967) pp. 56–7. O. W. Jones, *Isaac Williams and His Circle* (London, 1971) pp. 145–7, uses Allchin's work.
3. See, for example, on E. B. Pusey, Alf Härdelin, *The Tractarian Understanding of the Eucharist* (Uppsala, 1965) pp. 135–6.
4. Austin Farrer, 'Revelation', in Basil Mitchell (ed.), *Faith and Logic: Oxford Essays in Philosophical Theology* (London, 1957) pp. 84–107.
5. Austin Farrer, *The Glass of Vision* (London, 1948) p. ix.
6. H. D. Lewis, *Our Experience of God* (London, 1970) p. 156.
7. Farrer, op. cit., pp. 109–10.
8. For another discussion of the nature of divinely authorized images and stories, see W. A. Whitehouse, 'R. B. Braithwaite as an Apologist for Religious Belief', in Whitehouse, *The Authority of Grace: Essays in Response to Karl Barth*, ed. Ann Loades (Edinburgh, 1981) pp. 137–44.
9. Farrer, op. cit., p. 12.
10. Ibid., p. 94.
11. See Huw Parry Owen, 'The Theology of Coleridge', *Critical Quarterly*, 4 (1962) 60–1.

12. Lewis, op. cit., p. 163.
13. Ibid., p. 254.
14. Farrer, op. cit., pp. 127–8.
15. *AR (II)*, p. 3.
16. Helen Gardner, *The Limits of Literary Criticism* (Oxford, 1956) pp. 25–6.
17. Farrer, op. cit., pp. 136–45.
18. Gardner, op. cit., p. 29.
19. Ibid., p. 36.
20. David Pym, *The Religious Thought of Samuel Taylor Coleridge* (Gerrards Cross, 1978) p. 70.
21. In F. F. Bruce (ed.), *Promise and Fulfilment*; repr. in Austin Farrer, *Interpretation and Belief*, ed. Charles C. Conti (London, 1976) pp. 39–53.
22. Farrer, *Interpretation and Belief*, p. 53.
23. See, for example, M. Jadwiga Swiatecka, *The Idea of the Symbol* (Cambridge, 1980) p. 65.
24. *Confessions*, p. 13.
25. Frank Kermode, 'The Structures of Fiction', *Modern Language Notes*, 84 (1969) 891–915.
26. For a comment on Coleridge and structuralism, see above, Ch. 5, p. 96.
27. Kermode, op. cit., p. 904.
28. Helen Gardner, *In Defence of the Imagination*, the Charles Eliot Norton Lectures, 1979–80 (Oxford, 1982) p. 114.
29. Frank Kermode, *The Genesis of Secrecy: On the Interpretation of Narrative*, the Charles Eliot Norton Lectures, 1977–8 (Cambridge, Mass., 1979) pp. 63–4.
30. John Coulson, review of *In Defence of the Imagination*, in *Theology*, 86 (1983) 71.
31. Terence Hawkes, *Structuralism and Semiotics* (London, 1977) p. 18.
32. Farrer, op. cit., pp. 248–9.
33. Thomas Carlyle, *The Life of John Sterling* (1851) Part I, Ch. 8, in Alan Shelston (ed.), *Thomas Carlyle: Selected Writings* (Harmondsworth, 1971) p. 317.
34. *Church and State*, p. 26.
35. F. D. Maurice, *The Kingdom of Christ* (London, 1883) dedication to the 2nd edn, vol. 1, p. xi.
36. H. D. Traill, *Coleridge* (1884, London, 1909) pp. 205–6.
37. George Watson, *The Literary Critics: A Study of English Descriptive Criticism* (1962; rev. edn Harmondsworth, 1964) p. 130.
38. McFarland, *Coleridge and the Pantheist Tradition* (Oxford, 1969) pp. 142, 218, 231, 236, 244, 379–80, etc; and his *Romanticism and the Forms of Ruin* (Princeton, NJ, 1981) pp. 135–6, 281, 402–6, etc.
39. Paul Tillich, *Theology of Culture* (New York, 1964) 'The Nature of Religious Language', pp. 55–7.
40. See David Jasper, 'Supporting the Radicals: a Poetic Contribution', *The Heythrop Journal*, XXII (1981) 407–16; Don Cupitt, *The World to Come* (London, 1982) pp. 77–89.
41. Lord Coleridge (Geoffrey Duke, 3rd Baron), quoted in Kathleen Coburn, *In Pursuit of Coleridge* (London, 1977) p. 27.
42. 13 July 1834, *CL*, VI, p. 990.

Bibliography of Secondary Sources

Abrams, M. H., *The Mirror and the Lamp: Romantic Theory and the Critical Tradition* (New York, 1953)
——, 'The Correspondent Breeze: a Romantic Metaphor', in M. H. Abrams (ed.), *English Romantic Poets: Modern Essays in Criticism* (New York, 1960) pp. 37–54.
——, 'Structure and Style in the Greater Romantic Lyric', in F. W. Hilles and H. Bloom (eds), *From Sensibility to Romanticism* (New York, 1965) pp. 527–60.
——, *Natural Supernaturalism: Tradition and Revolution in Romantic Literature* (New York, 1971).
——, 'Coleridge's "A Light in Sound": Science, Metascience, and Poetic Imagination', *Proceedings of the American Philosophical Society*, CXVI (1972) 458–76.
——, 'Coleridge and the Romantic Vision of the World', in John Beer (ed.), *Coleridge's Variety: Bicentenary Studies* (London, 1974) pp. 101–33.
Agosta, Louis, 'Kant's Treasure Hard-to-attain', *Kant-Studien*, 69 (1978) 422–42.
Aldrich, Virgil, C., 'Tinkling Symbols', in John Hick (ed.), *Faith and the Philosophers* (London, 1964) pp. 40–53.
Allchin, A. M., 'The Theological Vision of the Oxford Movement', in A. M. Allchin and John Coulson (eds), *The Rediscovery of Newman: An Oxford Symposium* (London, 1967) pp. 50–75.
Allen, Peter, *The Cambridge Apostles: The Early Years* (Cambridge, 1978).
Allen, Richard Charles, 'The Habits of the Soul: Samuel Taylor Coleridge's Religious Thought and its Background, 1794–8' (University of Notre Dame, Indiana, unpublished PhD dissertation, 1980).
Allsop, Thomas, *Letters, Conversations and Recollections of S. T. Coleridge*, 3rd edn, 2 vols (London, 1864).
Anderson, Robert (ed.), *The Works of the British Poets*, 14 vols (London, 1793–1807).
Anon., 'David Hume charged by Mr. Coleridge with Plagiarism from St. Thomas Aquinas', *Blackwood's Edinburgh Magazine*, III (1818) 653–7.
——, 'The Religious Opinions of S. T. Coleridge', *Church Quarterly Review*, 54 (1889) 316–31.
——, 'Samuel Taylor Coleridge', *Atlantic Monthly*, LXXVI (Boston, Mass., 1895) pp. 396–413.
Appleyard, J. A., *Coleridge's Philosophy of Literature: The Development of a Concept of Poetry, 1791–1819* (Cambridge, Mass., 1965).
Astley, Jeff, 'Revelation Revisited', *Theology*, LXXXIII (1980) 339–46.

Baillie, John, *Our Knowledge of God* (Oxford, 1939).
——, *The Idea of Revelation in Recent Thought* (London, 1956).
Ballanche, Pierre-Simon, *Oeuvres complètes*, vol. 6 (Geneva, 1967).
Barfield, Owen, *What Coleridge Thought* (Middletown, Conn., 1971).
——, 'Coleridge's Enjoyment of Words', in John Beer (ed.), *Coleridge's Variety: Bicentenary Studies* (London, 1974) pp. 204–18.
Barnes, Sam G., 'Was *Theory of Life* Coleridge's "Opus Maximum"?', *Studies in Philology*, 55 (1958) 494–574.
Barth, Robert J., *Coleridge and Christian Doctrine* (Cambridge, Mass., 1969).
——, 'Symbol as Sacrament in Coleridge's Thought', *Studies in Romanticism*, XI (1972) 320–31.
——, *The Symbolic Imagination: Coleridge and the Romantic Tradition* (Princeton, NJ, 1977).
Beattie, James, *Essays* (Edinburgh, 1776).
——, *Essays on the Nature and Immutability of Truth – in Opposition to Sophistry and Scepticism* (Edinburgh, 1776).
Beer, John, *Coleridge the Visionary* (London, 1959).
——, 'Coleridge and Boehme's *Aurora*', *Notes and Queries*, CCVIII (1963) 183–7.
——, 'A Stream by Glimpses: Coleridge's Later Imagination', in John Beer (ed.), *Coleridge's Variety: Bicentenary Studies* (London, 1974) pp. 219–42.
——, *Coleridge's Poetic Intelligence* (London, 1977).
Benziger, James, 'Organic Unity: Leibniz to Coleridge', *Publications of the Modern Language Association of America*, LXVI (1957) pp. 24–48.
Bevan, Edwin, *Symbolism and Belief* (London, 1938).
Blake, William, *Complete Writings*, ed. Geoffrey Keynes (Oxford, 1966).
Bodkin, Maud, *Archetypal Patterns in Poetry: Psychological Studies of Imagination* (1934; Oxford, 1963).
Boehme, Jacob, *Vom dreifachen Leben des Menschen* (1619–20), trans. J. Sparrow, as *The High and Deep Searching Out of the Threefold Life of Man* (1650) (London, 1909).
Booth, Wayne C., *A Rhetoric of Irony* (Chicago, 1974).
Boulger, James D., *Coleridge as Religious Thinker* (New Haven, Conn., 1961).
——, 'Imagination and Speculation in Coleridge's Conversation Poems', *Journal of English and Germanic Philology*, 64 (1965) 691–711.
——, 'Christian Skepticism in "The Rime of the Ancient Mariner"', in F. W. Hilles and H. Bloom (eds), *From Sensibility to Romanticism* (New York, 1965) pp. 439–52.
——, 'Coleridge on Imagination Revisited', *The Wordsworth Circle*, IV (1973) 13–24.
——, *The Calvinist Temper in English Poetry* (The Hague, 1980).
Brinkley, R. Florence, 'Coleridge on John Petvin and John Locke', *Huntingdon Library Quarterly*, 8 (1945) 277–92.
Broicher, Charlotte, 'Anglicanische Kirche und deutsche Philosophie', *Preussische Jahrbücher*, 142 (1910) 205–33, 457–98.
Brooke, Stopford A., *Theology in the English Poets*, 2nd edn (London, 1874).
Brooks, Cleanth, 'Religion and Literature', *Sewanee Review*, 82 (1974) 93–107.
Byatt, A. S., *Wordsworth and Coleridge in their Time* (London, 1970).

Calleo, David P., *Coleridge and the Idea of the Modern State* (New Haven, Conn., 1966).

Campbell, J. D., 'Coleridge's Quotations', *The Athenaeum*, 3382 (1892) 259–60.

——, *Samuel Taylor Coleridge: A Narrative of the Events of His Life* (London, 1894).

Carlyle, Thomas, *Selected Writings*, ed. Alan Shelston (Harmondsworth, 1971).

Cayré, F., *La Contemplation Augustinienne: Principes de Spiritualité et de Theologie* (Bruges, 1954).

Chambers, E. K., *Samuel Taylor Coleridge: A Biographical Study* (Oxford, 1938).

Chayes, Irene H., '"Kubla Khan" and the Creative Process', *Studies in Romanticism*, VI (1966) 1–21.

Christensen, Jerome, *Coleridge's Blessed Machine of Language* (Ithaca, NY, 1981).

Coburn, Kathleen, 'S. T. Coleridge', in A. P. Ryan (ed.), *Critics Who Have Influenced Taste* (London, 1965) pp. 19–21.

——, 'Coleridge: a Bridge between Science and Poetry', in John Beer (ed.), *Coleridge's Variety: Bicentenary Studies* (London, 1974) pp. 81–100.

——, *The Self Conscious Imagination: A Study of the Coleridge Notebooks in Celebration of the Bi-centenary of his Birth 21 October 1772*, The Riddell Memorial Lectures, 1973 (Oxford, 1974).

——, *In Pursuit of Coleridge* (London, 1977).

——, *Inquiring Spirit: A New Presentation of Coleridge from His Published and Unpublished Prose Writings*, rev. edn (Toronto, 1979).

——, *Experience into Thought: Perspectives in the Coleridge Notebooks* (Toronto, 1979).

Cooke, Katharine, *Coleridge* (London, 1979).

Cooke, M. G., '*Quisque Sui Faber*: Coleridge in the *Biographia Literaria*', *Philological Quarterly*, L (1971) 208–29.

Cottle, Joseph, *Reminiscences of Samuel Taylor Coleridge and Robert Southey* (1847; Highgate, 1970).

Coulson, John, *Newman and the Common Tradition: A Study in the Language of Church and Society* (Oxford, 1970).

——, *Religion and Imagination: 'In aid of a grammar of assent'* (Oxford, 1981).

Coveney, Peter, *The Image of Childhood. The Individual and Society: A Study of the Theme in English Literature*, rev. edn (Harmondsworth, 1967).

Croce, Benedetto, *Aesthetic: As Science of Expression and General Linguistic*, trans. Douglas Ainslie (New York, 1955).

Cudworth, Ralph, *The True Intellectual System of the Universe: The First Part; Wherein All the Reason and Philosophy of Atheism is Confuted, and Its Impossibility Demonstrated* (1678), ed. Thomas Birch (London, 1743).

Culler, Jonathan, *Structuralist Poetics* (London, 1975).

Cupitt, Don, *Taking Leave of God* (London, 1980).

——, *The World to Come* (London, 1982).

Dekker, George, *Coleridge and the Literature of Sensibility* (London, 1978).

De Quincey, Thomas, *Confessions of an English Opium Eater* (1821), ed. Alethea Hayter (Harmondsworth, 1971).

——, *Reminiscences of the English Lake Poets*, ed. John E. Jordan (London, 1961).

De Vigny, Alfred, *Chatterton* (1835), ed. A. H. Diverres (London, 1967).

——, *Oeuvres complètes*, ed. F. Baldensperger, vol. 1 (Paris, 1950).

Differy, T. J., 'The Roots of Imagination: the Philosophical Context', in Stephen Prickett (ed.), *The Romantics* (London, 1981) pp. 164–201.

Dilthey, W., 'The Great Poetry of the Imagination', in *Selected Writings*, trans. and ed. H. P. Rickman (Cambridge, 1976) pp. 78–84.

Dorner, J. A., *History of Protestant Theology – Particularly in German, Viewed According to its Fundamental Movement and in Connection with the Religious, Moral, and Intellectual life*, trans. George Robson and Sophia Taylor, vol. II (Edinburgh, 1871).

Downing, F. Gerald, *Has Christianity a Revelation?* (London, 1964).

Duffy, John J., 'Problems in Publishing Coleridge: James Marsh's First American Edition of *Aids to Reflection*', *New England Quarterly*, 43 (1970) 193–208.

Dunn, W. A., *Thomas de Quincey's Relation to German Literature* (Strasbourg, 1900).

Eliot, T. S., *Selected Prose*, ed. John Hayward (Harmondsworth, 1953).

Elmer, M., 'Die Geschichte der Maria Eleonara Schöning und die charakteristik Luthers in Coleridges *Friend*', *Englische Studien*, XLVII (Leipzig, 1913–14) 219–25.

Emmett, Dorothy M., *Philosophy and Faith* (London, 1936).

——, *The Nature of Metaphysical Thinking* (London, 1949).

——, 'Theoria and the Way of Life', *Journal of Theological Studies*, n.s. XVII (1966) 38–52.

——, 'Coleridge on the Growth of the Mind', in Kathleen Coburn (ed.), *Coleridge: A Collection of Critical Essays* (Englewood Cliffs, NJ, 1967) pp. 161–78.

——, Coleridge and Philosophy', in R. L. Brett (ed.), *Writers and their Background: S. T. Coleridge* (London, 1971) pp. 195–220.

——, 'Coleridge on Powers in Mind and Nature', in John Beer (ed.), *Coleridge's Variety: Bicentenary Studies* (London, 1974) pp. 166–82.

Estlin, John Prior, *Evidences of Revealed Religion, and Particularly Christianity, Stated, with Reference to a Pamphlet Called the Age of Reason* (Bristol, 1796).

Everest, Kelvin, *Coleridge's Secret Ministry: The Context of the Conversation Poems 1795–8* (Sussex, 1979).

Fackenheim, E. L., 'Kant and Radical Evil', *University of Toronto Quarterly*, 23 (1954) 339–53.

Farrer, Austin, *The Glass of Vision*, the Bampton Lectures, 1948 (London, 1948).

——, 'Revelation', in Basil Mitchell (ed.), *Faith and Logic: Oxford Essays in Philosophical Theology* (London, 1957) pp. 84–107.

——, 'Inspiration: Poetical and Divine' (1963), repr. in *Interpretation and Belief*, ed. Charles C. Conti (London, 1976) pp. 39–53.

——, *Faith and Speculation* (London, 1967).

Fichte, Johann Gottlieb, *Versuch einer Kritik aller Offenbarung* (1792; 2nd edn 1793), trans. Garrett Green as *Attempt at a Critique of All Revelation* (Cambridge, 1978).

Fish, Stanley, 'Literature in the Reader: Affective Stylistics', *New Literary History*, 2 (1970) 123–62.

Fruman, Norman, *Coleridge: The Damaged Archangel* (London, 1972).

Frye, Northrop, *Anatomy of Criticism: Four Essays* (1957; New York, 1969).

——, *The Secular Scripture: A Study of the Structure of Romance* (Cambridge, Mass., 1976).

——, *The Great Code: The Bible and Literature* (London, 1982).

Furst, Lilian R. (ed.), *European Romanticism: Self-Definition* (London, 1980).

Gallie, W. B., *Philosophy and the Historical Understanding* (London, 1964).

Gardner, Helen, *The Limits of Literary Criticism: Reflections on the Interpretation of Poetry and Scripture*, the Riddell Memorial Lectures, 1956 (Oxford, 1956).

——, *Religion and Literature* (London, 1971).

——, *In Defence of the Imagination* (Oxford, 1982).

Gill, Frederick C., *The Romantic Movement and Methodism: A Study of English Romanticism and the Evangelical Revival* (1937; London, 1954).

Gillman, James, *The Life of Samuel Taylor Coleridge* (London, 1838).

Gingerich, S. F., 'From Necessity to Transcendentalism in Coleridge', *Publications of the Modern Language Association of America*, XXXV, n.s. XXVIII (1920) 1–59.

Grant, Allan, *A Preface to Coleridge* (London, 1972).

Gunn, Giles, *The Interpretation of Otherness: Religion, Literature, and the American Imagination* (New York, 1979).

Hall, Richard C., 'The Symbolic Relationship and Christian Truth', *Religious Studies*, 2 (1966) 129–36.

Halstead, John B. (ed.), *Romanticism* (London, 1969).

Happel, Stephen, 'Words Made Beautiful by Grace: on Coleridge the Theologian', *Religious Studies Review*, 6 (1980) 201–10.

Härdelin, Alf, *The Tractarian Understanding of the Eucharist* (Uppsala, 1965).

Harding, Anthony John, *Coleridge and the Idea of Love: Aspects of Relationship in Coleridge's Thought and Writing* (Cambridge, 1974).

Harding, D. W., 'The Theme of "The Ancient Mariner"', *Scrutiny*, IX (1941) 334–42.

Hare, Julius Charles, *The Mission of the Comforter*, 2 vols (London, 1846).

Harper, George McLean, 'Coleridge's Conversation Poems', in M. H. Abrams (ed.), *English Romantic Poets: Modern Essays in Criticism* (New York, 1960) pp. 144–57.

Hartley, David, *Observations on Man, His Frame, His Duty, and His Expectations* (1749), notes and additions by H. A. Pistorius, 3 vols (London, 1791).

Hartman, Geoffrey H., *Wordsworth's Poetry, 1787–1814* (New Haven, Conn., 1964).

Harvey, A. D., *English Poetry in a Changing Society, 1780–1825* (London, 1980).

Haven, Richard, 'Coleridge and Jacob Boehme: a Further Comment', *Notes and Queries*, CCXI (1966) 176–8.

——, 'The Ancient Mariner in the Nineteenth Century', *Studies in Romanticism*, 11 (1972) 360–80.

Hawkes, Terence, *Metaphor* (London, 1972).

——, *Structuralism and Semiotics* (London, 1977).

Hazlitt, William, 'My First Acquaintance with Poets' (1823), repr. in Edmund D. Jones (ed.), *English Critical Essays (Nineteenth Century)* (Oxford, 1968) pp. 139–61.

Hefling, Charles C., *Jacob's Ladder: Theology and Spirituality in the Thought of Austin Farrer* (Cambridge, Mass., 1979).

Helmholtz, Anna Augusta, *The Indebtedness of Samuel Taylor Coleridge to August Wilhelm von Schlegel* (Wisconsin, 1907).

Hill, John Spencer (ed.), *Imagination in Coleridge* (London, 1978).

Hobbes, Thomas, *Leviathan* (1651), ed. C. B. Macpherson (Harmondsworth, 1968).

Hodgson, Shadworth H., *The Philosophy of Reflection*, vol. 1 (London, 1878).

Hofer, Philip (ed.), *The Prisons [Le Carceri] by Giovanni Battista Piranesi: The Complete First and Second States* (New York, 1973).

Hofstadter, Albert, 'Kant's Aesthetic Revolution', *Journal of Religious Ethics*, 3/2 (1975) 171–91.

Hort, F. J. A., 'Coleridge', in *Cambridge Essays Contributed by Members of the University* (London, 1856) pp. 292–351.

Hough, Graham, *The English Mind* (Cambridge, 1964).

House, Humphrey, *Coleridge*, the Clark Lectures, 1951–2 (London, 1953).

Hugo, Victor, *Oeuvres poétiques*, ed. Pierre Albouy and Gaetan Pican, vol. 1 (Paris, 1964).

Hume, David, *Dialogues Concerning Natural Religion* (1779), ed. Norman Kemp Smith (Indianapolis, 1977).

Jackson, J. R. de J. (ed.), *Coleridge: The Critical Heritage* (London, 1970).

James, D. G., *The Life of Reason: Hobbes, Locke, Bolingbroke* (London, 1949).

Jasper, David, 'Supporting the Radicals: a Poetic Contribution', *The Heythrop Journal*, XXII (1981) 407–16.

Jaspers, Karl, *Plato and Augustine*, trans. Ralph Manheim (New York, 1962).

——, *Philosophical Faith and Revelation*, trans. E. B. Ashton (London, 1967).

Johnson, Samuel, *Pocket Dictionary of the English Language* (Halifax, 1861).

Jones, David, 'An Introduction to "The Ancient Mariner"' (1963–4), repr. in *'The Dying Gaul' and Other Writings*, ed. Harman Grisewood (London, 1978) pp. 186–226.

Kant, I., *De mundi sensibilis et intelligibilis forma et principiis* (1770), trans. G. B. Kerferd and D. E. Walford as *The Inaugural Dissertation: On the Form and Principles of the Sensible and Intelligible World*, in *Selected Pre-Critical Writings and Correspondence with Beck*, ed. G. B. Kerferd and D. E. Walford, with a contribution by P. G. Lucas (Manchester, 1968) pp. 47–92.

——, *Kritik der reinen Vernunft* (2nd edn 1781), trans. Norman Kemp Smith as *Critique of Pure Reason* (London, 1950).

——, *Kritik der praktischen Vernunft* (1788), trans. T. K. Abbott as *Critique of Practical Reason*, 6th edn (London, 1909).

——, *Kritik der Urtheilskraft* (1790), trans. James Creed Meredith as *The Critique of Judgement* (Oxford, 1928).

——, *Die Religion innerhalb der Grenzen der blossen Vernunft* (1793), trans. T. M. Greene and H. H. Hudson as *Religion within the Limits of Reason Alone* (New York, 1960).

——, *Vermischte Scriften* (Halle und Konigsberg, 1799–1807).

Kaufman, Gordon D., 'On the Meaning of "God": Transcendence without Mythology', *Harvard Theological Review*, 59 (1966) pp. 105–32.

Keats, John, *Letters*, selected by Frederick Page (Oxford, 1954).

Kemp, John, *The Philosophy of Kant* (Oxford, 1968).

Kermode, Frank, *The Sense of an Ending: Studies in the Theory of Fiction* (1966; Oxford, 1979).
——, 'The Structures of Fiction', *Modern Language Notes*, 84 (1969) 891–915.
——, *The Genesis of Secrecy: On the Interpretation of Narrative* (Cambridge, Mass., 1979).
Kessler, Edward, *Coleridge's Metaphors of Being* (Princeton, NJ, 1979).
Kirk, K. E., *The Vision of God: The Christian Doctrine of the Summum Bonum* (1931; New York, 1966).
Knight, G. Wilson, *The Starlit Dome: Studies in the Poetry of Vision* (Oxford, 1941).
Knights, Ben, *The Idea of the Clerisy in the Nineteenth Century* (Cambridge, 1978).
Knights, L. C., 'Ideas and Symbol: Some Hints from Coleridge', in Kathleen Coburn (ed.), *Coleridge: A Collection of Critical Essays* (Englewood Cliffs, NJ, 1967) pp. 112–22.
Kolnai, Aurel, 'The Thematic Primacy of Moral Evil', *Philosophical Quarterly*, VI (1956) 27–42.
Lamb, Charles, 'Christ's Hospital, Five and Thirty Years Ago', in *Essays of Elia* (1823; London, 1903) pp. 23–42.
Lamb, Charles, and Mary Anne, *The Letters*, ed. Edwin W. Marrs, Jr, 3 vols to date (Ithaca, NY, 1975–8).
Landow, George P., *Victorian Types, Victorian Shadows: Biblical Typology in Victorian Literature, Art, and Thought* (Boston, Mass., 1980).
Lash, Nicholas, *Theology on Dover Beach* (London, 1979).
Lazaroff, Allan, 'The Kantian Sublime: Aesthetic Judgement and Religious Feeling', *Kant-Studien*, 71 (1980) 202–20.
Lee, Kwang-Sae, 'Some Reflections on Apprehension, Reproduction and Production, and Recognition in *The Critique of Pure Reason*', in *Akten des 5: Internationalen Kant-Kongresses, Mainz 4–8 April 1981 1.1* (Bonn, 1981) pp. 237–44.
Lewis, H. D., *Morals and Revelation* (London, 1951).
——, *Our Experience of God* (1959; London, 1970).
Lindsay, Julian, 'Coleridge Marginalia in a Volume of Descartes', *Publications of the Modern Language Association of America*, XLIX (1934) 184–95.
Loades, A. L., 'Theodicy and Evolution: Aspects of Theology from Pierre Bayle to J. S. Mill' (University of Durham, unpublished PhD dissertation, 1975).
——, 'Coleridge as Theologian: Some Comments on his Reading of Kant', *The Journal of Theological Studies*, n.s. XXIX (1978) 410–26.
——'Immanuel Kant's Humanism', in Keith Robbins (ed.), *Religion and Humanism*, Studies in Church History, vol. 17 (Oxford, 1981) pp. 297–310.
Lockridge, Laurence S., *Coleridge the Moralist* (Ithaca, NY, 1977).
Lovejoy, Arthur O., ' "Nature" as Aesthetic Norm', *Modern Language Notes*, XLII (1927) 444–50.
——, 'Coleridge and Kant's Two Worlds' (1940), repr. in *Essays in the History of Ideas* (Baltimore, Md., 1948) pp. 254–76.
——, *The Reason, the Understanding and Time* (Baltimore, Md., 1961).
Lowes, John Livingston, *The Road to Xanadu. A Study in the Ways of the Imagination* (1927; rev. edn 1930; London, 1978).

Luther, Martin, *The Bondage of the Will* (1525), trans. J. I. Packer and O. R. Johnson (London, 1957).

Luther, Susan M., *'Christabel' as Dream-Reverie* (Salzburg, 1976).

McFarland, Thomas, *Coleridge and the Pantheist Tradition* (Oxford, 1969).

——, 'The Origin and Significance of Coleridge's Theory of Secondary Imagination', in Geoffrey H. Hartman (ed.), *New Perspectives on Coleridge and Wordsworth* (New York, 1972) pp. 195–246.

——, 'Coleridge's Anxiety', in John Beer (ed.), *Coleridge's Variety: Bicentenary Essays* (London, 1974) pp. 134–65.

——, *Romanticism and the Forms of Ruin: Wordsworth, Coleridge and Modalities of Fragmentation* (Princeton, NJ, 1981).

MacKinnon, D. M., *A Study in Ethical Theory* (London, 1957).

——, 'Coleridge and Kant', in John Beer (ed.), *Coleridge's Variety: Bicentenary Essays* (London, 1974) pp. 183–203.

——, *The Problem of Metaphysics* (Cambridge, 1974).

——, 'Some Epistemological Reflections on Mystical Experience', in Stephen T. Katz (ed.), *Mysticism and Philosophical Essays* (London, 1978) pp. 132–40.

——, 'Kant's Philosophy of Religion', *Philosophy*, 50 (1975) 131–44.

Macmurray, John, *The Self as Agent*, the Gifford Lectures, 1953 (London, 1957).

Marcel, Gabriel, *Coleridge et Schelling* (1909; Paris, 1971).

Marks, Emerson R., *Coleridge on the Language of Verse* (Princeton, NJ, 1981).

Marsh, James, 'Preliminary Essay' to *Aids to Reflection*, 2nd American edn (Burlington, 1840); repr. in *AR (II)*, pp. xxiii–lxxvi.

Martin, Bernard, *'The Ancient Mariner' and the Authentic Narrative* (London, 1949).

Martin, C. G., 'Coleridge and Cudworth: a Source for "The Eolian Harp"' *Notes and Queries*, CCXI (1966) 173–6.

——, 'Coleridge and William Crowe's "Lewesdon Hill"', *Modern Language Review*, 62 (1967) 400–6.

Martland, T. R., 'To Glorify: the Essence of Poetry and Religion', *Religious Studies*, 16 (1980) pp. 413–23.

Maurice, F. D., Dedication to the 2nd edn of *The Kingdom of Christ, or Hints to a Quaker respecting the Principles, Constitution, and Ordinances of the Catholic Church* (1842), 3rd edn, 2 vols (London, 1883) pp. ix–xxx.

Mellor, Anne K., *English Romantic Irony* (Cambridge, Mass., 1980).

Midgley, Mary, 'The Objection to Systematic Humbug', *Philosophy*, 53 (1978) 147–69.

——, *Beast and Man: The Roots of Human Nature* (London, 1980).

——, *Heart and Mind: The Varieties of Moral Experience* (Brighton, 1981).

Mill. J. S., 'Coleridge' (1840), repr. in J. B. Schneewind (ed.), *Mill's Essays on Literature and Society* (New York, 1965) pp. 290–347.

Milne, A. J. M., 'Coleridge and Bentham as Religious Thinkers' (University of London, unpublished PhD dissertation, 1952).

Morris-Jones, H., 'Art and Imagination', *Philosophy*, 34 (1959) 204–16.

Motekat, Helmut, *Ostpreussische Literatur Geschichte, mit Danzig und Westpreussen, 1230–1945* (München, 1977).

Muirhead, J. H., 'The Cambridge Platonists', I and II, *Mind*, n.s. 36 (1927) 158–78, 326–41.

——, *Coleridge as Philosopher* (London, 1930).

——, 'Metaphysician or Mystic?', in Edmund Blunden and Earl Leslie Briggs (eds), *Coleridge: Studies by Several Hands on the Hundredth Anniversary of his Death* (London, 1934) pp. 179–97.

Nahm, Milton C., 'The Theological Background of the Theory of the Artist as Creator', *Journal of the History of Ideas*, VIII (1947) 363–72.

Needham, J., 'S. T. Coleridge as a Philosophical Biologist', *Science Progress*, XX (1926) 692–702.

Newman, J. H., *Apologia Pro Vita Sua* (1864; London, 1959).

——, *Historical Sketches*, 3 vols (London, 1872).

Newsome, David, *Two Classes of Men: Platonism and English Romantic Thought* (London, 1974).

Nidecker, Henri, 'Notes Marginales de S. T. Coleridge', *Revue de Littérature Comparée*, 7 (1927) 130–46.

——, Notes Marginales de S. T. Coleridge: En Marge de Kant', *Revue de Littérature Comparée*, 7 (1927) 336–48, 521–35.

——, 'Notes Marginales de S. T. Coleridge', *Revue de Littérature Comparée*, 10 (1930) pp. 163–9.

Novalis (Friedrich von Hardenberg), *Gesammelte Werke*, ed. Carl Seelig, 4 vols (Zürich, 1945–6).

Orsini, G. N. G., 'Coleridge and Schlegel Reconsidered', *Comparative Literature*, XVI (1964) 97–118.

——, *Coleridge and German Idealism: A Study in the History of Philosophy, with Unpublished Materials from Coleridge's Manuscripts* (Carbondale, Ill., 1969).

Owen, Huw Parry, 'The Theology of Coleridge', *Critical Quarterly*, 4 (1962) 59–67.

Park, Roy, 'Coleridge and Kant: Poetic Imagination and Practical Reason', *British Journal of Aesthetics*, 8 (1968) 335–47.

Pater, Walter Horatio, 'Coleridge's Writings' (rev. 1889), repr. in Edmund D. Jones (ed.), *English Critical Essays (Nineteenth Century)* (Oxford, 1968) pp. 421–57.

Paton, H. J., *In Defence of Reason* (London, 1951).

Patterson, Jr, Charles I., 'The Daemonic in "Kubla Khan": Toward Interpretation', *Publications of the Modern Language Association of America*, 89 (1974) 1033–42.

Pfeiler, William K., 'Coleridge and Schelling's Treatise on the Samothracian Deities', *Modern Language Notes*, 52 (1937) 162–5.

Phillipson, N. T., 'James Beattie and the Defence of Common Sense', in Bernhard Fabian (ed.), *Festschrift für Rainer Gruenter* (Heidelberg, 1978) pp. 145–54.

Piper, H. W., *The Active Universe: Pantheism and the Concept of Imagination in the English Romantic Poets* (London, 1962).

Ploplis, W. M., 'The Great Name of God: a Study of the Element of the Kabbala in Samuel Taylor Coleridge's Theogony and its Influence on the Theodicy and Cosmogony of His Major Poetry' (Loyola University of Chicago, unpublished PhD dissertation, 1981).

Plotinus, *Ennead*, II, in Loeb Classical Library, ed. A. H. Armstrong (London, 1966).

Potter, George Reuben, 'Unpublished Marginalia in Coleridge's Copy of

Malthus's Essay on Population', *Publications of the Modern Language Association of America*, 51 (1936) 1061–8.

Pradhan, S. V., 'Coleridge's "Philocrisy" and His Theory of Fancy and Secondary Imagination', *Studies in Romanticism*, 13 (1974), 235–54.

Praz, Mario, 'Introductory Essay' to Peter Fairclough (ed.), *Three Gothic Novels* (Harmondsworth, 1968) pp. 7–34.

——, *The Hero in Eclipse in Victorian Fiction*, trans. Angus Davidson (Oxford, 1969).

Prickett, Stephen, *Coleridge and Wordsworth: The Poetry of Growth* (Cambridge, 1970).

——, *Romanticism and Religion: The Tradition of Coleridge and Wordsworth in the Victorian Church* (Cambridge, 1976).

——, 'The Religious Context', in Stephen Prickett (ed.), *The Romantics* (London, 1981) pp. 115–63.

Purser, J. W. R., 'Interpretation of "The Ancient Mariner" ', *Review of English Studies*, n.s. VIII (1957) 249–56.

Pusey, E. B., *Lectures on Types and Prophecies of the Old Testament*, written mainly in Jul–Aug 1836, bound manuscript in Pusey House Library, Oxford.

Pym, David, *The Religious Thought of Samuel Taylor Coleridge* (Gerrards Cross, 1978).

Rahme, Mary, 'Coleridge's Concept of Symbolism', *Studies in English Literature*, IX (1969) 619–32.

Raine, Kathleen, 'Traditional Symbolism in "Kubla Khan" ', *Sewanee Review*, 72 (1964) 626–42.

Rauber, D. F., 'The Fragment as Romantic Form', *Modern Language Quarterly*, 30 (1969) 212–21.

Read, Herbert, *The Forms of Things Unknown: Essays Towards an Aesthetic Philosophy* (New York, 1960).

Reardon, B. M. G., *Religious Thought in the Nineteenth Century* (Cambridge, 1966).

——, 'Kant as Theologian', *Downside Review*, 93 (1975) 252–68.

——, *Hegel's Philosophy of Religion* (London, 1977).

Richards, I. A., *Coleridge on Imagination* (London, 1934).

——(ed.), *The Portable Coleridge* (1950; Harmondsworth, 1977).

Ricoeur, Paul, *Essays on Biblical Interpretation*, ed. Lewis S. Mudge (London, 1981).

Ridenour, George M., 'Source and Allusion in Some Poems of Coleridge', *Studies in Philology*, 60 (1963) 73–95.

Rowell, Geoffrey, *Hell and the Victorians: A Study of the Nineteenth Century Controversies concerning Eternal Punishment and the Future Life* (Oxford, 1974).

Rule, Philip C., SJ, 'Coleridge's Reputation as a Religious Thinker: 1816–1972', *Harvard Theological Review*, 67 (1974) 289–320.

Sanders, C. A., 'Coleridge, F. D. Maurice, and the Distinction Between the Reason and the Understanding', *Publications of the Modern Language Association of America*, 51 (1936) 459–75.

——, *Coleridge and the Broad Church Movement: Studies in S. T. Coleridge, Dr. Arnold of Rugby, J. C. Hare, Thomas Carlyle, and F. D. Maurice* (1942; New York, 1972).

Sankey, Benjamin, 'Coleridge and the Visible World', *Texas Studies in Literature and Language*, 6 (1964) pp. 59–67.

Schenk, H. G., *The Mind of the European Romantics* (London, 1966).

Schiller, Friedrich, *Kleinere prosaische Schriften*, vol. 2 (Leipzig, 1800).

Schlegel, August Wilhelm von, *Kritische Schriften und Briefe*, ed. Edgar Lohner, vols 2 and 6 (Stuttgart, 1963, 1967).

——, *Vorlesungen über dramatische Kunst und Literatur*, trans. John Black, rev. A. J. W. Morrison, as *A Course of Lectures on Dramatic Art and Literature* (London, 1846).

Schlegel, Friedrich von, *Prosaische Jugendschriften*, ed. J. Minor, 2 vols (Vienna, 1882).

——, *Literary Notebooks 1797–1801*, ed. Hans Eichner (Toronto, 1957).

——, *Kritische Ausgabe*, vol. II: *Charakteristiken und Kritiken (1796–1801)*, ed. Hans Eichner (Munich, 1967).

Schneider, Duane B., 'Coleridge's Light–Sound Theory', *Notes and Queries*, CCVIII (1963) 182–3.

Schneider, Elisabeth, *Coleridge, Opium and 'Kubla Khan'* (Chicago, 1953).

Schrickx, W., 'Coleridge and the Cambridge Platonists', *Review of English Literature*, 7 (1966) 71–91.

Shaffer, Elinor S., 'Metaphysics of Culture: Kant and Coleridge's *Aids to Reflection*', *Journal of the History of Ideas*, 31 (1970) 199–218.

——, *'Kubla Khan' and the Fall of Jerusalem: The Mythological School in Biblical Criticism and Secular Literature, 1770–1880* (Cambridge, 1975).

Shelley, P. B., *A Defence of Poetry* (1821), repr. in Edmund D. Jones (ed.), *English Critical Essays (Nineteenth Century)* (Oxford, 1968) pp. 102–38.

Shepherd, John J., 'The Concept of Revelation', *Religious Studies*, 16 (1980) 425–37.

Snyder, Alice D., 'Coleridge's Cosmogony: a Note on the Poetic "World-view"', *Studies in Philology*, 21 (1924) 616–25.

——, 'Coleridge on Giordano Bruno', *Modern Language Notes*, XLII (1927) 427–36.

——, *Coleridge on Logic and Learning: with Selections from the Unpublished Manuscripts* (New Haven, Conn., 1929).

——, 'Coleridge on Böhme', *Publications of the Modern Language Association of America*, 45 (1930) 616–18.

Solger, Karl W. F., *Nachgelassene Schriften und Briefwechsel*, ed. L. Tieck and F. von Raumer, 2 vols (Leipzig, 1826).

Sontag, Frederick, *Divine Perfection: Possible Ideas of God* (London, 1962).

Stephen, Leslie, *Hours in a Library*, vol. III, 3rd edn 1879 (London, 1909).

Stirling, J. H., *The Secret of Hegel, Being the Hegelian System in Origin, Principle, Form and Matter* (Edinburgh, 1898).

Storr, Vernon F., *The Development of English Theology in the Nineteenth Century, 1800–1860* (London, 1913).

Strawson, P. F., *Freedom and Resentment* (London, 1974).

Stuart, J. A., 'The Augustinian "Cause of Action" in Coleridge's "Rime of the Ancient Mariner"', *Harvard Theological Review*, 60 (1967) 177–211.

Swiatecka, M. Jadwiga, OP, *The Idea of the Symbol: Some Nineteenth-Century Comparisons with Coleridge* (Cambridge, 1980).

Swinburne, A. C., *Essays and Studies* (London, 1875).

Tennyson, G. B., *Victorian Devotional Poetry: The Tractarian Mode* (Cambridge, Mass., 1981).

Tetens, J. N., *Philosophische Versuche über die menschliche Natur und ihre Entwickelung*, 2 vols (Leipzig, 1777).

Thomas, J. Heywood, 'Religious Language as Symbolism', *Religious Studies*, 1 (1965) 89–93.

Thompson, A. H., 'Thomson and Natural Description in Poetry', in Sir A. W. Ward and A. R. Waller (eds), *The Age of Johnson*, Cambridge History of English Literature Series, vol. X (Cambridge, 1932) pp. 93–115.

Thompson, E. P., Review of Coleridge, *Essays on His Times*, 3 vols (Princeton, NJ, 1978), in *The Wordsworth Circle*, 10 (1979) 261–5.

Tieck, Ludwig, *Nachgelassene Schriften*, ed. R. Köpke, 2 vols (Leipzig, 1855).

Tillich, P., *Theology of Culture* (New York, 1964).

Traill, H. D., *Coleridge* (1884; London, 1909).

——, 'A Pious Legend Examined', *Fortnightly Review*, n.s. XXXVII (1885) 223–33.

Trickett, Rachel, 'Imagination and Belief', in A. E. Harvey (ed.), *God Incarnate: Story and Belief* (London, 1981) pp. 34–41.

Tulloch, John, *Movements of Religious Thought in Britain during the Nineteenth Century* (1885; Leicester, 1971).

——, 'Coleridge as a Spiritual Thinker', *Fortnightly Review*, n.s. XXVII (1885) 11–25.

Van Peursen, C. A., *Leibniz*, trans. Hubert Hoskins (London, 1969).

Vaughan, William, *Romantic Art* (London, 1978).

Vermes, Pamela, *Buber on God and the Perfect Man* (Providence, RI, 1980).

Vidler, Alec R., *F. D. Maurice and Company: Nineteenth-Century Studies* (London, 1966).

Wackenroder, W. H., *Herzensergiessungen eines kunstliebenden Klosterbruders* (1797), ed. A. Gillies (Oxford, 1948).

Waples, Dorothy, 'David Hartley in "The Ancient Mariner"', *Journal of English and Germanic Philology*, 35 (1936) 337–51.

Warmington, Eric H. and Rouse, Philip G., *Great Dialogues of Plato*, trans. W. H. D. Rouse (New York, 1956).

Warnock, Mary, *Imagination* (London, 1976).

——, 'Imagination – Aesthetic and Religious', *Theology*, LXXXIII (1980) 403–9.

Warren, Robert Penn, *A Poem of Pure Imagination: An Experiment in Reading* (New York, 1946).

Watson, George, *The Literary Critics: A Study of English Descriptive Criticism*, rev. edn (Harmondsworth, 1964).

Wellek, René, *Kant in England* (Princeton, NJ, 1931).

——, and Warren, Austin, *Theory of Literature*, 3rd edn (Harmondsworth, 1976).

Werkmeister, Lucyle, 'The Early Coleridge: His "Rage for Metaphysics"', *Harvard Theological Review*, 54 (1961) 99–123.

Wesley, Charles, *Short Hymns on Select Passages of the Holy Scriptures* (London, 1796).

Whalley, George, 'The Bristol Library Borrowings of Southey and Coleridge, 1793–8', *The Library*, IV (1949) 114–31.

——, 'Coleridge's Poetic Sensibility', in John Beer (ed.), *Coleridge's Variety: Bicentenary Studies* (London, 1974) pp. 1–30.

Wheeler, K. M., *Sources, Processes and Methods in Coleridge's 'Biographia Literaria'* (Cambridge, 1980).

——, *The Creative Mind in Coleridge's Poetry* (London, 1981).

Whitehouse, W. A., *The Authority of Grace: Essays in Response to Karl Barth*, ed. Ann Loades (Edinburgh, 1981).

Wicker, Brian, *The Story-Shaped World. Fiction and Metaphysics: Some Variations on a Theme* (London, 1975).

Willey, Basil, *The Eighteenth-Century Background: Studies on the Idea of Nature in the Thought of the Period* (1940; Harmondsworth, 1967).

——, 'Coleridge on Imagination and Fancy', *Proceedings of the British Academy*, XXXII (1946) 173–87.

——, 'Coleridge and Religion', in R. L. Brett (ed.), *Writers and their Background: S. T. Coleridge* (London, 1971) pp. 221–43.

——, *Nineteenth-Century Studies: Coleridge to Matthew Arnold* (1949; Harmondsworth, 1969).

——, *Samuel Taylor Coleridge* (London, 1972).

Wilson, John (attrib), 'Some Observations on the *Biographia Literaria* of S. T. Coleridge, Esq. – 1817', *Blackwood's Edinburgh Magazine*, II (1817) 1–18.

Wimsatt, W. K., 'The Structure of Romantic Nature Imagery' (1954), in M. H. Abrams (ed.), *English Romantic Poets: Modern Essays in Criticism* (New York, 1960).

Woodring, Carl, 'The Mariner's Return', *Studies in Romanticism*, 11 (1972) 375–80.

Wordsworth, William and Coleridge, S. T., *Lyrical Ballads* (1798), ed. W. J. B. Owen, 2nd edn (Oxford, 1969).

Wordsworth, William, *Poetical Works*, ed. Thomas Hutchinson, rev. Ernest de Selincourt (1936; Oxford, 1969).

——, and Dorothy Wordsworth, *Letters: The Middle Years*, ed. Ernest de Selincourt, rev. Mary Moorman, vol. 1 (Oxford, 1969).

Yates, Frances A., *The Art of Memory* (Harmondsworth, 1969).

Index